MW00526133

Branch Rickey in Pittsburgh

Branch Rickey in Pittsburgh

Baseball's Trailblazing General Manager for the Pirates, 1950–1955

by

ANDREW O'TOOLE

McFarland & Company, Inc., Publishers
Jefferson, North Carolina, and London

Front cover: Branch Rickey with his arm around manager Bobby Bragan. *Back cover:* Branch Rickey with wife, Jane, at Forbes Field.

All photographs courtesy of the Pittsburgh Pirates unless otherwise noted.

Library of Congress Cataloguing-in-Publication Data

O'Toole, Andrew.
    Branch Rickey in Pittsburgh : Baseball's trailblazing general manager for the Pirates, 1950–1955 / by Andrew O'Toole.
       p.   cm.
    Includes bibliographical references and index.
    ISBN 0-7864-0839-1 (softcover : 50# alkaline paper) ∞
    1. Rickey, Branch, 1881–1965. 2. Baseball managers — United States — Biography. 3. Pittsburgh Pirates (Baseball team)
I. Title
    GV865.R45 O76   2000
    796.357'092 — dc21
    [B]   00-33861

British Library cataloguing data are available

©2000 Andrew O'Toole. All rights reserved

No part of this book may be reproduced or transmitted in any form or by any means, electronic or mechanical, including photocopying or recording, or by any information storage and retrieval system, without permission in writing from the publisher.

Manufactured in the United States of America

McFarland & Company, Inc., Publishers
 Box 611, Jefferson, North Carolina 28640
  www.mcfarlandpub.com

For my brothers,
Michael and Terry

Acknowledgments

"Judas Priest, what a character!" an editor once wrote of Branch Rickey in the pages of *The Sporting News*. Though others have used different terminology when expressing their opinion of the baseball great (both laudatory and defamatory), that single passage in the pages of "Baseball's Bible" best defines the wondrous Rickey. It is his engaging personality that makes a book possible, for which the subject is a last-place dynasty.

I must acknowledge a debt of gratitude to the men who chronicled the Pittsburgh Pirates on a daily basis for the city's three newspapers — Jack Hernon of the *Post-Gazette*, Les Biederman of the *Press*, and Charles "Chilly" Doyle of the *Sun-Telegraph*. In addition to those three beat writers, the work of a number of other newspapermen helped document this era of Pittsburgh baseball: Al Abrams, Davis Walsh, Harry Keck, Jimmy Jordan, Myron Cope, and Chester Smith.

Though this book is for the most part a contemporary account, I did conduct several interviews for the text. I would like to thank the following for kindly giving of their time and patiently answering my questions: Joe L. Brown, Clyde Sukeforth, Thomas P. Johnson, Howie Haak, Branch Rickey III (who generously allowed the reprinting of letters and other papers from the Branch Rickey collection), Curtis Roberts, Jr., and Christine Roberts.

I was deeply saddened to learn of the passing of Christine Roberts as this book was being prepared for publication. I had the pleasure of spending an afternoon with her at her home in Reno, where she regaled me with stories of her life with her beloved husband. Though I met with her for just a brief period of time, I was profoundly impressed and have thought of our encounter often. She lived her life striving to make a difference, and she will be sorely missed by all whose lives she touched.

I would also like to thank Sally O'Leary and Mike Gordon of the Pittsburgh Pirates organization. Sally and Mike were of great assistance in locating several interviewees and they generously allowed me to browse the Pirate archives for the photographs used in these pages.

Thanks must go to Bruce Markusen of the National Baseball Hall of Fame Library, whose encouragement helped convince me to pursue the project.

Several people helped mold the manuscript into a coherent work. Todd Catchpole, Linda Harper, Heidi Shaw, and Scott Cole, your advice and criticism were sorely needed — thank you.

And finally, my bride Mickie, whose love brightens my every day … You are the everything.

Contents

Introduction:
From Small Things,
Big Things One Day Come

This book has its origins in the summer of 1997. My wife, Mickie, and I had gone to the District of Columbia on vacation that July, and while in the capital I made a point of visiting the Library of Congress to peruse an aggregation that I had read about, the Branch Rickey Collection, which is held in the manuscript division of the library.

Though I'm extremely interested in the life and work of Rickey, as any fan of baseball's history rightfully should be, I was hoping to locate information on a particular player who had crossed paths with Rickey — Curtis Roberts. I had recently written an article for *Pittsburgh History* magazine on Roberts, the first black man to play for the Pittsburgh Pirates, and for curiosity's sake I was hoping to find something, any smidgen, of information on Roberts.

While I was busy flipping through file after file, Mickie was leafing through the papers I had discarded, and she brought several documents to my attention. The first was a fifteen-page epistle from Rickey to Pirates owner John Galbreath dated March 21, 1952. The letter was a mesmerizing diatribe — a brilliant piece of baseball literature which centered solely on the shortcomings of Pirate star outfielder Ralph Kiner. I asked Mickie to photocopy the more interesting pieces for me to browse at a later time.

Though I found each memorandum educational, and in its own way entertaining, I must admit that the idea of doing a book on Rickey did not immediately come to mind. The thought of researching a book on Rickey's Pittsburgh years did not come to me for several months. When it did, since I had already riffled through his files, I was convinced there was enough previously unpublished material to warrant an effort.

There have been two full-length biographies written on Rickey. Branch's friend Arthur Mann wrote *Branch Rickey: American in Action* in 1957 and Murray Polner had his work, *Branch Rickey,* published in 1982. Both volumes are full-length studies of Rickey. I was aiming for something different, something more specific. Though his career had been written upon extensively in books other than Polner's and Mann's, namely his part in the racial integration of baseball, Rickey's tenure in Pittsburgh has largely been ignored, and some would say for good reason. Rickey's five year stay as the Pirate's general manager was anything but successful on the field. A seventh place finish (in an eight-team league) was followed by four consecutive eighth place finishes. A losing dynasty is usually not a prime subject for a book. Yet I believed that Rickey, as evidenced by the material gathered by my wife in Washington, D.C., was an exceptional subject. Certainly one of the greatest characters the game has ever known, Rickey is arguably its greatest genius.

While other participants in the National Pastime became specialists of individual aspects of the game, with Rickey, baseball had a man whose aptitude was not compartmentalized. Branch educated, participated, and opined on virtually every realm of organized ball. Scouting, managing, inventing, playing, broadcasting, and front office management — Rickey didn't just dip his toe into these matters; he would dive in, determined to conquer even the most minute details confronting baseball.

Branch's major league playing career was far from spectacular. Four seasons, 118 games, and a lifetime batting average of .239, certainly isn't the reason we remember him today. Nor was his ten-year managerial term, spent with the St. Louis Cardinals and Browns, all that striking, which his won-loss record of 597–669 will affirm. It was in the second stage of his managerial career, when functioning in the dual role of general manager/field manager for the Cardinals, that Rickey became *Branch Rickey*. The Cardinals captured five National League pennants while under his guidance, but all of the first place finishes occurred after he stepped aside as the Redbirds field manager and concentrated on the front office machinations of the ball club. St. Louis' success can be attributed, almost completely, to Rickey's ingenious innovation: the "farm system." This system allowed the Cardinals to compete with the wealthier clubs in the league, and before long, the Redbirds were regularly finishing ahead of the "rich" teams.

Branch remained in St. Louis until 1942, when he had a falling out with Cardinal owner Sam Breadon. But Rickey landed on his feet and quickly found employment in Brooklyn where he was given the authority needed to build a winner for the Dodgers. Rickey constructed a championship-caliber club in Brooklyn much the same way that he had in St. Louis, through the farm system. During his time in Flatbush, Rickey won two pennants, but the Bums added five more with the fruit of his labor in the immediate years after he left Brooklyn.

So beloved were these successful teams in St. Louis and Brooklyn that they were dubbed, and forever immortalized, as the "Gas House Gang" and the "Boys of Summer," respectively. Contrarily, Rickey's Pittsburgh creations were cruelly, but perhaps accurately, tagged "Rickey's Rinky Dinks."

October 13, 1960, 3:36 P.M.: the defining moment in Pittsburgh sports history. At that instant Bill Mazeroski sent a Ralph Terry delivery sailing into Schenley Park giving the Pirates their first world championship in thirty-five years. As Maz festively rounded the bases, wildly windmilling his helmet wielding arm, the whole of Pittsburgh spontaneously exploded in a celebration of unabashed orgiastic joy. The Golden Triangle, the city's downtown district, was awash with reveling fans snake dancing along the town's one-way boulevards.

The accredited pilot behind the champion teams' rise was their general manager, Joe L. Brown. The World Series victory came virtually five years to the day that the then thirty-seven-year-old Brown was named as Rickey's successor in Pittsburgh. The club that Brown had inherited resembled anything but pennant winners. The dismal teams led by Rickey amassed a record of 269 victories and 501 losses, an astounding 224.5 aggregated games out of first place. Pittsburgh's beloved Bucs, to paraphrase Dr. Theodor Geisel, "Stink ... Stank ... Stunk!"

Rickey had come to Pittsburgh in November 1950 full of vim and poised to repeat the ample success he had previously encountered. Branch found the prosperity he enjoyed with the Cardinals and the Dodgers not easily repeated. Rickey employed his timeworn methods while striving to build a winner for Pittsburgh, which curiously meant stripping the Pirates of every player with any semblance of talent and starting from scratch. The rebuilding process would begin at the bottom ... in the farm system.

Though the standings in those years don't reveal anything but failure, among the sad sack Rickey teams were some golden prospects. Vernon Law, Bob Friend, El Roy Face, Bill Mazeroski, Dick Groat, Roberto
Clemente, and Bob Skinner all were key members of the '60 Bucs who
had either been members of Rickey's lackluster teams or, as in the case
of Mazeroski, were signed by Branch's scouts and reached the major
leagues subsequent to Rickey's tenure. Not all these men were the product of Branch's farm system. However, Maz, Skinner, and Groat were
brought into professional ball by Rickey's scouts. Friend and Law were
members of the Pirate organization prior to Rickey's term, and Face and
Clemente both were plucked from the Dodgers' roster in the major
league draft — Face in 1952, Clemente in 1954.

Despite the fact that the core of the 1960 championship team was
put together and nurtured by Rickey, following the Series victory no
credit was granted his administration either in the press, or by the public. By 1960 Branch was a forgotten man in the city of Pittsburgh. In the
minds of most Bucco fans, Rickey's contribution to the team and its city
was an elongated misery, his rule a frightful nightmare.

Rickey's pursuit for baseball supremacy while in Pittsburgh was
hindered from the start. The conflict in Korea was taking young men
from professional baseball at a rapid rate, and the Pirates, because of the
youth movement incorporated by Rickey, were affected by the selective
service more so than their competitors.

Branch encountered another significant obstacle. The Pirates, though
Rickey didn't know it when he took the position, were effectively broke.
Pittsburgh was a "small market" town before the term even existed. A
common viewpoint held by nostalgic baseball fans is that the fifties were
a golden age for baseball. For a few annually successful organizations that
perception was true, but in most major-league cities the season was over,
competitively, before it began.

The decade was dominated by the three New York entries to the
major leagues. Fourteen of the twenty participants in the World Series
during the 1950s called New York City home. The Yankees won eight
American League pennants, while the Dodgers and Giants won four and
two flags, respectively. Five times in the decade two Gotham City clubs
battled each other in a "Subway Series." Only once, 1959, did neither
Series combatant hail from New York, and that fall classic pitted the *Los
Angeles* Dodgers against the Chicago White Sox.

Leveling the playing field between the "haves" and the "have-nots" was high on Rickey's priority list during his Pittsburgh tenure. When not busying himself with the rehabilitation of the Pirate's pennant prospects, Rickey strenuously campaigned for a more equitable playing field for both the rich and poor teams.

Rickey, a man of enormous intellect, certainly would have succeeded in any field he chose, but baseball, his enduring passion, was the beneficiary of his sagacity. One could forcefully argue that no individual was more influential to the game than Branch Rickey. His authoritative and provocative presence can still be felt throughout organized baseball today. The innovation of the minor league farm system and the racial integration of professional baseball were just the most prominent of the many gifts that Rickey bestowed upon the game.

Even in Pittsburgh, the sight of Branch Rickey's first "failure," the repercussions of Rickey's foresight were still being enjoyed well into the 1980s. Pirate teams of the sixties, seventies, and eighties were well known for their wealth of quality Latin American players. The organization's foray into the Caribbean market began with a 1955 Rickey directive to his favorite scout, Howie Haak. The result of Haak's detective work wasn't felt during Branch's incumbency, but what began as a sprinkling of Latino talent in the late fifties became a flood by the early sixties. Joe Christopher, Rennie Stennett, Julian Javier, Manny Sanguillen, Tony Pena, John Candelaria, and Omar Moreno among others were products of Haak's brilliant scouting. Again, as with the case with the 1960 championship, credit was not granted for Rickey's initiative.

One part hustler, one part evangelist, Branch Rickey was a paradox. He could be verbose, philosophical, condescending, and humorous. Even reporters who found Rickey undesirable flocked to him, for Branch was a living, breathing quote machine. Ask him a question, or simply offer a salutation, and a flurry of words — entertaining, educational, or purely rhetorical — were sure to emanate from Branch. From his very first day in Pittsburgh, Branch repeatedly expressed, indeed emphatically asserted, that Pittsburgh fans would soon be frolicking through the streets, rejoicing a Pirate pennant. Sometimes, though, even the best-laid plans are tardy in coming to fruition.

Monetary concerns plagued Rickey's decision making process and hampered his club's progression. Undeterred, Branch continued to build the foundation of a team that would one day culminate in a World Championship. But it would be a long, arduous climb. Still the anguish that accompanied the failed aspirations didn't deter Branch. His timetable may have been skewed, but the Pirates, as Branch promised, eventually realized his vision.

"Luck," the wise Rickey once declared, "is the residue of design." And though he didn't author the cliché, Rickey would certainly advise, "Patience is a virtue."

1. A Five Year Plan

"We're pointing toward 1955. That's when the bells will start ringing and the red wagon comes down the street. That's when Pittsburgh folks will shout, 'By George, this is it.'"

The date was November 3, 1950, and the clairvoyant speaker was Branch Rickey. On that bright fall day Rickey was named the general manager of the Pittsburgh Pirates at a press conference held within the confines of Forbes Field. It mattered little that Pittsburgh's three daily newspapers were on strike, and Branch's words would reach a limited audience. Superfluous verbiage continually flowed from Rickey. Whether he was speaking to a crowd of one or a group of a hundred, Branch was never at a loss for words nor too shy to express his bounty of opinions. Despite the media work stoppage, two dozen members of the city's sporting press, including writers from the Pittsburgh *Press,* the Pittsburgh *Post-Gazette,* and the Pittsburgh *Sun-Telegraph,* were present for the introduction of Rickey to the western Pennsylvanian burgh.

Rickey came to a city rich in baseball tradition, but long starved for a winner. Pittsburgh last captured a pennant in 1927, and the most recent seasons had seen the Bucs customarily finish in the second division. Branch's vow to turn the hapless Pirates into winners was music to the ears of the Iron City's hardworking fans.

"Pittsburgh," a journalist wrote of Rickey's new home, "is smoke and dirt. Pittsburgh is raw and alive. Pittsburgh is poverty and railroad tracks. It's also the home of extreme wealth — big, brick houses in residential districts, far away from the game and the smog. Pittsburgh is

"The Mahatma"

crowded, noisy, scrappy. But most of all, Pittsburgh is a working man's town. The working man built it. His speech is heard everywhere, rough and honest. And baseball is his game."[1]

With successful stays in his previous baseball homes of Brooklyn and St. Louis, the fans of Pittsburgh were hoping Rickey would be the antidote for their Bucs' recent woes. He was nicknamed "the Mahatma" by a New York writer, after that reporter had read John Gunther's portrayal of Mahatma Gandhi, "a combination of God, your father, and Tammany Hall," a description which many observers believed was apt concerning Rickey. Even his detractors would be forced to admit that Rickey's baseball genius was beyond reproach. Along with his formidable knowledge of the game, Branch was bringing with him to the Steel City his sizable ego and eccentricities. The Mahatma, awash with personality and character, was sure to entertain the Pittsburgh masses for the next five years.

Rickey, after a distinguished and successful reign in Brooklyn, dropped anchor in Pittsburgh subsequent to losing a bitter power struggle with Walter O'Malley.

Rickey and O'Malley—two names indelibly linked in Brooklyn Dodger lore. Only the Bums' rivalry with the hated crosstown Giants could match the furious relationship these two baseball titans endured. As O'Malley's visibility steadily increased following his 1943 purchase of Dodger stock, it became quickly apparent that Flatbush wouldn't be large enough for the dueling egos.

"Walter O'Malley is the most devious man I have ever met,"[2] Rickey once confided to Dodger broadcaster Red Barber.

O'Malley's contempt for his adversary was every bit as heartfelt. "A psalm singing faker"[3] was how O'Malley viewed the sometimes pious Rickey.

Subsequent to 1948, when his initial five-year contract ran its course, Rickey worked on a year-to-year basis, thus easily leaving him open for removal by the power-hungry O'Malley. The opportunity for the Irishman came when John Smith, a strident O'Malley supporter and Brooklyn stockholder, died in July 1950. O'Malley quickly swooped in and convinced Smith's widow to turn the administration of her husband's stock in the Dodgers over to the Brooklyn Trust Company which O'Malley, incidentally, represented.

With the majority of stock now in his control, O'Malley quickly moved to rid the Dodgers of his nemesis. Rickey's contract officially was to end on October 28, but the writing was on the wall well before that, as O'Malley had no intention of retaining Rickey for another season. Rickey had taken a dreadful financial loss on a stock he held in margin, Air Reduction, and had borrowed to the limit on his life insurance. He would be without a paycheck and in dire need of employment. John Galbreath offered Rickey the opportunity of running his Pittsburgh club when the Brooklyn contract ran its course. League rules, however, prohibited Rickey from working for another club as long as he held his Brooklyn stock.

O'Malley was banking on Rickey's acute need for income and hoped he would accept virtually any offer for his Dodger stock. Rickey had paid $346,667 for the stock, which is precisely what O'Malley offered. However, the man who orchestrated the entire coup de grace did not figure on a William Zeckendorf entering the picture.

The forty-five-year-old Zeckendorf was the president of Webb and Knapp, Inc., an immense New York real estate firm. Galbreath and Zeckendorf became acquainted when the latter purchased a large portion of Hoboken, New Jersey. Zeckendorf certainly was not one to shy away from colossal transactions. He was the man who assembled the real estate that would become the United Nations. For his friend Galbreath, Zeckendorf stepped out of his role as a real estate mogul, and came forward to offer $1,000,000 for Rickey's Brooklyn stock.

O'Malley was infuriated; why would anyone tender such an exorbitant sum just to be a silent partner? O'Malley correctly theorized that

Galbreath worked as an intermediary, bringing his two friends together for what assuredly was a bogus bid. Still the furious Irishman couldn't take the chance that Zeckendorf's proposal wasn't legitimate, and reluctantly upped his own bid to match.

It wasn't bad enough that O'Malley had to meet Zeckendorf's bid: under the terms set in the 1943 Brooklyn partnership agreement, he was required to pay $50,000 to the person he outbid. When his canceled check returned, O'Malley was appalled to discover Rickey's signature directly beneath Zeckendorf's endorsement. Not only was he forced to fork over substantially more than he desired for Rickey's stock, his $50,000 also found its way into his antagonist's pocket.

O'Malley released a statement to the press expressing his sadness at the departure of his colleague. "I would like to say for the record that over the seven years that I have been with Mr. Rickey ... I have developed the warmest possible feelings for him as a man. I have admired his intense devotion to his family. I do not know of anyone who can approach Mr. Rickey in the realm of executive ability in baseball. I am terribly sorry and hurt personally that we now have to face this resignation."[4]

In Pittsburgh, Thomas P. Johnson, a Pirate vice-president, wasn't fooled by the sentiments put forth by O'Malley. "Walter hated him thoroughly," Johnson said. "Walter was so pleased to see his ass out of Brooklyn that he would have kissed him good-bye."[5]

For nearly half a century, Barney Dreyfuss, or his heirs, owned and operated the Pittsburgh Pirates. The dynasty ended August 8, 1946, when Dreyfuss's son-in-law, William Benswanger, working for the interests of Barney's widow, sold controlling interest in the club to a conglomerate headed up by Frank McKinney. McKinney, an Indianapolis banker, also purchased Forbes Field and its property in the name of the Pittsburgh Athletic Club as part of the transaction.

McKinney's partners included real estate investor and horse breeder John Galbreath, Pittsburgh attorney Thomas P. Johnson, and Hollywood star Bing Crosby. The quartet had acquired a disgruntled lot mired in mediocrity. Pittsburgh had not seen a pennant winning club for two decades, but McKinney vowed that with an infusion of capital, Pirate fortunes would certainly brighten. With the initial investment, sorely needed cosmetic upgrades to their ballpark could occur. Long thought to be one of the most aesthetically pleasing parks to the eye, Forbes Field was given a facelift. Prior to his first full season as the Pirates' owner, McKinney gave a rundown of the ownership group's early expenditures.

Left to right: Attorney David M. Lewis, Tom Johnson, and Frank McKinney.

"We have expended $518,000 rehabilitating Forbes Field, building new rest rooms, clubhouses and offices, and installing new seats. Add to this $100,000 for new concession stands and the installation of electronic refrigeration,"[6] the Pirate president reported.

Even though neither he nor any of his partners had prior baseball experience, McKinney understood that cosmetic upgrades to the ballpark would not be enough. The quality of play on the field, in the end, would determine if Pirate fans would venture to Forbes Field.

"To acquire players we have spent $238,000 in purchase prices alone," McKinney said. "The development of our farm system, that is, payment for outright ownership and working agreements comes to $200,000. We have fourteen clubs in the system and we mean to have twenty."

The new ownership quickly found that, in post–World War II baseball, buying talent was a difficult proposition. In the immediate postwar years teams held fast to aging players and resolutely refused to part with younger prospects. The Bucs did, however, have at least one "friend" who was willing to deal, and he could be found in the borough of Brooklyn, New York.

Though McKinney was the regulating partner and Roy Hamey was the team's general manager, John Galbreath would, to put it politely, on occasion play Branch Rickey's stooge. Over the course of four-and-a-half years since the McKinney takeover, Rickey sold Pittsburgh more than $2 million worth of forgettable talent. In addition to selling the Pirates his Dodger castoffs, Rickey stole gems like Preacher Roe, and Billy Cox away from Galbreath's stable. One particular transaction saw Rickey send five nondescript players to the Bucs for $300,000 and outfielder Al Gionfriddo.

"Why throw in Gionfriddo?" one scribe asked.

"Rickey needed him to carry all that gold back to the Dodgers," came the wisecrack reply.

Galbreath was browbeaten so boisterously in the local newspapers as a result of these trades that he told Rickey, "Branch, I have made my last deal with you. I like your company, but I just cannot buy another ballplayer from you ever again."

"Oh yes you will," Rickey assured his favorite pigeon. "In fact I'll bet on it." So sure that he wouldn't be duped by the old master again, Galbreath leapt at the opportunity to place a wager on this declaration. The two men laid the details of the bet. To win, Rickey would have to sell Pittsburgh a player of "more than $50,000 in value." The transaction would have to be within a year or the triumphant party would be awarded a new suit of clothes.

Before twelve months had passed, the Pirates had acquired a Dodger farm hand by the name of Monty Basgall. The price for Mr. Basgall and the 110 hits he collected over the course of three seasons as a Buccaneer was a cool $50,001. Following the deal, Rickey was wont to sport the suit he won from Galbreath and reveled in the opportunity to spin the tale of how he procured the clothing.

The honeymoon for the new Pittsburgh administration was short-lived. Four seasons under McKinney's control saw the Pirates finish eighth, fourth, sixth, and eighth again. Soon relationships among members of the ownership group were strained. "We had two prima donnas in McKinney and Galbreath, and it soon became apparent that they weren't going to hit it off," Thomas Johnson said. "I was caught in the middle, and Bing, of course, wasn't paying attention."[7]

Johnson contended that McKinney's stake in the minor league Indianapolis Indians, which was then a Pirate affiliate, often conflicted with the interests of the Pittsburgh club. "McKinney tended to run our team as a farm club for Indy," Johnson alleged.

"They would get our players and win their pennant and we'd finish eighth. It angered both Galbreath and myself. I was much younger than both so I was in the middle when they were taking pot shots at each other. Galbreath [soon] came to me and said, 'You've got to get rid of Frank.'"[8]

Johnson and McKinney sat down in Chicago at the site of the 1950 All-Star Game and discussed the uncomfortable situation. McKinney, it turned out, wanted to shed himself of what had became a burden and agreed to sell his share of the Pirates to

Thomas Johnson

Johnson and Galbreath. "Galbreath was a little better healed than myself, and bought a little more stock than I," Johnson said. "We had essentially the same amount of stock, but because of the age difference, I deferred to Galbreath as president, and I was vice-president. Bing didn't pay much attention to the business aspect."

Once knowledge of Rickey's pending availability became public, Galbreath, in his new role as president, quickly set his sights on bringing the Mahatma into the fold. "I want to make one thing clear before I talk about Mr. Rickey," Galbreath told the assembled newsmen on November 6. "Rickey approached me last summer and asked if I would be interested in helping him buy the St. Louis Browns. I told him I wasn't interested — I was completely satisfied with the Pittsburgh franchise."[9]

Galbreath was not dissuaded by Rickey's interest in returning to the Midwest. Pittsburgh had much to offer, and he was determined to convince Branch that it would be the perfect situation for him to express his baseball prowess.

"It was a hard job to sell Rickey on the idea of coming here," Galbreath explained. "We tried to sell him on the fact that we have a one-team city and a greater opportunity than in any other city. Two days later, on November 1, he agreed to come to Pittsburgh." John Galbreath then proudly introduced the latest members of the Pirate family, Branch Rickey, and his son, Branch Jr., who was following his father to Pittsburgh.

"What is your position?" Vince Johnson of the *Post-Gazette* asked following Rickey's opening statement.

"Executive vice-president and general manager," Branch replied. "I have a five-year contract with an option of a five-year renewal."

"Are you buying stock?" came Johnson's next question.

"No."

"Would you like to divulge the terms of your contract?"

"I would not."

"Are you going to give us double talk around here?" Al Tederstrom asked the notoriously garrulous Rickey.

"You know, I've been accused of that, but most of the time it isn't true," Branch claimed. "There are occasions when a man isn't free to say what he wants to say, and he must be evasive."

Jim Hilton quizzed the new Pirate general manager. "Why did you come to Pittsburgh?"

"This is a challenge," Rickey replied. "I very seriously considered other baseball offers but here you have a wonderful sports city. I would much prefer to take hold of a second division team when I change jobs than to latch onto a first division team, and rise."

Not to dispute Rickey's reasoning, but the generosity of John Galbreath certainly helped sway him to Pittsburgh. Branch's contract with the Pittsburgh Athletic Club called for him to be employed as its executive vice-president and general manager for a period of five years, commencing November 1, 1950, and ending October 31, 1955. It also decreed that Rickey would be employed in an advisory capacity for an additional period of five years, beginning November 1, 1955, and ending October 31, 1960. Compensation for the management period of the contract would be $100,000 annually. Rickey would then be paid $50,000 per year during the advisory portion of the agreement.

With Rickey's arrival in the Steel City, the Pittsburgh Pirates found themselves with two general managers, an oddity, if not a completely unique situation in the long history of baseball. Roy Hamey would be retained in his position, in name at least. However, there was little doubt that whatever trace of power he previously may have had was now surely gone. Though many in Pittsburgh viewed Rickey as a savior for their beloved Bucs, not everyone was enthralled with his entrance to the local baseball scene which pushed the hardworking Hamey aside.

"I was very upset that Galbreath didn't inform me of his intentions of bringing in Rickey," Tom Johnson complained. "John had been playing footsie with Rickey unbeknownst to me. Galbreath gave Hamey a lot of bullshit, telling him that Rickey was just coming in here as a part of ownership. I was very loyal to Hamey and felt that he had done a wonderful job for us. He [Galbreath] thought Rickey was the greatest thing since sliced cheese, and the old phony showed up here."[10]

Rickey sought to convince all who would listen that Hamey's status with the club would not be altered. "He will remain as general manager," Rickey said at the November 6 press conference. "If there is any change involving Roy, it will be in the form of a promotion."[11]

Despite that assurance, Hamey was fully aware that with the Mahatma in the picture, he was now nothing more than a figure head with no real authority. "Since Rickey entered the Pirate scene, Hamey has had nothing to do except sit around at Forbes Field." Jack Hernon reported in the *Post-Gazette*. "His only duty since the Mahatma took charge was a request from Rickey to look up the playing record of Bob Dillenger."[12]

Hamey had too much pride to stay with the Pirates and be little more than Branch Rickey's errand boy. On November 19, Roy announced his resignation from the position he had held since August 8, 1946. Though his contract was due to run through January 1952, Hamey asked that the Pirate owners release him from his obligation so he might accept an offer with the New York Yankees where he would be an assistant to general manager George Weiss.

"I very much dislike leaving here, but I just couldn't pass up the opportunity the Yankees offered," Hamey confessed. "It will give Rickey a clear road. Perhaps if I waited until my contract ran out after next year I would be a forgotten man."

A farewell party was held for the well liked Hamey at the Pittsburgh Hotel on November 27. Well-wishers, including the city's mayor, David L. Lawrence, braved the blizzard-like conditions of an early season snowstorm to pay homage to Hamey.

Speaking to the gatherers, which were comprised primarily of members of the Pittsburgh Chapter of the Baseball Writer's Association of America, the outgoing Pirate general manager discussed his successor. "Not that I have to speak for him," Hamey said. "Because, in a way, he's sort of Mr. Baseball. If anybody can give Pittsburgh a first rate ball club, he can. He has more connections, and knows more about what goes on in baseball in all leagues, than anyone else in the game. He's been around so long that there's hardly a club anywhere that doesn't include in its ranks someone who at one time or another has worked for, or with, Mr. Rickey."[13]

Hamey also optimistically informed the crowd that the Pirate minor league system was on the verge of bearing fruit. "We have considerable promising talent planted in our farm system, and it will start trickling through," Hamey pledged to his listeners. "Some of the best of it is at the bottom, perhaps several years removed from reaching the top. In the next year or two you'll be hearing from the youngsters who started out in our system a year or two ago. Once the Pirates are able to let them mature naturally they'll be all right."[14]

Who would guide the 1951 club on the playing field was still in question. Bill Meyer, manager of the Bucs since 1948, was one season into a two-year contract but Rickey was making no promises. "As of now," Branch said in the middle of November. "Bill Meyer is still the manager of the Pirates. But I will have final word about this job at the winter meetings at St. Petersburg, December 12."

Though he made some overtures to former Cleveland Indian great Lou Boudreau about the possibility of managing the Pirates, Rickey did not conduct an excavating search for Meyer's replacement. En route to the winter meetings, Rickey stopped off in Knoxville, Tennessee, to meet briefly with Meyer. Still in the dark, and not knowing if he would return to Pittsburgh, Meyer boldly pressed the Pirate general manager. "You give me the ballplayers, and I'll run the club," Meyer told Rickey, "and when I tell you I can't use a certain fellow, I want your support. You stand behind me and my ballclub won't have any disciplinary problems."

Meyer had good reason to make such demands. Though most local writers found him to be a perfectly capable strategist, the Pirate skipper still found himself under fire in the Pittsburgh dailies. A prevalent criticism among the scribes contended that Meyer was too "easy going," and "the club had gotten away from him."[15] Both complaints were common phrases in baseball vernacular which implied Meyer's players lacked proper respect for their leader.

Meyer's insistence that he retain control of the club on the field stemmed from the frustration of working under a meddling Frank McKinney. "I went to Frank McKinney during the 1950 season," Meyer told Rickey, "and asked him to get rid of a half dozen players who weren't doing me any good. Frank refused. He said he had too much invested in the players. Well, the players knew I was stuck with them, so they had me on the spot. Hell, who could have discipline?"

The Pittsburgh manager wasn't the only member of the Pirate family to have his hands tied while working under McKinney. Roy Hamey, an astute baseball man, was little more than a figurehead in his position as general manager. "At times, when Roy was the Pirates' general manager, we couldn't do some of the things we wanted, but not because Hamey didn't try," Meyer related. "He was just blocked by a higher official at times. That situation was cleared up when Mr. Galbreath brought Rickey to Pittsburgh."[16]

Surely Rickey had already made his decision prior to setting sail for Knoxville, but the old man most certainly was pleased with the confidence and honesty excised by Meyer. After a brief pause, Rickey stuck out his hand and declared, "Bill, you're my man."[17]

Rickey wanted to assure his manager that, despite numerous reports to the contrary, he did not manage the club from the front office. "Running the team is your department," he told his field general. "I'll run the office, and you run the field."[18]

Rickey's decision to retain Meyer was met with cynicism by New York *Post* columnist Jimmy Cannon, "The continued employment of Billy Meyer as [the] manager of Pittsburgh," Cannon penned, "not only appeals to Branch Rickey's stinginess, but grants him the perfect fall guy who can be tripped up and dumped if the team flops."[19]

From Knoxville Rickey continued on to St. Petersburg, where he spoke to a gaggle of newsmen and rationalized his decision of retaining Meyer for the upcoming campaign. "I have spent much time pondering the decision, and it was only after I considered all possible angles to the eighth place Pirates of last season," Rickey explained.

"The Pirates ran into a defeatist psychology, and as manager Meyer should have fought it more vigorously. He permitted himself to drop into a similar frame of mind. There was no extension, or new contract for Meyer," he emphasized. "In forty years of baseball none of my managers was ever given a contract for more than one year's duration."[20]

The reporters hurled a volley of questions at the invariably cooperative Rickey, including one concerning the prospects of obtaining a working agreement with Hollywood of the Pacific Coast League. "Pittsburgh just doesn't have the materials to supply another roster." Rickey replied. "Supplying players to Indianapolis [then the Bucs top farm club] would be difficult enough."

Because of Rickey's tendency in the past to dispose of high priced players most scribes had already assumed that the Pirates' premier and highest paid player, Ralph Kiner, was as good as gone. "We don't have enough Kiners on the Pittsburgh club, so why would I trade the one I have? We don't intend on trading Kiner," Branch insisted.

In fact, Rickey didn't anticipate much action in St. Petersburg. "I never saw so much reluctance on the part of people to discuss trades. At Pittsburgh we do not have much trading material. Pittsburgh finished in last place on merit."[21]

Rickey's efforts to right the Corsairs' ship was hindered by events much larger than the game of baseball. The conflict in Korea was looming over the country and, subsequently, professional baseball. Though few doubted that President Truman would request that organized baseball desist for the duration of the war, many wondered how the game would be affected. Reporters that greeted Rickey's arrival in Florida asked for the Mahatma's thoughts on the subject.

"We can make quick and proper adjustments in case of total mobilization," Rickey answered. "Baseball and the government were able to adjust things for the last war and we should be able to tackle the job once more."

"But," he cautiously added, "baseball would stop instantly if not properly related to the all-out effort of the war."[22]

"Sport in a nation reveals more accurately the characteristics of its people than does war," Rickey lectured. "In these days of international unrest, it is good that our continent finds in competitive sport its basic preparation for the unknown national emergencies that may face us. Sport has most of the virtues of war, and none of the vices."[23]

Baseball commissioner Albert "Happy" Chandler also chimed in on the topic. "I don't know what we will be asked, or whether we'll even be approached," baseball's leader told reporters in St. Petersburg. "But if we are, we are prepared to do anything asked of us. Baseball never has, and never will, ask for any special favors. I don't know whether we will have total mobilization. Even if we did, I have no idea what the consequence will be. Nobody does."[24]

Chandler had recently met with President Harry Truman and informed the commander in chief that the world of baseball would do anything asked of it. The fiery Truman assured Chandler that every effort would be made not to disrupt the National Pastime. "There was total mobilization in the last war," the commissioner reminded listeners, "and baseball survived it. I know the machinery for total mobilization has been set up ... in the event of total mobilization it could have the effect of stopping baseball."

Because of the comparative youth of the Pirates, Rickey, more than most general managers in the league, had to consider the implications of the draft while preparing to mold his club for the upcoming season. The drafting of Catfish Metkovich from the Oakland Oaks, and the signing of Pete Reiser as a free agent were two such preparatory transactions. Both men were thirty years old and therefore relatively safe from the selective service draft.

"Some things are going to be done with the Pirates [that] don't fit into our plans for a championship team," Rickey clarified after bringing in Metkovich and Reiser, two men who had certainly seen their best playing days pass. "But we are definitely going to have in mind a war time ball club if the occasion arises."[25]

"We're taking precautions for wartime," Rickey explained. "I'm tripling our scouting staff. I'm confident that unless we have an all-out war, I will be able to show some progress in a couple of years. If there is an atomic war, it will last ten days. If we win, baseball will go on to still greater heights. If we lose, well we must not think in those terms. If contrary to my beliefs it develops into a long war, the job of baseball will be even more vital than it was in World War II, insofar as the stay at homes are concerned."[26]

The draft status of the Pirate forty-man roster at the major league meetings was as follows: Shortstop Danny O'Connell and pitcher Bill MacDonald had already been called into service. A half dozen other men on the forty-man roster were susceptible to be called up before the season began. The only player among the six thought to be a starter, Gus Bell, was married and had one child. Dale Coogan, Al Grunwald, and Bob Thompson were also eligible, although Thompson was also married with a child. Rookie hurlers Paul Pettit, who was recently wed, and Bob Friend, were also prime draft age.

Three players, Ed Fitzgerald, Clyde McCullough, and Ray Mueller were veterans of World War II, married, and with children. Pitcher Harry

Fisher was also a veteran and a Canadian citizen. Four Buc fly chasers were single and veterans, including Kiner, who was a member of the Naval Reserves. It was unlikely that any of the twenty-eight would be recalled for active duty.

One thing was certain: no ballplayer would be classified 4-F and be allowed to continue his professional career. George Marshall, the Secretary of Defense, declared that professional athletes with physical defects, unlike World War II, would not be permitted to be labeled 4-F. In some cases these men would be called for limited duty.

"If an athlete has a punctured eardrum he will be inducted because men with punctured eardrums are taken," Assistant Secretary of Defense Anna Rosenberg explained. The new policy required 4-Fs in all professionals to be called for non-combat duty ... if they were deemed qualified.

Complaints were lodged during the second World War when seemingly able-bodied men played baseball for a living, yet were not qualified for the armed forces because of their 4-F status. This was not the fault of professional baseball, but the policy of the selective service. The chairman of the House Armed Services Committee, Carl Vinson, expressed what many felt. "There is reason to be disturbed when we see a great baseball player, a great football player, or some prize fighter, is 4-F, and able to draw $10,000 a year, do all the hard work of a star athlete, but never the less can't carry a rifle, throw a grenade, or do kitchen police work because he isn't able," Vinson said.[27]

Another decision brought about because of the war would directly affect major league players. The Wage Stabilization Board placed the salaries of baseball players under government control. This decision would place a ceiling on the top level players on each major and minor league team. Lesser players could be given merit raises, provided the increase did not exceed the salary of the team's highest paid player in 1950.

The player most affected by this ruling was the Cardinals' Stan Musial, who was given a $35,000 raise over his $50,000 salary of the previous year. National League president Ford Frick thought the ruling was essentially the same as the one enforced during World War II. "It means," Frick explained, "that any club can raise a player's salary up to the maximum amount paid by that club during 1950 without asking for permission. In the case of contracts calling for more money than was paid the top star in 1950, it will be necessary to obtain permission. The money would be held in escrow until the case could be settled."[28]

While in Florida, Rickey attended and spoke at a dinner held in the honor of Commissioner Chandler. Addressing the assemblage he eloquently explained in heartfelt and patriotic tones why baseball, even in a time of war, was still vital to the health of the republic.

"Baseball is an American game — integral part of our life in this country," Rickey began. "Professional baseball is a business, but if it is anything worth-while at all, it is a business of service.

"And now the war is taking our young men. It should — it must. The war took young men in the first World War, and baseball adjusted its business quickly and effectively. It continued with the full approval of the Government. The teams were made up of old men and under age boys.

"The Government in that war, and in the last one, at great expense and with careful planning and thorough organization, undertook to relax the tension of the man in uniform. The stage, the movies, indeed the artists of this country in the field of literature and music, gave diversion and entertainment to the men in the camps and even in the trenches. The athletic program was actively promoted by the Army, Navy, and the Air Forces.

"Recreation is as essential as you can make it when a man's mind is continuously directed toward learning 'how to kill.' It is good for boys to seek and find recreation and to be recreated as much as they can.

"And it's good for a people to work hard, to toil and sweat, but they work better if they can so manage their time that they can throw some sway, so to speak.

"If we can help it, tears must not be continuous, and sorrow must not be broken. Habitual distress may lead to a sense of futility, and anything that tends to break that up is a good thing. It is therefore important that we keep the morale of our people high. You can't win games or a war without a high morale. If baseball doesn't sense that obligation, it should not be.

"All sports, everywhere, must adjust to the war effort. It must really be conducive to an early and favorable ending.

"This game of baseball is typically American and it must, and will, lend itself freely and unselfishly to the overall purposes of our Government. We are all loyal citizens of our country and that means we must be willing servants of our country. I think on this basis baseball can properly endure."[29]

2. Heaven Help the Pirates

John Galbreath expressed no concern that expenses would increase exorbitantly with Rickey at the helm. "We have the money," Galbreath assured, "and should we run out, we'll get some more."[1]

The Pirate president was in Wilmington, Delaware, on business when an Associated Press reporter caught up with him. The enterprising writer was trying to verify reports that Rickey was attempting to gain controlling interest in the Pittsburgh ball club. "I am not considering selling controlling interest in the Pirates," Galbreath emphatically stated. He admitted, however, that Rickey purchased a small amount of stock as a token investment, which gave the general manager a place on the Pirate Board of Directors.

The newest Pirate stockholder took to the road as the new year began. On January 8, Rickey was in Montreal, making one of his numerous off-season appearances where he spoke before the Canadian Club. There writers questioned Rickey about a column written by Jimmy Powers of the New York *Daily News*. Powers alleged that Rickey was behind a movement at the major league meetings in St. Petersburg to oust Commissioner Chandler. "[Rickey] engineered the action with the help of Bob Carpenter of the Phillies and Bill DeWitt of the Braves," Powers wrote.

"A complete fabrication, manufactured nothingness," Rickey said, as he vehemently denied Power's assertion. "I didn't even attend any of the meetings where Chandler's dismissal was discussed," Rickey claimed.

He wouldn't divulge to the newsmen, though, how the Pittsburgh club voted on the Chandler matter. "It was a secret ballot," he said, "and the clubs weren't at liberty to divulge how they voted."

From Montreal, Rickey flew to Buffalo where he sat before the annual sports-writers and sportscasters March of Dimes dinner, held at the Hotel Statler. "In many of our colleges and universities, no sound knowledge of American history is required for entrance," Rickey preached to the audience. Branch complained that some college professors he had met accepted "the Communist ideology without having read the speeches

John Galbreath

of Jefferson or Madison, and without fundamental knowledge of the Bill of Rights, or the Declaration of Independence."[2]

If Rickey was anything, he was a staunch believer of inherent American ideals, and he proudly wore his patriotism on his sleeve. Nothing was more un–American than Godless Communism, and Rickey gladly appropriated any forum to preach the perils of its tenets.

Montreal and Buffalo were just two stops on Rickey's winter itinerary which saw him make numerous addresses to audiences across the land. The subject matter of his speeches varied widely, from the state of baseball to the state of the country, and everything in between. Given a microphone and an attentive congregation, Rickey could sermonize on any topic under the stars.

"Words sprang from his lips, endless and countless, like water in a foamy pirouette before the multi-colored lights of a fountain," was one writer's description of Rickey in action.[3] The Mahatma would use his propensity for eloquent verbiage to his advantage when discussing contracts with his players. He could string a dizzying torrent of words to great effect when seated across from one of his players. The less educated the listener, the more transfixed the listener would be.

His loquacious commentaries weren't necessary for his first contract negotiations of the season. Pirate coach emeritus Honus Wagner was the first member of the club to visit Forbes Field and discuss his contract for the upcoming season. "He is, without a doubt, the best player baseball ever knew," Rickey testified. "I'm glad I never had to talk salary with him, as I probably would have offered the ballpark to have him play for me,"[4] Rickey admitted with a chuckle.

The soon to be seventy-seven-year-old Wagner had been with the club in a coaching capacity since 1933, but he no longer had any tangible duties. Out of respect for the old Dutchman's brilliant career and affectionately engaging personality, Honus was permitted to "have the run of Forbes Field as long as he lives."[5]

"Imagine this," an astonished Rickey relayed, "during our talk, Honus asked if I would mind if he didn't accompany the Pirates to spring training this year. 'It's a little too much for me now,' he said."

Rickey continued, "Well for a minute I didn't know what to say. The only answer I could give Honus was to tell him anything he wanted to do was all right with me."

Signing Wagner was merely a formality as Honus had been working for the same token salary for years. For Rickey, the real test of his negotiating prowess would commence after he mailed player contracts for the upcoming campaign. Rickey was notorious in baseball circles for his proclivity toward low-balling his players come contract time. Jimmy Powers had little appreciation for Rickey's methods and would often deride the then Dodger general manager. "A tightfisted man who paid his players coolie salaries," Powers wrote of the Mahatma. The New York *Daily News* columnist also stuck Rickey with the defamatory tag, "El Cheapo." Warranted or not, it was a designation that stayed with, and infuriated, Rickey.

"Money isn't anymore important to Rickey than legs are to Betty Grable," Jimmy Cannon wrote in the New York *Post*. "But his flunkies brag he seldom has the price of a newspaper on him when he makes his incessant pilgrimages of enlightenment among the hicks. Traveling empty is supposed to qualify him as an impractical dreamer who has the unselfish impulses of the pure at heart seized by a holy cause."[6]

The "El Cheapo" tag was born in 1943 after Rickey had rid the

Dodgers of several veteran players, including Joe Medwick, Dolph Camilli, and Whitlow Wyatt. Shortly after the unpopular deals, Powers unveiled the nickname, and Rickey was hung in effigy in front of Borough Hall in Flatbush. Some of Rickey's transactions were simply good baseball decisions, while others were monetarily motivated. Trying to substantiate Power's allegation one must first separate myth from fact. Unfortunately the two often meld together, and some stories of Rickey's actions take on legendary standing.

Bill Veeck, a baseball executive who spoke from the experience of numerous dealings with Rickey, insisted the Mahatma had a foot pedal under his desk that would activate a bell which caused a telephone to ring.* Rickey would be in the course of contract deliberations with a player when the phone would ring. On the other end of the line would be one of Rickey's scouting directors, who as fate would have it, was phoning to inform the boss about a magnificent prospect, who, by chance, happened to play the same position as the young man with whom Rickey was currently engaged. At the conclusion of the telephone call, the player in question invariably would sign for the terms presented by Rickey, lest he lose his job to an upstart.

The cartoonist employed by the New York dailies profited from Rickey's penny pinching reputation and never failed to capitalize on the material. Caricatures of Rickey as Scrooge offering a naïve country boy the option of a new shotgun, a choice fishing rod, or much-deserved cash were popular. Other lampoons depicted Rickey as the overseer on his "plantation" of young prospects.

His reputation as a skinflint had certainly preceded him to Pittsburgh, but the writers in that city were giving Rickey the benefit of the doubt. The new Pirate general manager put on a facade for the newsmen, feigning apprehension as he embarked upon negotiating with Pirate players for the first time. "I have not had a holdout in many years, but I have not had a last place club in a great many years ... thirty two to be exact."

Rickey had the full intention of using the Pirate's futile 1950 season to his advantage. "How could they possibly be asking for more money when the team finished so poorly?" Rickey would sermonize the petitioners. He intended on using this psychological approach when dealing

---

*Others told tales similar to Veeck, but believed Rickey had his secretary ring him at a preordained time.

with any Buc who might believe the contract offered by management was inequitable. Ideally, the player would walk out of the Mahatma's office thankful that his salary was cut *only* ten percent, such was the effectiveness of Rickey's persuasive negotiating maneuvers.

Rickey quickly learned that these, and some of his other time worn tactics, lost none of their potency in his new locale. During a three-day period in the last week of February, Rickey came to terms, *his* terms, with six different Pirates for the ensuing season.

Clyde McCullough came to Pittsburgh from his home in Roanoke, Virginia, and the thirty-four-year-old backstop left his sit-down with his new Pirate boss pleased with the outcome. "He's a finer man than I ever thought," the major-league veteran of nine years gushed. "My new contract is better than I bargained for. We talked for three hours, but it only took a few minutes to reach an agreement. I never talked with a finer person. I've been in baseball sixteen years and nobody ever showed such an interest in me."[7]

Stan Rojek was another Buc that left Rickey's Forbes Field office with a smile on his face, another disciple witnessing at the feet of the Mahatma. "Mr. Rickey is the fairest man I ever dealt with," Rojek said. "He treated me like a father. I can't understand all the talk of Mr. Rickey being tightfisted. I played for Mr. Rickey in Brooklyn, and when I walked in on him the other day at Forbes Field he greeted me like a long lost son. He made me feel at home. Made me feel important, as though signing me was the biggest event of his life."

Rickey's bombastic charm clearly swayed the men with whom he negotiated. Rojek's account of his conference with Rickey was akin to the account other players gave of their negotiating sessions. Business was, more often than not, a secondary topic of conversation. "I spent a little more than two hours with him, but I don't think our actual contract talk lasted two minutes," Rojek revealed. "We talked of everything, the war, his grandchildren, my milk business. He asked me to place myself in his position, and we actually changed chairs. I impersonated Mr. Rickey, and he impersonated Stan Rojek. I even smoked one of his cigars, but I couldn't use the big words he does, and I couldn't make my eyebrows dance like he can."

Rickey did such a brilliant job of courting his subjects that his players would walk out of his office satisfied, regardless of the conditions agreed to in their contract. Cynics would even suggest that it wouldn't be too far fetched to believe that a naïve player under Rickey's spell could be convinced to *pay* the club, such was the privilege of playing big league ball.

"How did I do with him?" Rojek replied to Les Biederman's question. "I came down here to fight against a twenty-five percent cut. In exchange for the same terms I received for 1950 (which for Rojek was a fifteen percent cut from 1949) I pledged complete loyalty, one-hundred percent co-operation, and my promise that I would do better in 1951 than I did in 1950.

"Not many people understand Mr. Rickey. He kept impressing me on that he faced a terrific challenge with the Pirates and insisted he must have a winner. Knowing him as I do, it can't be any other way while he's top man here."[8]

Rickey used the inept play of the 1950 Pirates to strengthen his bargaining position. That group of Buccos, according to Les Biederman of the Pittsburgh *Press*, lacked hustle, were absent of spirit, and generally had a lackadaisical attitude. For the privilege to don a Pittsburgh uniform in 1951, Rickey's subjects gave an oath of commitment to expunge

Rickey gives a spring training talk to his troops.

the sins of the previous season and excise the stigma attached to the Pirate organization. This approach proved successful as Rickey had no holdouts, and his minions excitedly charged into the upcoming campaign determined to gratify their new mentor.

Pomp and Circumstance abounded as the Bucs pulled into California for the first spring training of Rickey's regime. The San Bernardino High School Band was at the train station to merrily greet the club's traveling party when they arrived on the morning of February 28. With brass horns blaring, the band marched through the boulevards of San Bernardino leading the Pirate team bus and the accompanying police escort to the California Hotel where a large banner saluted the team, "Welcome Pirates, We Want You in '52," it read.

Meyer would not have a repeat of the debacle of 1950. Before his team would take to the field for the first time, Bill gathered his troops and laid down the law. He informed them of some new regulations that would be strictly enforced. Meyer deeply resented the accusation in the press that he was too "easy going." The reward for his evenhanded managerial approach was a last place finish. Now, with Rickey fully supporting him in the front office, Meyer felt comfortable in becoming much more of a taskmaster. If his ballclub was going to finish in last place, it would not be because he was running a loose ship.

"You must be in your room at 11:30 every night. All lights out by midnight," Meyer commanded. "Any violation of that rule and you'll find yourself in a jam. You'll find me tough if you disobey. And by order of Rickey, absolutely no drinking will be permitted. On the question of drinking intoxicants I can tell you he is strict, so let my warning be your guide."[9] Previously the Bucs had been allowed to consume beer in the clubhouse or have a cocktail on the team train. No longer, though, would these vices be indulged by the club.

"Most of you know that everyone on the Pittsburgh club fell down in 1950. I am including myself in this report. I made mistakes and will try to correct them in the coming race. In other words, the last place finish was partly my fault, and of players here now. This is a good time to say that things must change. If we hustle for the next six months, everybody on this club will be happy when the race ends."

While Meyer was meeting with his players, Rickey was speaking with several writers asking the newsmen to please steer clear of the lectures he intended to give to his new club. "If you boys sat through the meetings, I might have to hold myself back with the players," he explained. "It would handicap you boys in the future, even though I know you would keep my confidence."[10]

"Today, March 1, 1951, the Pittsburgh club is not looking forward to finishing in seventh place, nor sixth, fifth, fourth, or anywhere else. We are shooting for first place.

"Now you fellows know it won't be this year," Branch assured the gathered scribes as laughter reverberated throughout the room, "but these boys are going to be impressed with the thought of setting their sights on only one spot, first place. We'll get there. When we will reach that objective is the problem we start working on today.

"When I finish my talks with the players, they will start thinking in terms of first place... We're on our way boys so stick around and see the fun."

The title of the much ballyhooed lecture would be, "Why Finish Last?" Though they weren't welcome in the meeting, the press reported widely on the address, gathering information from the players present.

"Analyze things for yourself," Rickey advised his men. "Think back on how many of you are endowed with better than average abilities as hitters, runners, and throwers. Then think how many times you've tried to improve yourselves in a department where you may not even be average. This game is one of perfection. A player must try to excel in every department."[11]

A few Bucs demonstrated the apathetic attitude of the 1950 team and wandered into the lecture tardy. These recalcitrant Pirates were greeted with a damning glare from Rickey, who most certainly made a mental note of the derelict parties. Refocusing on the attentive gathering, he continued by pointing out to his "boys" that there were a number of similarities between themselves and their opponents in the senior circuit.

"You have the same number of eyes, ears, arms, and legs," Rickey informed the youthful, and apparently unworldly, group. "You compare favorably with their weight and age. So why last place?"

Rickey did not pause before launching into a tale of a traveling man who engaged another traveler in a game of chess. "At that game the men were fairly even," he told the players. "So the first man challenged his rival to a game of checkers.

"Quickly reaching into his bag, the first man pulled out a checker board and prepared to play a game, but the second man refused to be suckered into a match that obviously was his opponent's best game.

"That is the way baseball is in some cases," Rickey explained after telling the yarn. "A team will have one or two players who are near great in some department, while the opposition may be average. But their efforts to excel at everything will overcome the few individuals."

"Think it over boys, and see if I'm not right. Of course the last place finish wasn't solely the players' fault. Maybe it was the manager, or the front office. Regardless of where the blame lies, we are going to find out and remedy the mistakes.

"I want to make one thing clear," he advised his men. "I'm here to get better acquainted with you fellows and I want you to know me better. I don't think I'm as bad as I've been painted." Then, to clarify an opinion often expressed by his critics during his tenure in Brooklyn, "I'm not trying to manage this club. We have a very able manager in Bill Meyer. But I do know there are a couple of New York columnists who will read of this meeting and immediately say, 'Oh, oh, Rickey is taking charge already.'

"As you may know, I don't pay attention to won-lost averages. I watch the innings pitched, hits allowed, and the strikeouts, and base on balls. That's my guide, and on that basis I can see why you might have finished last."

In spite of vowing to leave the on-field decisions to his manager, Rickey suggested that Kiner be moved from left field to first base. Meyer didn't see the recommendation as meddling, but rather good advice from a wise baseball man. "We need more power in the infield, and shifting Kiner there could solve the problem," the Buc manager said.

Kiner disagreed with the conclusion, but had little choice but to follow along faithfully with the dictate. "I got the chance to talk to other players, the first base coaches, and the umpire," Kiner reported of his new social surroundings. "Maybe when I get into a slump, I won't have much time to think about it if I continue at first base."[12]

Rickey also advised Meyer on another roster move. Unlike the Kiner proposal, the suggestion that the twenty-five-year-old Dale Long be given a chance to back up Clyde McCullough behind the plate was unconventional. Long was a southpaw.

"Why not a left-handed catcher?" Rickey asked anyone within earshot. Suffering from the remnants of a bout with the flu, Branch wore a stylish beret for protection from the elements as he strolled about the fields pitching his latest idea. "I think a reliable left-handed thrower can be a major-league player in any position except shortstop. I admit a southpaw would be in a jam trying to field a smash in the hole."[13]

The knowledgeable baseball veteran of five decades cited his theory as to why a left-handed receiver was an anomaly in the game. "The reason we're accustomed to right-handed catchers is because when the game started almost every batter was right-handed. Later Ty Cobb showed what a left-handed hitter could do and more followed. Now we have lineups that can produce four or five, or maybe six left-handed batters in a game. Why not a left-handed catcher?" the old man asked again, as if he were trying to convince himself as much as his audience that his was a sound idea.

"He would be in a better position to throw to first base with a left-handed hitter at bat. He could be in a better position to throw after fielding bunts. The only objection I can see is that it would be against custom. It seldom has been done. But why shouldn't we try it? My main reason for trying this idea was that I'm thinking in terms of the future. Not necessarily 1951, or 1952, but 1953."

Long, a native of Springfield, Missouri, was introduced to Rickey for the first time in San Bernardino. "What's your father's name?" Branch asked.

Without missing a beat Long replied, "Mr. Long, sir."

The exuberant Long cared not one iota at which position his manager penciled his name, "I want to play ball in the majors, and I'll play anywhere," he dutifully said. "I actually caught a game in high school, but I had to use a glove made for a player's left hand."[14] Long would have a glove to fit his right hand. Rickey made sure that his player had the correct equipment by requesting to the Rawlings Company that they prepare two mitts for the left-hander.

Once the press caught wind of Rickey's latest experiment, photographers descended on the Bucs' camp from the media-heavy city of Los Angeles to document the unusual sight of a southpaw receiver.

Perhaps publicity was Rickey's end goal with the Long machination. Pittsburgh had been deprived of substantial notice in the national sport pages since the early days of the McKinney administration. The new ownership group had been greeted with much fanfare in 1946 — not solely because the men were replacing the Dreyfuss dynasty in Pittsburgh, but thanks in large part to the inclusion of Bing Crosby.

Crosby, in addition to being a best-selling recording artist, was also a star on the silver screen, having appeared in numerous movies. Perhaps most notable among Bing's films were the "Road" movies with sidekick Bob Hope. His inclusion in the McKinney group was Crosby's third stab at ownership of a major league franchise. His first attempt, a bid for the Boston Braves, was stymied by then commissioner Kenesaw Mountain Landis, who disapproved of Crosby's horse racing interest. Several years later, following Landis' death, Crosby was part of a conglomerate that tried to acquire the Cleveland Indians. That group fell short in the bidding process, losing out to another aggregation which included Crosby's pal, Bob Hope.

After McKinney, through Tom Johnson, invited Crosby to join their purchase of the Pirates, the comic duo had a new stage from which they dispensed their act. "There's one thing certain," Hope smirked when he heard the news of the new Pittsburgh owners. "Crosby can't hurt the Pirates. They're dead already."

Pausing for a rim shot heard only in his own mind, Hope wisecracked, "I've finally found out why Crosby sold his horses during the meat shortage. It was because he had a new racket in mind. He'll probably use Frank Sinatra as a bat."[15]

Crosby returned the barbs to his screen partner, "I don't think Bob Hope's Indians will ever play the Pirates," he declared. "After all, we throw overhand in this league."

The one-liners flowed hard and fast, "I don't know how much money Bob Hope put into the Cleveland Indians, but it couldn't have been much after they cut open his underwear."

"Hope says he used to be a ballplayer himself. I tried to look up his record, but there isn't much data on that era. Hope had one great talent as a player. He was the only man who could steal second base with his nose without taking his feet off first. The trouble was that nobody could figure out a way to get him to first base."

The proximity of the Bucs' training camp in San Bernardino to Crosby's home in Hollywood coaxed "Der Bingle" out to the ballpark for an exhibition game between the Pirates and Hope's Indians. The world famous singer was treated to a dose of humility when the ticket taker at the ballpark didn't recognize him and insisted that Bing fork over $1.25 for his ducat. Bob Rice, the Pirates' traveling secretary, was informed of the faux pas and refunded the money to Crosby. The misunderstanding inspired a writer to quip, "Passes are about the only dividend Bing can collect for his $250,000 investment in the Pirates."[16]

The following afternoon Crosby took in a game with Rickey and his wife during which he was given a discourse from the master. "You may be sure I derived considerable benefit out of the opportunity to sit with you and talk and get first hand your personal views of some of the aspects of the Pittsburgh situation," Crosby wrote in a letter to Rickey. "I was also considerably edified by your disclosure of your aims and intentions, and although my opinion on baseball is practically worthless, I am adult and quasi-intelligent, and I don't believe I have to be a baseball expert to appreciate that you are on the right track, and that your goal or an approximation thereof will certainly be achieved within the time you have allotted yourself. I am with you a thousand percent and if there is any-

Branch with wife, Jane, at Forbes Field.

thing I can do out here at anytime, don't hesitate to call upon me and if it is within my power I shall certainly do it."[17]

The Pittsburgh Pirates version of the "era of good feeling" was in full bloom. For the time being Rickey's word was taken on faith as Pittsburgh ownership, the team's players, the city's press, and fans of the club, were hypnotized by Rickey's exhortations of the good times that lie ahead. Reality, however, quickly caught up with Rickey's hyperbole. With training camp came the true state of the Pirate ballclub as Rickey witnessed firsthand the shortage of quality players on the Pittsburgh roster. The evaluations became more evenhanded, yet optimism was still abundant, as Rickey urged that salvation was just around the corner.

"Last place clubs should be adventurous," Rickey declared during his first interview with Pittsburgh beat writers. "We can take chances with the young fellows, where a pennant contender couldn't afford to do that, but second division clubs can."[18]

The newsmen were pleased to finally have the opportunity to speak with Rickey. Throughout the spring, scribes had attempted to nail down the Mahatma for a brief chat, but were continually frustrated in their efforts. "He moves too fast, and the phones ring too often," moaned Les Biederman of the Pittsburgh *Press.*

The initial group interview took place in the midst of a car ride from San Bernardino to Los Angeles where Rickey was to attend a luncheon in honor of outgoing commissioner Happy Chandler. The beat writers leapt at the chance to join the commute, an ideal, if not unorthodox venue for an interview. In a moving vehicle, the scribes reasoned, Rickey couldn't be interrupted by a ringing telephone or visitors dropping in during the conversation.

"We're going to use as many of the kids this year as we possibly can," Rickey told his companions. "We're thinking of rising and when we do reach a contending position, we'll remain there, not recede."[19]

Rickey's sunny outlook was not based on the reality of the talent he possessed, but in the firm conviction that he could build a productive farm system for the Pittsburgh organization. The Pirates roaming the San Bernardino ballfields were a ramshackle fusion of has-beens, several legitimate prospects, a number of suspects, and a sprinkling of actual viable major-league players.

Wally Westlake, the Pirates' right fielder, was the only player on the roster that would bring value on the trade market. Kiner, though considered a star and desired by several teams around the league, would not bring enough talent and cash in return to justify the loss at the gate a Kinerless team would spell. Branch had vastly underestimated the job that awaited him when he agreed to join up with Galbreath. In addition to a major league roster that deservedly finished in last place, the farm system was almost totally void of talent.

At the close of spring training, Rickey sat down to pen his impressions of the men who would represent the Pirates on the playing field. More a commentary than scouting report, these observations present Rickey at his most irreverent:

McCULLOUGH, Clyde
> I believe McCullough is overbearing and perhaps bombastically so. With certain people he is domineering. His tendency is to tear down an individual, and not ever to build him up. It is said by one who is generally considered a conservative and competent observer that he is the most destructive influence on the Pittsburgh club, a morale breaker. Another chap, Rip Sewell, told me that the greatest service I could render the club would be to get McCullough off the

team for the sake of producing a winning club; that he is a show-off;
a pretender, — likes him personally, and has never had any difficulties at anytime with him....

REISER, Pete

Without a doubt, a confirmed neurotic. Ability today, and none
tomorrow. As volatile as alcohol and seeks an easy and common level
as conveniently as any fluid. He can hit and run, and throw passi-
bly, — as great, indeed, as probably his neuroticism will permit. I
leave your curiosity at this point for oral exposition. He reminds me
of the fellow who jumped out of the 20th story window. In the games
to date, he has passed the 10th floor and he is all right so far....

DICKSON, Murry

Dickson is a scatterbrain, which may explain a scatterarm.... A
pitching staff of ten Dicksons would finish about mid-way in the
race.

He reminds me of the fellow in the army who complained of
every job given to him and was unsatisfactory in all of them and
finally was given the job of sorting potatoes. At the end of two days,
the sergeant asked him how he liked his new work, and he said, "Terrible, I don't like it all, — it almost worries me to death." "What worries you?" said the sergeant, and the reply was, "The damn decisions."
I will say Dickson reminds me of that chap. He ought to be a really
great pitcher....

CHAMBERS, Cliff

He could have been the Illinois democrat politician who supported Lincoln and came to General McClernand whom Sherman
fired. Later, McClernand wrote his "memoirs", and asked Uncle Abe
to write the preface and Uncle Abe did write it, and this is what he
said. "This is a good book for those who like this kind of book."...

PETTITT, Paul

He could be an embryonic neurotic. Complains a great deal.
Ailing so frequently — fearful all the time lest, for example, his elbow
will get sore "again".... One day "he has it." The next day he
doesn't....

PIERRO, Bill

A blatherhead. Typical low grade Brooklynese. Hedonistic. A six
footer or more with a paper thin body, a troublesome but transparent head, who can throw a ball harder and with more skills than his
150 pounds entitle him to do. Certain functional organs dominate

him to such an extent that his judgment, practices, and consequent habits are completely subordinated. In other words, he does not put duty or fidelities to his job or to other people first. He does not care enough about success in his work....

ROJEK, Stanley
   If it be true that God's universal redeeming grace is proved by salvation of one soul that was lost, then Rojek is the evidence. The lost lamb has returned to the moral fold. I do not think he should be classed as a matrimonial coward. Outside of his physical virility, I doubt if he has much to offer.[20]

One month of exhibition games was more than enough time to evaluate the sorry state of the Pirate pitching corps. "Our pitching simply isn't good enough," Rickey said, "and we would like to take on some additional men in this department. I doubt if one man on this club feels sure of himself as a major-league pitcher."
   The quartet of moundsmen who would take on the bulk of the workload, Cliff Chambers, Murry Dickson, Bill Werle, and Vernon Law, had a combined ERA that approached 4.50.
   The dearth of quality arms on the club concerned Rickey greatly. "We need help there, plenty of help," he confessed to Al Abrams of the Pittsburgh *Post-Gazette*. "We don't have any depth. A ballclub needs pitching to get anywhere."[21]
   Other than Kiner and Westlake, the starting eight for the Pirates was adequate at best. The great majority of the position players on the club had seen better days. With Danny O'Connell, who was just twenty-four, called into the service, only David "Gus" Bell among the team's regulars, could be considered, in baseball terms at least, young. The year 1950 saw a twenty-one-year-old Bell enjoy a solid, if not spectacular rookie season when he batted .282 and drove in 53 runs in only 111 games. The Bucs, however lacking in playing ability they may have been, tried to make up for those deficiencies with All-Star-caliber characters.
   "Pistol" Pete Reiser was well on his way to the Hall of Fame, and very well may have found himself in Cooperstown had the outfield walls in National League ballparks not kept getting in his way. In 1941 Reiser led the league in doubles, triples, runs scored, batting average, and concrete walls crashed into. Then with the Brooklyn Dodgers, he played center field as if there were no enclosed boundaries, hell-bent to catch anything within the confines of the ball yard. Concrete and brick walls,

however, are immobile, which Reiser unfortunately discovered the hard way. His meteoric rise was curtailed by too many collisions with the stationary borders. The Pete Reiser that came to Pittsburgh during the winter of 1951 was a shell of the phenom who wore Dodger blue a decade earlier, and for the Bucs he would be little more than a bench player.

Danny Murtaugh, while never an All-Star in any of his eight major league seasons, could claim to be a perennial member of the league's all-ugly team. "A stock gent with two black mops for eyebrows, and a beard that produces five o'clock shadow by noon," is how one writer described the Irishman who hailed from Chester, Pennsylvania.[22]

Like the majority of major-league players of his era, Murtaugh served his country during World War II. While in Czechoslovakia with his platoon, he happened upon a dozen eggs in an abandoned farm-house. Murtaugh gently placed the eggs under his helmet and began, with the rest of his platoon, down a country road. A German sniper opened fire on the Americans as they marched down the dusty path. Murtaugh's mates quickly sought cover, and from there they witnessed Danny carefully removing his helmet and gently placing the fragile eggs on the road before diving headfirst into a ditch while bullets swirled per-ilously close overhead. Then his pals saw a hand slowly emerge and reach for the precious eggs, which were then retrieved one by one.

Murtaugh was slated to be the regular second baseman for the Bucs in 1951, a fact which repudiated the dire straits in which the team found itself . "[Murtaugh] has lost both ability and running speed, as well as power in hitting ... the only way Murtaugh can help the Pittsburgh club to win the pennant is with his head," was Rickey's frank appraisal.[23] A new player on the team, George "Catfish" Metkovich, was one of the few members of the Screen Actor's Guild in the major leagues. (Johnny Berardino, who played with the 1950 Bucs was also a member of SAG.) Metkovich was given his nickname while playing under Casey Stengel in Boston. It seemed that Metkovich was injured while trying to remove a hook from a catfish. Among the films that "Catfish" had appeared in was *The Jackie Robinson Story, The Stratton Story,* and *Million Dollar Mermaid,* which starred Esther Williams.

Catfish was among a contingent of Bucs who took a break from training camp when they had the opportunity to visit Esther Williams on the set of the film *Texas Carnival,* which co-starred Red Skelton. Skel-ton entertained the boys with several humorous stories and a few jokes before sending them back to the harsh realities of baseball in the world of the Pittsburgh Pirates.

With Opening Day looming, there was little positive that the Pirate fan could reasonably anticipate. Rickey's abundant promises of pennants arriving in Pittsburgh by the truckload wisely never included the 1951 season. Other than root Ralph Kiner on to another home run title, the wise baseball aficionado knew there'd be little joy for the local nine during the upcoming season. But, as happens every spring, with Opening Day comes a rebirth, and for even the worst team in the game there is always a glimmer of hope for baseball glory. That is, however, until they actually prove their unworthiness on the field.

The Pirates had no bigger booster than their radio announcer Rosey Rowswell. Rosey was unabashed in his love for the game and his "Buccos." Even the most pessimistic Pirate follower could be warmed by Rosey's loving prose.

"Love for the game moves in early youth and ceases only when the Great Umpire has called the final decisions," Rowswell penned. "Down through the years every boy cherishes the hope of someday being up there in the big leagues. Only the graying of the temples and the slackening of his pace compels him to abandon the ambition that has owned him since his first game of rounders on the old hometown lot.

"Once the dream is buried, there is born anew a baseball fan and whether he be a man or boy, his interest in and love for the great American game is ever increasing and never waning. Baseball to him is part of his heritage: his father loved it, his grand father loved it, his uncles, his cousins, his neighbors all talked about it. It was one topic of conversation in which everyone was allowed to participate.

"Baseball is the key that unlocks the heart of the fellow sitting next to you out in the bleachers, or the banker sitting along the first base line … the Senator, the Governor, or the mayor who has taken the afternoon off to watch the Buccos take on the Giants. Baseball is the leveler that makes us all kin to one another."[24]

Despite dire forecasts, the Pirates went on to win the 1951 pennant. The club started poorly, sometimes resembling a troupe of extras on loan from a Marx Brothers film. On occasion the bumbling Bucs would bounce off each other in pursuit of fly balls or embarrassingly arrive at a base only to find two teammates already occupying the same bag. The familiar looking crew, despite playing their home games at Forbes Field and wearing identical uniforms to Rickey's brood, these Pirates weren't

Father and son, Branch Jr.

piloted by Bill Meyer; instead they received their marching orders from Guffy McGovern.

McGovern was a fictional character from the motion picture *Angels in the Outfield*. The movie was filmed at Forbes Field and the surrounding Oakland neighborhood during the last two weeks of April. The fictitious Bucs, and the Hollywood production cast and crew that accompanied them to Pittsburgh, produced a great deal more excitement in the city than the real-life Pirates. The original screenplay had included a different team in the story line but Rickey convinced the producer of the film, Clarence Brown, to use the Pirates instead with the hope that the movie would be excellent exposure for the city and the club. The film did give the organization some positive publicity, but the actual Pirates still had to take the field and, as one scribe cracked, "Only in the movies could the Pirates win a pennant."

Much like their silver screen counterparts, the non-fiction Bucs started slowly, but without the assistance of the "Heavenly Choir Nine," the authentic Pirates progressively went downhill. On June 1, Rickey sent a telegram to Meyer; it read, "I just want you to know that whatever changes you make in your movements of players will have my complete support. Do whatever you think is best and I will share responsibility of any and all criticism. Besides, I do not think that either of us should fear criticism. Anyhow, I am behind you in every way."[25]

Why Pirate management would come under fire was readily apparent. They had lost eight in a row, and fourteen of the previous fifteen contests. During that stretch Pirate pitchers had allowed close to ten runs a game. As often happens when a team's luck goes south, unconfirmed rumors appeared in the press suggesting that the manager's job was in jeopardy. Meyer was not spared this tradition. Rickey, upon reading of his manager's imminent dismissal, phoned Meyer at the Kenmore Hotel in Boston where the club was scheduled to play the Braves.

"Don't worry," Rickey assured Meyer. "you're still the manager of this team. I'm more concerned that you retain your good health than anything else."[26]

Meyer had recently been hospitalized where it was learned that he was suffering from an ulcer. "Branch Rickey is the finest man I ever worked for, and that statement will stand even if I'm fired tomorrow," Meyer said shortly after Rickey's telephone call. "He stood behind me all spring and what's important, he's a baseball man and he understands our problems. He never interferes with his managers. During spring training, I told him I thought this was a last place club and he didn't agree. Later, in spring training, he told me that I was completely right in my judgment."[27]

Last place was foreign to Branch Rickey. Whatever his pre-season apprehensions, the actuality of a losing ballclub was disheartening. While his adversaries were surely pleased with the prospect of Rickey lording over an eighth place club, his numerous supporters believed a Rickey-led team couldn't possibly remain at the bottom of the standings for long.

Wid Matthews, the Cubs general manager and protégé of Rickey, offered an anecdote that gave witness to the Mahatma's tenacity. "There used to be a barbershop near the office of the Cardinals in St. Louis," the former major league outfielder said, "and Rickey dropped in every morning for his shave. One day he spotted a checkerboard. He asked who played checkers, and the barber replied that he had tried the game a few times but wasn't very good at it. Almost before his face was dry, Branch challenged the barber who promptly beat him five straight."

"Rickey was wild," Matthews offered with a laugh. "He stormed into his office and yelled for his secretary, Miss Murphy. 'I want you to drop everything right now and get me a book on how to play checkers,' Rickey said to his secretary. 'I want the best book you can find, and I don't care if you take all day to get it.'

"Miss Murphy did as she was told. When she came back with the book, Rickey studied it between his most pressing baseball duties. A week later he marched into his office and sang out triumphantly, 'Well I can hold my head up down there again. I beat the barber two in a row.'"[28]

The Pirates' season wasn't totally void of highlights:

Ralph Kiner led the National League in home runs for the fifth consecutive season with forty-two.

Cliff Chambers would forever be known as "No-Hit" Chambers following his May 6 masterpiece against the Braves. Chambers' performance against the Braves was the first no-hitter for a Pirate since 1907, when Nick Maddox beat the Dodgers 2–1.

With little else to cheer for, the Pirates welcomed the idea brought forth by the Croatian Society of Western Pennsylvania. On July 27, prior to a contest against the Braves' George Metkovich, the only Croatian in the National League, was honored. Catfish was presented with a wristwatch by the Croatian Society, and Danny Murtaugh represented the club while giving Metkovich a silver chest. The Duquesne TamBoritza Orchestra entertained during the festivities.

If the Metkovich celebration wasn't enough excitement for Pirate fans, the 1925 Pirates were asked by Rickey to come to Pittsburgh to help celebrate the seventy-fifth anniversary of the National League. Rickey took the dais at the Hotel Schenely, where a luncheon was held for the last Pittsburgh championship club. "It's wonderful to have you all back to renew old times," he said to the old ballplayers. "You will all be invited back to Pittsburgh every time the Pirates win a pennant. And it might be sooner than a lot of people think. I'm just sorry you have to see a last place team perform now."[29]

Rickey empathized with those who were forced to endure the Pirate's pitiful on-field exploits. "I can get up and leave whenever I please," he commiserated with his manager, "but you have to sit through this day after day."[30] Most Pittsburghers agreed with Rickey's assessment as they stayed away from Forbes Field in mass. On September 6 only 4,222 fans showed up to watch the replay of an April 19, 1–1 ten inning tie between the Bucs and the Reds. It was the smallest crowd in the history of night ball at Forbes Field. Six days later, a paltry 2,364 were in the stands for an afternoon contest. It would be the second lowest mark of the year, besting only the July 5 turnout of 2,212.*

Pittsburgh, thanks to the Chicago Cubs, was able to finish the season out of the cellar. The Pirates, with their 64-90 record, ended the year a distant 32.5 games behind the Giants, and in seventh place. A dreary Rickey confessed to Al Abrams that success for the Pirates was not as close at hand as he first believed. "I'm afraid that Pittsburgh will have to bear with us at least one more season before we can offer them a respectable ballclub.

"It will take at least that long, maybe well into 1953, before we can realize the fruits of our labor on a farm system that we have to build up in a gradual fashion. I can tell you this much, however, that barring heavy war calls, we will bring up some likely looking prospects within the next two years."[31]

Rickey insisted that he wasn't disappointed with the club's performance. "No, I somewhat expected we'd be in last place, or thereabouts. We don't have a good ballclub, and there's no use trying to believe that we do."

"I was disappointed, however, in not being able to provide more help from the farm system than we did. I thought that by September 1 we would be able to bring up some good material, but it didn't develop. We called in some fair boys the past two weeks but they weren't what I originally anticipated.

"I have great hopes for our pitching. I want you to know that in another two years we'll have the finest crop of young pitchers to come up that I have ever seen in major-league baseball. Unless I miss my guess, it will even outdo the number of good arms we developed in St. Louis back in the early thirties when Bill Lee, Paul Dean, and a couple of others jumped to the big time."

During the course of the season he had made several transactions which changed the makeup of the club markedly. On May 26, the Pirates obtained Rocky Nelson† and Erv Dusak from the Cardinals for Stan Rojek.§ The left-handed catching wonder of the spring, Dale Long, and

---

The poor turnout on July 5 could partially be ascribed to the fact that Ralph Kiner was out of commission that afternoon as he was serving the third day of a three-day suspension.

†*They later, on September 20, lost Nelson on waivers to the White Sox.*

§*Following the trade of Rojek, Rickey referred to the recently* (continued on p. 44)

outfielder Dino Restelli were both claimed on waivers by the St. Louis Browns and Washington Senators, respectively. June 15 saw Rickey make his biggest deal as Pirate general manager to date when he traded "No-Hit" Chambers and Wally Westlake to the Cardinals for catcher Joe Garagiola, pitchers Ted Wilks and Howie Pollet, infielder Dick Cole, and Bill Howerton.

Despite his invocation to the contrary, Rickey was dissatisfied with the yearlong struggle he and his club had suffered through. He was able to mask his frustration while sitting down with the editor of the *Post-Gazette* because the interview was taking place on the eve of Rickey's latest innovation. Baseball's greatest thinker had come up with an idea that would speed up the process of developing minor-league players — the fall baseball school. This "school" was scheduled to open in DeLand, Florida, on October 1 and the Mahatma could scarcely contain his excitement.

On September 5, Rickey sent out telegrams to more than seventy of the organization's top prospects inviting them to "a one month school."[32] "It will be an invitational school and limited to a comparatively small number," the message read. "It is our belief that we may be able to save one year in the player's advancement... I will have personal charge assisted by George Sisler and a very competent staff. You will receive more personal attention than can be given in spring training."

Rickey confirmed that his seventy-three-year-old mind was still fertile when he unveiled his instructional school. Baseball's most imaginative man had no doubt that other clubs would emulate his initiative and have schools of their own in short order, "For $1,000 to a doughnut, I say [they] will," Rickey predicted. "I expect it will spread next year. I just hope Pittsburgh has the jump on them and they don't follow our example for five years."

The school would open on October 1 and run for thirty days. Rickey left no question as to who would be running things in DeLand. "I'm going to take charge," Rickey told Al Abrams, while firmly poking a finger into his own chest. "This is my job and I'm going to run the works for a full thirty days. I want to see how good some of these boys are, and how soon they'll be ready to move up the ranks. I have a general idea on short observation and reports, but this way I can make certain on how we stand."[33]

---

departed Buccaneer as, "a third rate shortstop." Just three years prior, upon completing the sale of Rojek to the Pirates from the Dodgers, the Mahatma declared, "I made a pennant contender out of the Pirates by trading them that boy."

"I am not missing the World Series for nothing," he added. "It is the first Series I have missed in I don't know how long. And the other men here with me are also making the same sacrifice." Rickey was speaking of the fifteen Pirate employees who forsook a month's vacation and received no pay in return for participating at the DeLand camp as instructors. Instead of the fifteen to twenty acceptances he anticipated, Rickey was pleasantly astonished to find nearly seventy positive responses. "When we got more requests than we could handle, we halted the invitations,"[34] a pleased Rickey reported.

DeLand's intention was in tutoring the youthful participants, unlike spring training which Rickey believed played to an individual's strength with very little time spent on teaching. "Spring training camps are mass attendance camps where not too much is accomplished in individual instruction," Rickey wrote. "Conditioning periods, lack of instructors, and pressures of exhibition games interfere with any sort of teaching programs. As a matter of fact, spring training is very largely a time for dividing the sheep from the goats."[35]

The daily curriculum at DeLand began at 8:30 A.M. with a lecture from Rickey. At 10:00 A.M. players and instructors took to the diamonds where practice would commence until noon when they adjourned for an hour lunch. "Classes" then resumed at 1:00 with a ballgame on one field, while other position players would practice with batting machines and pitchers would throw through string targets. Kenneth Blackburn, Branch's secretary, followed Rickey's every move throughout camp furiously jotting down his boss' thoughts and observations which were later passed on to instructors.

Rickey wholeheartedly believed in the primary directive of the school, abbreviating time spent in the minors, which he hoped would be reduced by a year. "Very few of the players were over nineteen years of age, most of them eighteen," Rickey penned to John Galbreath, giving the Pirate owner a summary of DeLand. "The average time of service of regular major-league players in the minor leagues is approximately four years. If we could reduce this period to three years, it would mean that several of these boys, assuming, of course, that they are potential major leaguers, would be members of the Pittsburgh Club in 1954 instead of later."[36]

Rickey was especially gratified with what he saw in the Pirate pitching prospects. "We now rate eighteen young pitchers, none of whom is a present member of the Pittsburgh roster, as definite major league

Branch demonstrates the proper pitching motion to an enthralled audience.

probabilities. Personally, I believe that several of these will be members of the Pittsburgh Club not later than 1953. I do not know of anyone connected with the school, either players or staff, who doesn't believe that the work with pitchers alone justified not only the sacrifice of everyone, but the total expense as well."

Galbreath received a brief analysis of individual players from his general manager. As usual, Rickey's critiques are far more entertaining than the usual fare found in baseball scouting reports:

> Dick Hall, he has exceptional aptitude and might eventually be a first baseman. He is a "catawampus," pregnant with ability in every pore in his body. He can be defeated only because of the possible reaction of a sensitive gentleman to fan or press criticism. That COULD lick him. Surely nothing else.
>
> Another first baseman is a Pittsburgh kid, 5'9", 152 pounds, his name is Tony Bartirome. His father, according to the boy, is engaged

in the "numbers racket" but is very "quiet" just now because "they're after 'em." He does not have much "background" of education or culture, but he is a piece of greased lightning in handling a baseball. He was a bit of a bench jockey. He asks no quarter and he certainly gives none.

The best all-around athlete in the school was a Pittsburgh boy who has had for some years a Damon and Pythias relationship with Bartirome. His name is Del Greco. You will understand the confidential nature of this report when I tell you that Del Greco is eighteen years of age and can neither read nor write. He has, of course, come from nowhere, yet he is baseballically very smart. One of the staff has protested placing the boy immediately under a tutor, to learn to read and write, "because," said the coach, "the army cannot take him as long as he is that dumb. We would be sure to have him, and he can be the center fielder in Pittsburgh in 1952." I believe the coach is right about him. However, we are giving him a tutor quietly, in fact secretly. The boy is sensitive about the matter and would be the butt of ridicule, from the opposing bench unbearably. Not only that, but it would be a great reflection not only on the boy, but on baseball and the Pittsburgh Club, and the City of Pittsburgh and the United States too, if we were to present a major league player of considerable ability, who was completely illiterate. It will be our immediate loss to make him eligible to the Government, but, of course, it must be done.

The wildest man in the entire group is a boy by the name of Bill Bell, a right-hander, scared to death. Possibly a proper subject for a practical psychiatrist. Young, even below his years, but a chap to be patiently handled for he has unlimited greatness as a future major league pitcher.

Law [Vernon], our young Pittsburgh pitcher, has a chance for the outfield. He is highly intelligent, a good athlete, a good runner and very adventurous. Could easily be the best base runner in the Pittsburgh organization. He has never had an opportunity of hitting very much for he has always been a pitcher.

The school, from Rickey's point of view, was an unqualified success. "We accomplished so much in such a short time with rookies that the results are overwhelming," Rickey excitedly relayed to a reporter upon his return to Pittsburgh. "The biggest single purpose of the school is that the school was to find out the difference between a ball and strike for everybody, and I'm certain we achieved our goal. The by-product of the school is that the second division teams will be younger than the first division teams simply because they will spend more time with the rookies and hasten their development."[37]

On the final day of camp, October 27, Rickey addressed the players and coaches prior to the morning session and informed them that he and Meyer had agreed to conditions allowing for the Bucs' skipper to return in 1952. With the pronouncement came a roar of approval from Rickey's audience. The applause lasted almost two minutes before the Mahatma called for order.

The rookie camp cost the organization approximately $40,000, which included transportation, food, and lodging. Though the $40,000 was money well spent, it was just a fraction of the cash Rickey drained from the club's coffers during 1951. Branch spent an astounding sum of $496,000 on players during his first full year in Pittsburgh. The extravagance rankled many in baseball. At the winter meetings, a ranking administrator with the New York Yankees was heard to comment, "Who do they think they are?" with incredulity. "They're kidding nobody but themselves, Pittsburgh just doesn't have that kind of money."[38]

3. Rickey Dinks

Rickey's ecstatic appraisal of DeLand was soon tempered as he encountered the truths facing the Bucs. For all intents and purposes, the Pittsburgh Pirates were broke. Rickey discovered this fact shortly after the fall instructional league, when he and Tom Johnson ventured to a Pittsburgh bank hoping to secure a loan for the club. It was there that Rickey "received a shock, the like of which I do not recall ever experiencing before."[1]

Because of massive debt, the financial institution would not grant the Pirates a loan. Any influx of cash to the organization would have to come from within. In a letter to John Galbreath, Rickey scarcely veils his frustration in not knowing the economic status of the team when he took over.

"I now feel very regretful that I was unable to say to you and to the Board, immediately upon my taking over the job in Pittsburgh, that there was doubtless in front of us, at that time, a great expenditure of money for contracts of new players. I did not, and could not know this at that time."

Rickey continued, "The program was undoubtedly in my mind, at that time, and, of course, there was never a moment that I was not thinking about, and discussing with anyone and everyone the plans for the finding of new players, but to present it formally in a challenging manner did not occur to me. Indeed, as time went on, the costs far exceeded my expectations or plans. Even then, it did not occur to me that there was any doubt whatever, about the club's ability to meet the current

49

expenses and it never did occur to me at anytime that there was anything but complete approval of procedures and expenses. I felt that we were doing a great job and that the players were worth very much more than what we were paying for them, everything considered, and that we were using the most direct and fastest means to produce a pennant winning team in Pittsburgh. I still so believe."[2]

It was as if the carpet had been pulled out from under him. Rickey's boundless designs for the future of the Pirates, for the most part, had to be scrapped. Instead, he was saddled with the burden of discovering means of curtailing expenses and increasing revenues. In the same letter to Galbreath, Rickey set down an outline proposing means to help the club become solvent.

I Bonuses

These have amounted, in the past twelve months, to a half million dollars… We can reduce the bonuses beyond the amount now shown on our budget, viz, $200,000. As a matter of fact, since the first of October we had, until a few days ago, spent practically nothing for bonuses to players. Or, indeed, we can wipe out all bonuses, regardless of amounts. That would indeed affect the next subject.

II Scouting

If we cut out all bonuses, then we do not need our present scouting staff. The cost of scouting could be reduced very much indeed. Our scouting program has been given considerable thought and we have planned to make very systematic and extended effort in the field of young Negro players in America. Also a plan in the field of commission scouting and the commission scouting program has for some months been held up partly due to our financial situation. We believe the "commission scouting" will produce more players, and at less cost per player. But the overall scouting expense could within one year's time be considerably increased. If the "commission scouting" program were to develop as it could develop and as it should, it will eventually increase the need of more manpower, more scouts. Therefore, we are holding up on it. We are going through with the program of Negro scouting, although that too could and might necessitate the turning of all our present scouts into the field for half the summer, or, perhaps, all of it. The justification of this quality, with comparatively little bonus problem. The fact is that the young American Negro scouting field has scarcely been touched at all by professional baseball.

The work of the past year has, very largely, almost completely excluded Negro scouting.

III *Dispose of All Non-Profit Ownership Clubs*

The ownership of minor league clubs has very great advantages over the working agreement arrangements.

Ownership of B, C, and D clubs are generally more expensive than working agreement clubs. In our organization, at the present time, we have ownership clubs as follows.

New Orleans — AA
Charleston — A
Waco — B
Brunswick, Ga. — D

As against the four ownership clubs, we have eleven working agreement clubs.

Hollywood — Open Classification
Denver — A
Burlington, NC — B
Billings, Mt. — C
Hutchinson, Ks. — C
Modesto, Ca — C
St. John's, Quebec — C
Bartlesville, Ok. — D
Batavia, N.Y. — D
Bristol, Va. — D
Mayfield, Ky. — D

The sale of our non-profit ownership clubs, allowing for a working agreement expense of $30,000 per year, according to our estimates, would save $20,000 each year.

IV *Reduce Managerial and Coaching Expense*

Changing personnel is not always pleasant or easy, and it has seemed to me that it was not desirable in our case. A change of manager and coaches CAN mean a savings of approximately one half of the present cost. There was a time in baseball when the manager would use extra players for coaches. They were generally not qualified, as a matter of fact, incompetent. But we can save $25,000 per year by getting rid of the coaches and we can save another $10,000 easily enough by changing the manager. If it were a matter of solvency or insolvency, even more drastic reductions can be made.

V *Reduce Administrative Expenses*

VI *Deal High Priced Players*

This has to do with both saving expenses and increasing income. On the one hand, you get rid of the high salary. On the other hand, you realize on the sale price. We have been undertaking for some-time past to make player moves, but we do not have many players attractive to the market. Other clubs approach us only on one of our players and for several reasons we have not found ourselves in a posi-tion to give serious consideration to any deal for this player. But we could come to that. If we were to adopt a policy of full retreat, it would then become consistent to blow up the bridges rather than surrender.

VII Sell New Orleans
We have $350,000 tied up in the New Orleans property, approx-imately $100,000 in a major rehabilitation program, which has been completed, and we owe approximately $250,000 on a mortgage cov-ering the purchase of the land.

I do not like the idea at all of selling the New Orleans property. Why not? Well, simply because I feel that the New Orleans club can be operated at a substantial profit... However, it has a value over and above profits, viz, the acquiring and developing and assigning of players. It is an ideal "farm" property, in fact just as valuable as AAA or the Pacific Coast League.

In any event, I hope we can reserve decision on the sale of New Orleans, if possible, until mid-season of 1952.

VIII Increase Admission Income
[Although it was too late for the Pirates to increase the price of tickets for the '52 season, Rickey wanted to investigate the possibil-ity of doing so for the '53 season.]

IX Get Rid of Concession Contract
It is a very conservative estimate, made by people in position to know, that we are losing approximately $150,000 per year on account of our concession contract. When we consider that the contract includes our advertising as well as our refreshment sales, the esti-mate, I am very sure, is too low. [The concession contract was with the Jacob Brothers.]

X Sell Fence Advertising
[For esthetic reasons the Pirates had never littered the fences of Forbes Field with advertisements as many other clubs did.] If we could get rid of the concession contract, and if further we wish to do so, we could possibly increase our net income by not less than $50,000 if we were to sell fence advertising.

XI Promotion

XII Sell Hollywood Stock
The purchase of the Hollywood stock is a good investment. It

rivets a relationship with a league now unclassified and having the advantages of no salary limit, and indeed, gives advantages to Pittsburgh in many respects that other major league clubs cannot acquire except by part or complete ownership. In addition, our personal relations are very friendly with the Hollywood people and this relationship in itself is valuable.

If necessary this can be sold [Pittsburgh's stock in the Stars], but I firmly believe that apart from prospective dividends the advantage of the California territory as enhanced by our Hollywood identification, will have more influence and effect upon the future playing strength of the Pittsburgh Baseball Club than any investment we can possibly make for a like amount of money in any direction.

XIII Television

We are now considering the possible telecasting of sixteen of our mid-week day games. Personally, I believe that the telecasting of these sixteen home games would be stimulating to attendance (I know that you and Tom feel different about it). If we could get $4,000 per game, say $65,000 net to us for these telecasts, I think we would be well ahead in money.

I do not regard it as embarrassing at all, nor a matter of adverse criticism to the club if we were to telecast the sixteen week day games this year and then not telecast at all in the future. It is said that television may, perchance, offer a solution to all baseball that will make gate receipts inconsequential.

I am not at all positive that my judgment may not be sub-consciously influenced by our need of money.

XIV Refinancing

I have complete faith in the future of the Pittsburgh Club. On the field, artistically, it will win; and off the field, financially. It will pay all its debts as surely as a reasonably short time goes by, because our present debts and any ensuing debts are payable before taxes. This is a firm belief based upon facts, experience, and a faith that is a part of me and must become a part of everyone connected with the Pittsburgh Club if we are to continue to operate aggressively.

I regret more than I can tell you how difficult it has been for me to approach what seems to be the utter necessity of writing this letter. I am unhappy about it because I feel that I am so largely to blame for our present circumstances. This letter, as indicated, is written to you in the most personal and confidential manner. Only Kenneth [Blackburn] knows about it and I trust him fully.[3]

In early February, Branch, under duress, reached into his own pocket and invested $200,000 into the struggling franchise. Tom Johnson, who accompanied Branch to the bank for the transfer of funds, remembers a very reluctant contributor. "I met with Rickey in his Forbes Field office," Johnson recounted. "I sat with him for over six hours listening to his bullshit. Finally I started folding my papers.

"'Where are you going?' he asked me.

"'Well Mr. Rickey, I think you gave your answer, you're not going to put the money in.'

"'I didn't say I wasn't going to put my money in,' he told me. 'I don't *want* to put the money in.' We had run out of cash and we desperately needed the capital, which I finally got out of him, but it was like pulling teeth from the old bastard."[4]

Of course, Rickey's telling of the account differed a great deal from Johnson's.

"There came a time when we were in desperate need of money," Rickey told Joe Brandis of the Associated Press. "I had told John Galbreath at the time I came to the team that sooner or later, I would invest in the Pittsburgh club as much as $200,000 worth of stock from the present stockholders. The stock at the time I purchased it had no book value whatever. It was nil. However, I paid the average price for the stock that represented the cost to the original stockholders, and the price I paid was approximately $209 a share. This I take it had some evidentiary value in showing that I had great faith in the future of the Pittsburgh operation. I was willing to put $200,000 into something that had no book value whatever. I would do it again under the same circumstances, and although at this date when the situation is worse than when I bought the stock, if I had the money I would put another $200,000 into it. Why? Because I thoroughly believe that the club has both artistic and gate future. Eventually it will win and eventually, therefore, it will win at the gate. Pittsburgh is a jealous city. By and large from the lowest employee in a filling station on up to the President of the United States Steel Company, there is a jealous regard for the good name of 'Pittsburgh,' not only in industrial and social and cultural activities, but there is a civic pride held to very tenaciously by everybody hereabouts in everything that bears the Pittsburgh name. And that means that a good team in Pittsburgh will be generously supported."[5]

For the Pirates' general manager, the off-season could elicit an even more frenzied pace than the summer months held for him. The last week of January gives testimony to the bustling nature of a week in the life of Mr. Rickey:

Sunday: A speaking engagement in Buffalo.

Monday: An appearance at an open house at U.S. Steel in Pittsburgh.

Tuesday: A speaking engagement in Connelsville.

Wednesday: A speaking engagement honoring Jim Thorpe in Canton, Ohio.

Thursday: Boston, where he was a guest speaker at a sportswriters' banquet.

Friday: A number of appointments at his Forbes Field office.

Saturday: A trip to New York for a league meeting.

Sunday: A banquet at the William Penn Hotel where he was a guest of the Pittsburgh baseball writers.

One man who could definitely identify with the hurried pace that Rickey kept was his secretary, Kenneth Blackburn. "You might take a small bag, figuring on two days away from home, and not get back for ten or fifteen," Blackburn said of his excursions with the unpredictable Rickey.

Blackburn told a tale of Rickey's whims that took place in March of 1951 at a Pirate tryout school in Anaheim. "We were sitting there watching the kids in their workout," Blackburn recounted. "When I spied Mr. Rickey heading for center field. I caught up with him near the fence and inquired as to where he was going.

"'Wait around and I'll show you' he said, then

Branch dictating to his secretary Kenneth Blackburn.

proceeded to climb the fence and head for a lunch stand across the street"[6]

Branch Jr. sympathized with Ken Blackburn. He too, for a time, acted as his father's secretary. "Sometimes dad would start dictating while shaving," the younger Rickey remembered. "There I would be in my shorts, taking down notes while he shaved and dressed. Then he'd be ready to eat and would tell me to hurry.

"He'd leave and, say he'd order breakfast. While I sent the wires and got dressed, dad would be starting on his breakfast. Many's the time I had a cold breakfast."[7]

The admirable work habits of not only Rickey but also, his son, "the Twig," paid off for the Buc's in early 1952. It was a personal policy of Rickey not to send out contracts until February 1, but in 1952 he made an exception by getting his offers in the mail several weeks early. By early January, six players had already agreed to terms thanks to the work of Rickey and Branch Jr. No one on the club need worry about receiving a contract with a reduced salary according to Rickey. "I never cut any player I intend to keep."[8]

One notable player not yet under contract was Ralph Kiner, though Rickey fully expected to sew up the star outfielder to suitable terms personally when he traveled to California on Valentine's Day.

"There's no sense in wasting correspondence with Kiner," Rickey told reporters. "I'd prefer to talk to him personally. And you might add that we certainly have no thought of trading him. Ralph is a person of high intelligence, and he's reasonable. He has more than arms-and-legs value. He has gate value too."[9]

Although Rickey proclaimed that the club wouldn't request any of their players to accept a decrease in salary, some in the front office were shocked when Kiner asked for an increase in 1952. "We didn't think Kiner would ask for a raise," a nameless spokesman for the club was quoted as saying in *The Sporting News*. "After all, we finished seventh and our attendance fell off."

Kiner had signed a two-year deal following the 1949 season, a year in which the slugger had 54 home runs and 127 runs batted in. "But," the Pirate official said, "last year he hit 42 home runs and batted in 109 runs. We thought he would be perfectly satisfied with a renewal of his contract."[10]

The request seemed perfectly reasonable to Kiner. Moreover, according to Kiner, the deal was all but finalized. "I talked to John Galbreath at the World Series," Kiner rationalized, "and although nothing was agreed upon, we were pretty well agreed on what I would receive in 1952. In the past, Mr. Galbreath and I have settled most of our contract matters prior to signing, and I don't see why it should be different this year."[11]

Kiner's desire to bypass Rickey to negotiate his contract certainly did little to ingratiate him to the general manager. Branch, though, kept his brewing resentment toward his outfielder off the sports pages. He quietly stepped aside and allowed Kiner to come to terms with his pal Galbreath. The Bucs offered Kiner a one-year deal for $75,000 with no bonus. After mulling over the proposition for several days, Kiner acceded to the submitted terms and handed the signed contract over to Rickey following the Bucs' exhibition game with the San Francisco Seals on March 15.

There would be no red carpet treatment for Rickey's peach-fuzzed youngsters as they arrived in the Golden State on February 18. Instead of a banner reading, "Welcome Pirates" and brass bands triumphantly broadcasting their arrival, the rookie representatives for the Bucs stepped off their train in San Bernardino to the deafening silence of indifference and a streamer that ominously declared, "This is National Crime Prevention Week."

The rookie camp was an extension of the DeLand School, and Rickey was sure to be on hand to personally instruct the invitees. Also in San Bernardino to assist the old man were George Sisler, Danny Murtaugh, Sam Narron, and Clyde Sukeforth. Sukeforth had performed as an aide to Burt Shotton in Brooklyn before becoming the latest of Rickey's Dodger protégés to land in Pittsburgh in December of 1951.

Bill Meyer was not included in the assembly of coaches aiding Rickey with rookies, but before the first week of camp was concluded he had received a wire at his Tennessee home instructing him to pack for California.

"These boys have such exceptional ability that it wouldn't be fair not to allow Bill Meyer to judge them," came the explanation from Rickey for cutting short Meyer's winter vacation. "I want Bill to observe them and form his opinion on just which players should remain to work out with the regulars."[12]

"We have as fine a crop of youngsters as I've ever seen in baseball," he also said. If, and when, some of our boys return from the service and these youngsters progress, we'll be feared."[13]

Much like the "Why Finish Last?" lectures of the previous spring, Rickey engaged the rookies every day with his spellbinding elocution. Each morning at 8:30 sharp Rickey would begin his talks with camp attendees. His lectures ran the gamut — from baseball, to morals, to life's learned lessons. The morning meanderings of the Mahatma attracted a number of prominent San Bernardino citizens who, upon learning of the orations, asked to sit in and listen. Rickey's strong suit was certainly not his humility, and he was delighted to expand his audience.

"It's the history of this country that men are what they make themselves," Rickey told his congregation. "We don't pay attention to the color of the man or the last three letters of his name in this business of baseball.

"Your education never stops. You're always learning.

"Reserve judgment on your fellow man. Look for the best in everybody, but don't allow first impressions to sway you. Don't allow personal things to influence your judgment.

"Make public appearances all your life. Be part of your community life. Give something of yourself. Men who do only what they want to do can become very narrow.

"A man who isn't alert is usually in the second division, and that's where he belongs. It's a good thing to be overconfident if you can hold it. Rogers Hornsby was a supreme egotist as a hitter, but he was worthy of it.

"Nine times out of ten a man fashions his own destiny. You get out of life only what you put into it. You pay men in baseball and out of baseball for unseen things.

"The more a man makes excuses, the more chance he has of winding up in the second division.

"Discipline should come from within, and be self-imposed. It's more effective that way. Hornsby would never go to a movie because it MIGHT hurt his batting eye. He wasn't sure, but he wasn't taking any chances. The same way with smoking and drinking, as far as Hornsby was concerned. Drinking will affect your keenness, loss of sleep and loss of senses. And I have yet to meet the first man who benefited by drink.

"Men who don't want to be right don't last long."[14]

If one can determine the worth of Rickey's eloquent speeches by his ability to maintain the interest of a room full of post-pubescent young adults, then his morning meetings were a success. Ron Necciai wholeheartedly endorsed the seminars. "Mr. Rickey is the only man I've ever listened to for more than fifteen minutes without falling asleep."

Pittsburgh severed its association with Indianapolis at the conclusion of the 1951 season. The termination of the relationship was not, however, without complications. The Pirates, as their agreement allowed, attempted to purchase eight players from Indianapolis only to be rebuffed. When the time came for the selection of these players, they found that three of the eight were "frozen" and not subject to selection by the Pittsburgh club until after such players had been subjected to the draft. Indianapolis had clearly reneged on their agreement, and Rickey fully believed that Frank McKinney was behind the transgression.

"This case will doubtless come before the commissioner," Rickey informed Galbreath. "I think it absolutely necessary for you to see Ford Frick personally and lay the case before him. It is my understanding that Mr. McKinney has done some talking about it and I am also informed that he has talked to Ford (Frick) about it. It is said generally that Frank is a clever politician; whether he is or not, his presentation can bring about an early test of the new commissioner's good sense and fairness. I will, of course, present our side of it upon proper opportunity. In the meantime, I think you should make a point to see Ford."[15]*

The Pirates were in need of a high classification affiliate. Branch did not have to search for long as the Hollywood Stars were eager to join into a partnership with the Bucs. Branch engineered a deal in which Pittsburgh would buy stock in the Hollywood club. This purchase of sixteen percent of the Stars upset many prominent members of the Pacific Coast League (PCL).

"I cannot understand it," a frustrated Rickey said when he heard that the six independently owned clubs of the Pacific Coast League were angered by the stock purchase. "I did not come into this league to hurt it. And I have always been welcome wherever I have gone in baseball. Never have I been accused of being a bad partner in any enterprise. I went into the Stars on behalf of the Pirates because I deemed it a good investment and because of my friendship for the people in the Hollywood picture. It must be something personal, although my acquaintanceship throughout the Coast League has been a good and friendly basis, so far as I have been aware."

Rickey had maintained a friendship with the owner of the Stars, Bob Cobb, since Hollywood had arranged a working agreement with Brook-

---

*Commissioner Frick decided in favor of the Pirates, and the team was awarded the players in question for $5,000 apiece.

lyn in the mid-forties. The good will between the two men was only solidified when Cobb decided to end the arrangement with the Rickey-less Dodgers and signed on with the Bucs for the forthcoming campaign.

"Never did it occur to me that there would be opposition to the deal I made with Bob Cobb," Rickey said. "Our share of the Stars is a small one, and another club in the league, Los Angeles, is completely owned by the Chicago Cubs without ever having aroused any ill feeling."[16]

Cobb, in addition to being the principal owner of the Stars, was the owner of the famous Brown Derby restaurants, a position he achieved after beginning as the head waiter. He was equally mystified by the response to the stock purchase. "I needed ballplayers, I needed advice, and I needed money. So I simply went to the outstanding man in baseball, Branch Rickey," Cobb reasoned. "My greatest desire is that the Pacific Coast League become the third major league, and I know of no quicker way than to enlist the support and counsel of Branch Rickey. Moreover, I am proud to be associated with him. I have nothing to regret and nothing to hide. Besides, I don't have to obtain any official approval in transferring title to a minority chunk of stock."[17]

The relationship between Pittsburgh and Hollywood would be no different than any other big league / minor league arrangement, Rickey insisted. The association would be mutually beneficial. "We would like to share and share alike," he conveyed, "but we shall never seek to own fifty-one percent or more. If and when the Coast League goes major, we will not embarrass the Stars by trying to retain an interest in the club. We'll sell out at a fair price."[18]

The prospect of the Pacific Coast League integrating with the major leagues was not preposterous. The possibility had been seriously debated since 1946, and in the months previous to the Hollywood stock transfer, the discussion was renewed with increased vigor.

If an issue was pertinent to the entity of organized baseball, Rickey undoubtedly would be found somewhere in the mix. The controversy over the PCL's aspiration to gain entrance into the major leagues was no different.

Ford Frick, the former National League president, was elected to replace the dismissed Happy Chandler as baseball commissioner on September 21, 1951. Frick did not campaign for baseball's top job, but vowed to expend all his energies on the various questions that faced the game.

"I didn't seek this job," Frick said shortly after his appointment. "I didn't particularly want it, but now that I have it, I am going to give it the best I have and I'm going to be the commissioner twenty-four hours of the day."[19]

One of the issues greeting Frick as he stepped into his new position was the desire of the Pacific Coast League to be granted "open classification," which the league believed would boost their chances of joining the majors. "Nothing stands still, and it is the same with baseball," Frick reasoned. "There has been no change in the major-league map for fifty years. I am not saying changes at present are desirable or necessary, but in the past half century there have been vast changes in the size and importance of American cities. Changes in baseball's structure are inevitable."[20]

Frick narrowed the scope of his discourse and addressed the qualifications of the Pacific Coast League specifically. "Of course they have cities out there which would qualify for the majors," Frick said. "They have the people and the interest. But, I am thinking of this thing from a larger sense. There are other cities in the East and Middle West which also feel they have claims to higher classification. We must give them the same consideration as we give Los Angeles and San Francisco."

"The Coast League does not demand major recognition," Frick clarified, as 1951 came to a close. "But it wants a chance to keep its players and build up to major rating. I'm very sympathetic toward that ambition."

If the Pacific Coast League were granted the "open classification" it desired, the league's players would be free from the major-league draft for five years, instead of four. Additionally, the draft price would be $15,000 instead of the $10,000 it was at the end of 1951 for Triple A teams. Also, teams in an open class league could not have working agreements with major league organizations and could refuse to take players from the big leagues on option.

The president of the Pacific Coast League, Clarence Rowland, believed that with open classification status, the league would be prepared to join the majors in short order. "At present our physical plants are not adequate to handle major-league crowds," Rowland admitted. "Granted five years to build them up, we could get ready to step into the major league family.

"This [open classification] gives us assurance that the integrity of the Pacific Coast League will be recognized, and that when it advances, the advance will be made by all eight clubs as a whole."[21]

Rickey agreed with the general consensus that the West Coast was a natural area for the majors to progress into and, like Rowland, he believed that bringing the entire Coast League into the fold would be the most appropriate decision. "I would say the Coast League's chances of gaining major status are good, but whether soon, or at a distant date remains to be seen. It is the logical, natural development, rather than to have one or two clubs go up. And to the best of my knowledge, no efforts are being made by any team to transfer its franchise to the West Coast at this time. Such a move, in the future, is possible, of course, but not very probable."[22]

"My heart bleeds for Los Angeles people who want major league baseball," Rickey said. "If I were a resident of Los Angeles, I am sure I would feel as they do. But the complexities of baseball laws would recommend that Los Angeles become big league through graduation of the Coast League.

"Los Angeles and Hollywood, or both, should first ask and secure permission of the Coast League to formally petition for a major-league franchise. The same procedure would apply to the Bay area — San Francisco and Oakland — if the owners so desired.

"Such permission, I realize, would be difficult to obtain. Possibly, it could be secured by the four clubs buying out the other PCL mentors. I have been told such cities as Denver, Salt Lake City, Vancouver, and Spokane are capable of supporting Coast League teams so that the league would not be broken up, merely reorganized."

Rickey then suggested that another option might be for an already existing franchise to relocate to the Coast. "There's always the chance some major-league owners might want to move their franchise, and draft the Los Angeles or Bay territory," he explained. "Under baseball law [this] could be done. Dan Barnes of the (St. Louis) Browns had the machinery all set to move his club before World War II started and travel became restricted."

He then addressed the issue that transportation to the coast would be a problem. "Why I left New York by plane at 10 o'clock this morning and arrived here (in Los Angeles) at 5 o'clock this afternoon. Teams can fly from New York to Los Angeles a lot quicker than they can get from St. Louis to Boston by train. Few, if any, clubs have real objection to air travel anymore."

Last in his argument was the commonly held theory that there weren't enough quality players to supply expansion teams. "Why, there is going to be the greatest growth of major league talent the next ten years that baseball has ever seen. The rapid growth of Little League for young-sters all over the country insures that,"[23] Rickey predicted.

The PCL did approve the measure that would take effect following the 1952 season: the league would not accept players on option from major league teams anymore by rule. This decision, Rickey believed, would be disastrous if acted upon. "If the Coast League refuses optioned players next year from the majors, the league will suffer terrible disinte-gration. It simply wouldn't last long."[24]

Whatever his feelings about the resolution that was passed by the PCL, Rickey didn't vary from his intention to develop a trustworthy relationship with their new partner in the league, the Hollywood Stars. The Pirates, Rickey maintained, would assist the Hollywood club in any fashion. Perhaps, as the Mahatma's critics would later suggest, the Pirates' relationship with the Stars was too cozy. "We will give manager Fred Haney players who can help him right now," Rickey said from San Bernardino, "not players we wish to develop for the future. So most of the fellows he gets will come from our regular squad, not this kid group here today."[25]

Surely the Hollywood club would accept any and all assistance offered by Pittsburgh, but Rickey's statement smacked of a conflict of interest. Though his commitment to the Stars made in San Bernardino attracted little interest at the time, this policy would, as the summer wore on, draw the ire of sportswriters and fans alike.

The rookie camp was deemed a success, and seventeen of the kids were invited to remain in San Bernardino when the veterans arrived on March 3. Bill Meyer greeted his team as the major-league manager with the longest tenure with the same club — five years. Since Rickey's takeover of the Bucs, Meyer had made an about-face from an easygoing "one of the guys" manager to a tough task master. Most witnesses credited the metamorphosis to Meyer's general manager.

The change in disposition was certainly noticed and commented upon during the '51 season, but any delusions the Bucs may have held that they could muscle their manager were rebutted during training camp. The first player to endure the wrath of Meyer was Gus Bell, who made the grave mistake of traveling with his wife and child from their home in Louisville to San Bernardino. Meyer was clearly, and perhaps unreasonably, frustrated with Bell, who he believed was being distracted from the business at hand by his family.

"I told Gus he had to do one thing or the other," Meyer said. "He

Bing Crosby with manager Bill Meyer.

has a fine career ahead of him, and he can't afford to fool around. I just told him it was either stick to getting in shape to play or else forget about baseball."[26]

Bell reluctantly relented to his manager's wishes and sent his family back East. Just one day after they left California Bell's wife became ill and Gus left camp to tend to his wife and baby in El Paso. Placing his family's welfare above that of his burgeoning baseball career did not sit well with the Pirate hierarchy. Logic would assert that Pirate brass would have been pleased that their young right fielder was adhering to Rickey's strict training rules and was accounted for every evening. Instead, Bell was browbeaten until he complied with Meyer's dictate. Ironically, shortly after Meyer chastised Bell for being a good family man, he suspended another of his men for breaking training rules.

Over the previous quarter-century as a minor and major league manager, Meyer had fined only two players, Pirate left-handed hurler Bill Werle would up that total to three. Werle was fined $500, suspended indefinitely, and immediately shipped back to Pittsburgh. Werle's transgression took place at the tail end of spring training in Beaumont, Texas, as the Bucs played their way to St. Louis for Opening Day. The Bucs asked for waivers on the thirty-year-old left-hander, but rather than lose a player that the club had invested $50,000 into following the 1948 season, Rickey futilely attempted to trade him.

The infraction that led to Werle's punishment was addressed in a correspondence he sent to his wife, who in turn released the letter to the press.

"As to the mess I'm in," Werle penned his wife, "it's the greatest mix up and piece of information that I've heard of. When I left Beaumont, I hadn't any idea as to why I had been fined and suspended, but I had heard a few rumors."[27]

The note explained that the Pirate hurler went to his general manager and requested an explanation. "I asked if it had something to do with a woman supposedly [being] in my room, and Rickey said, 'Well it's true isn't it?' I swore on my father's grave that it wasn't, and that someone is a damned liar."

Left out of his communication with his wife was the fact that Werle, along with all his teammates, had been warned about the club's training rules. What's more, Werle specifically had been told that he was being observed intensely, and just one misstep could cost him his major-league job.

The incident resulted with short-lived disorder in the team's clubhouse when Werle began pointing fingers at teammates when he was accused of being equally guilty of breaking Rickey's rules. "If I was suspended for merely being late, there were others who could also have been suspended," the unrepentant Werle professed, "and that's all I did."

The suspension was repealed in time for Opening Day, but Werle's stay with the Pirates was all but over. Just two weeks into the season Rickey shipped the troublesome Werle off to St. Louis in return for pitcher George Munger.

Perhaps the liveliest character in uniform for the Bucs during the exhibition season was a twenty-three-year-old Puerto Rican pitcher named Ramon Salgado. Pittsburgh had purchased Salgado's contract from Texas City of the Gulf Coast League the previous fall for $7,500.

Doc Jorgensen, the Bucs' trainer, purchased an English-Spanish dictionary with the hope of improving communications with Salgado. The well-meaning Jorgensen would have been better off to save his money. "He cannot speak a word of English and cannot understand a word of English," according to Rickey. "As a matter of fact, he knows very few words in Spanish. He states to an interpreter that he has never had time to learn to read or write very well because of his interest in baseball."

Language difficulties aside, Ramon was a joy to watch perform. "Salgado is a showman, and takes over the crowd immediately,"[28] Rickey wrote after observing the pitcher.

Though he couldn't read or write, Salgado did manage to fill out an expense report. For his trip to San Bernardino from his home in Puerto

Rico, Salgado wished to be reimbursed for the cost of a "woman" who traveled along with him. Pressed on the matter, Ramon agreed to "settle for half."

Rickey sincerely believed that, with some seasoning, Salgado would certainly reach the big leagues. He was ticketed to spend the 1952 campaign with New Orleans, with the hopes of reaching Pittsburgh the next year.*

The Bucs struggled the entire spring. More often than not the club resembled a squad of little leaguers who infiltrated the Pirate clubhouse and commandeered the big leaguers' uniforms. Even when most men in his position would be either cringing or taking a stiff drink, Branch kept his chin up. On the eve of the new season Rickey saw reason for Pirate fans to be as energized as he himself was. He recognized Pittsburgh's long and, more often than not, successful history and refused to suspend his belief that these Bucs too, would soon be mentioned in the same breath with the great Pirate teams of the past.

"It is only in the last six years that Pittsburgh has shown a tendency to stay low in the race, and that is a condition which the present owners and directors of the club are striving through spring, summer, autumn, and winter to eliminate.

"Now comes another playing season in the major loops, the second under the supervision and direction of the directors," Branch continued. "And when I say sunlight is beginning to peer through the darkness always in evidence just before dawn, I know that our scouts, coaches, minor-league associates and others, who have been giving their great efforts toward building up a pennant contender for Pittsburgh, anticipate, as we do, the full sunlight of a brighter day..."[29]

And then, because league regulations insisted, they took the field. "We got off to a slow start," Pirate catcher Joe Garagiola reported. "We lost ten out of the first fourteen, and then had a slump."

What the 1952 Pirates couldn't produce in victories, they more than made up for in belly laughs. Garagiola himself was able to forge a career which, in large part, was based on humorous anecdotes describing the follies of the 1952 Bucs.

"They talk about Pearl Harbor being something; they should have seen the 1952 Pittsburgh Pirates," came Garagiola's gibe.[30]

In retrospect, perhaps humor was present during the awful perfor-

---

*Salgado never did reach the majors.

mance of the '52 Bucs. Still, as the horror unfolded each day that fateful season, smiles were few and far between around Forbes Field. To call the ballclub terrible would be charitable. Their play bordered on criminal, which is represented by their frighteningly bad record of 42 wins and 112 losses. Their ineptitude, and the club's extraordinary youth, earned them several unflattering nicknames. "Rickey Dinks" and "Operation Peach Fuzz" aptly captured the essence of the '52 Pittsburgh squad.

The decidedly politically incorrect tag of "Rickey's Singer Midgets" was befitting to the diminutive crew that Meyer let roam the field. The starting infield for the April 21 contest against the Cub's epitomized the Lilliputian band of Bucs. At first base, manager Meyer penciled in five-foot-nine Tony Bartirome, five-foot-eleven Johnny Merson manned second, the shortstop was five-foot-six Clem Howerton, and five-foot-eight Dick Hall was at the hot corner. One veteran shook his head and sighed, "If they let the grass grow, we'd lose one every time."[31]

Meyer knew that he was in the midst of a struggle which he had little chance of winning. "Our boys are battling them with sticks and stones," he cried, "while the other fellows are using swords and guns."[32]

The Bucs' top three pitchers, Howie Pollet, Murry Dickson, and Bob Friend, amassed but one victory in their first nine combined starts. At the plate Pittsburgh's production was equally anemic. A joke floating around the ballyard was that the Pirates' tiny players weren't big enough to hold a bat, let alone swing one.

"I'm disappointed, sure, but not discouraged," was Rickey's typically quixotic outlook. "I can still see daylight. This young team will go through a period of depression, then recover. We may have to jockey some of these kids along, perhaps send some out for further work, but in the long run you'll see we're on the right track."

Flowery quotes were no longer soothing the masses. Despite his persistence that the Pirates were "on the right track," the press, the fans, and some of the Bucs themselves were beginning to vent their disgruntlement with Rickey's determination to "force feed" the big league club with youngsters who should have been honing their skills in the bushes.

Reports of dissension on his team didn't vex Rickey. "If the players are dissatisfied, it's a good sign," he said with a shrug. "I wouldn't want them to be satisfied with last place. If there are any players who are unhappy with us we'll be glad to arrange for their transfer to some other club that will take them. I don't mind the players fighting among themselves in their efforts to win, but I do not like unhappy players."[33]

Pirate fans, with their wallets and voices, expressed disgust with the play they witnessed on the field. On Memorial Day, the Bucs sat with 8 wins and 32 losses, leaving them an astounding twenty-and-a-half games out of first place. The afternoon before Memorial Day, only 1,070 fans clicked through Forbes Field's turnstiles to witness the hapless Bucs. Many believed the dire straits the Pittsburgh club faced was due to the general manager pinching pennies. The "El Cheapo" accusation was given new life by Rickey's critics who contended the Pirates were dumping high salaried ballplayers in lieu of rookies that were paid the major league minimum. This was a charge that infuriated the Mahatma. "Now isn't that downright ridiculous?" he bristled. "I wonder what they would say if they knew that in an eleven-month period up to late last year, the Pirates paid out $496,000 in bonuses to sign young ballplayers. And that only recently we gave an eighteen-year-old boy $35,000 to sign a contract. That $496,000 was for bonuses alone, and did not include expenses of scouts or any other costs.

"Now if we spend that much money just to sign players who may produce for us at some future date, does it make sense that we would want to get rid of established players who are worthy of good play? Mark this and mark it well: when you're in baseball your highest salaried player is your cheapest player. He gets the big pay because he draws at the gate and gets it back for you."[34]

Rickey's saving grace was his inability to find any takers for Ralph Kiner. He had begun shopping his number one gate attraction during Kiner's spring holdout. As long as Pittsburgh's number four player remained in the home whites, Rickey could keep the wolves at bay. However, the newsmen in the press box weren't nearly as easy to appease as the paying customer (whom the Pirates were already struggling to pacify). The scribes were fully aware of Rickey's frantic efforts to deal not only Kiner, but several other veterans as well.

The Mahatma's continual justification of his use of unseasoned youths was insulting to most writers. If Rickey was being up-front when telling listeners that the Pirates were playing the youngsters because of a lack of veterans on the club, why then attempt to trade off the few experienced men remaining?

Gus Bell was one of the few Pirates who actually belonged on a major league field, yet he seemingly could do little to please Branch.

Bell's critics, of which Rickey certainly could be counted as one, felt he was "lazy," and that the right fielder lacked ambition. Both the general manager and field manager were frustrated in their efforts to bring out Bell's potential. Rickey hoped that a threat to send Gus back to the minor leagues might motivate him, and so he requested that both Bell and his wife come into his Forbes Field office for a chat.

Normally a big proponent of wedded bliss, Rickey was surprisingly agitated with Bell's devotion to his family. "Perhaps Mrs. Bell should handle the night time feeding, which would allow Gus to get his proper rest,"[35] the grandfatherly general manager suggested.

Rickey's distaste for Bell was unreasonable by most any measurement. His censure of the Bell family was not only out of his jurisdiction, but was also unfounded for the most part. He questioned the couple's respect for the dollar, which the Mahatma certainly had in spades. The Bells squandered money, Rickey believed, as Mrs. Bell, along with the couple's baby boy Buddy, occasionally would travel with the club on road trips. Rickey was also outraged to learn that Mrs. Bell would toss Buddy's soiled diapers in the trash because she did not want to launder the linen.

Unknown to Rickey, Mrs. Bell's father was a conductor on the Louisville & Nashville railroads, and she was able to obtain tickets for free, which, on occasion allowed her to travel on the same trips as the Bucs. A relatively new item on the market, disposable diapers, cleared Mrs. Bell of Rickey's charge that she was not fulfilling her duties as a housewife.

The twenty-three-year-old Gus Bell came to Pittsburgh from Indianapolis on Memorial Day, 1950. He finished his rookie season with an average of .282, and he followed that respectable showing with a percentage of .278 the next year. Production and potential be damned, the boy had to show more devotion to the game or off to Hollywood he would go. "Mr. Rickey and I did everything we could to make Gus see the light, but we couldn't arouse any fighting spirit in him," Meyer lamented. "I even told him what to say to Mr. Rickey, that he considered himself a big league player, and didn't want to be sent back to the minors. But when Mr. Rickey told him he had in mind sending him away, Gus just took it in stride. He didn't fight back."[36]

The vigorous battle Rickey and Meyer hoped to see out of Bell never surfaced. In fact, the prospect of returning to the minor leagues was "all right by me."[37] This response earned Bell a trip to Hollywood the next day, April 21, where he was sent on a twenty-four-hour option.

Rickey counted off three reasons to justify his decision to ship Bell to the Stars:

"1) I want to win a pennant, 2) I want fellows on the club who can help me win it, 3) Bell can help me win it. He's capable of more ability than he's showing. It isn't that he's not trying. There are several things he has to get straightened out."[38]

Bell would benefit from the tutelage of Stars manager Fred Haney. "I expect him to be back a better ball player who will fit into my plans better than he's able to do now," Rickey anticipated.

On May 12, after turning in a good effort with Hollywood, Bell was recalled by the Pirates. He immediately tested the patience of his supervisors by not reporting to the club until the fifteenth. Prior to catching up with the Bucs in Boston, Bell took his wife and kids to Toronto where Mrs. Bell would be staying with her aunt. When Bell finally reached the Hub he told reporters that he "enjoyed" his stay in Hollywood, but added, "there's no place like the majors."[39] Rickey could do little more than shake his head upon hearing Bell's comments ... shake his head, and begin working the phones.

No man in baseball history was more savvy when it came to the "art of the deal" than Branch Rickey. Trade discussions with Rickey were a unique experience, even for a veteran of the game.

Buzzie Bavasi, who worked under the Mahatma in Brooklyn, found the process both educational and exasperating. Bavasi had moved up the Dodger chain and filled the general manager's position left vacant by Rickey's departure. He approached his mentor in the hopes of acquiring a pitcher for his squad.

"Mr. Rickey, whom do you rate as your number one pitcher?" Bavasi threw out as an opener.

"Young man," Rickey replied, "he's the greatest pitcher in baseball today. There's no one finer. Murry Dickson, naturally."

The Dodger executive nodded, "That's fine Mr. Rickey, but we don't want him. Now who is your number two?"

"Young man," came the answer, "he's my friend, he's Bob Friend. A splendid prospect."

"I suppose, Mr. Rickey, that Ted Wilks would be your number three?" Bavasi guessed.

"That," Rickey concurred, "is precisely correct."

"Well Mr. Rickey, I don't want number one, two, or three. I'll take number four, Howie Pollet," Bavasi offered.

"My dear Buzzie, Howard is, without a doubt the best pitcher I have ever had working for me on any team."

Rickey then sized up his protégé and moved in for the kill. "Young man, you really can help us out with a first baseman," he crooned. "Hodges?" Rickey asked of the slugging Brooklyn first sacker. "What will it take for him?"

Bavasi, though, had learned from the master. "You can have Hodges, Mr. Rickey. You can have him even up for John Galbreath."[40]

No deal was consummated between the Bucs and the Bums. Rickey had little to offer Bavasi, and what few marketable players he did possess, he asked for too much in return. He did have some kids that brought interest on the open market, but Rickey would not deviate from his program of building from within.

He could scarcely contain his enthusiasm for prospects, namely Tony Bartirome, Clem Koshorek, Dick Hall, Lee Walls, Ron Kline and most of all, Bobby Del Greco.

Del Greco, was a product of Pittsburgh's Hill District (as was Bartirome), and was, according to Rickey, "one of the finest instinctive outfielders I've seen since Terry Moore."[41]

Regardless of the potential Rickey's boys may have possessed, their production continued to make the Bucs a laughingstock. "We'll have some of these teams crying before long,"[42] Rickey sang out, refusing to allow himself to be deterred by the tragic play of his "Singer Midgets." He continued to put in fourteen to sixteen hours a day trying to improve his team in any way possible, leaving no stone unturned in his quest. Rickey's boundless energy was to be admired; the question was being asked, though — were all his efforts in vain?

In his DeLand report to Galbreath on November 26, Rickey digressed momentarily from the subject at hand to inform the Pirates' president about a senior at Duke University that he had his eye on. "He could be the Pittsburgh shortstop and needs never to go to any minor league club, all, of course, provided we can get him."[43]

The young man in question was Dick Groat, a native of Swissvale, Pennsylvania. Groat was an All-American at Duke, not only in baseball, but also basketball, his first love. He captured the interest of several major league teams following his graduation from Duke, and chose to sign with the Pirates on June 16. Though not officially confirmed, the media speculated that Groat received upwards of $75,000 to go with the Pirates.

"We won't talk about that," Rickey said with a wave of the hand, "any more than the salaries or bonus payments to any other player in the Pirate organization. I suppose there will be a number of guessing contests concerning it, but officially the figures will not be known."[44]

Just three days after signing his professional contract, Groat fulfilled the prophecy Rickey made to Galbreath the previous November and played his first major league game without spending a moment in the minors. Groat's debut at the Polo Grounds was one of the rare Pirate victories as the Bucs bested the Giants 8–1. The newcomer contributed to the victory with two hits, a run scored, and two runs batted in. He also fielded his position at shortstop flawlessly.

Groat was endorsed by Pirate coach Milt Stock. "The boy knew what he was doing out there," Stock appraised. "He did everything, 'big league.'"[45]

The Pirates were able to land Groat thanks to the "bonus rule." The rule, in effect, was no rule at all, as baseball allowed teams to bid with no artificial parameters placed on the teams. This practice obviously put the poorer clubs at a great disadvantage, but it wasn't until Rickey began running a cash-deprived team that he began to speak out against status quo.

"Something has to be done about the bonus rule," he urged. "First off it is harmful to the boy: It gives him something for nothing, a vicious thing in itself. Then, when the major league clubs hire a player, not on a basis of what he can do, but what was your offer, it puts the game on a shaky commercial basis."[46]

"It will ruin baseball if it isn't curtailed. The way it is written now, it will make permanent second division teams out of the clubs lacking the finances to compete in the bidding for some of these youngsters.

"There are clubs now which send their scouts out with instructions to the youngsters, that regardless of what bid they might receive, to come back to the scout and he will improve by a thousand dollars on the highest offer. There is nothing wrong with that, but that is ruining the chances of the clubs lacking capital to compete. Consequently they can't compete.

"The Pittsburgh club is definitely out of the big money market. And our boys [the Pirate scouts] have done quite well without big bonus outlays. We have paid some money, but not quite half what we paid out in our first year of operation."[47]

Rickey had a plan that he hoped to implement in place of the current situation. "I have a plan patterned after the football league draft, but the other clubs so far believe it's too complicated.

"Lump all the players into a huge pool, then let baseball clubs select the ones with whom they may deal with exclusively," Rickey suggested. "After the major leagues have selected up to their player limit, then the AAA clubs move in and take their picks. Then the AAs, then the As, and the Bs, and the Cs, and the Ds in order.

"By that system only can the lower minors have a chance to sign the good youngsters. The lower leagues being closer to the source might actually get the good ones."[48]

By July 4, the Pirates had been in nineteen one-run games and had come out on the short end fourteen times. They had also lost eighteen contests in which they led after the sixth inning, and had been shut out nine times.

The Boston Braves were perennially in the second division of the National League, but even their players were in awe with the consistently dreadful team the Pirates placed on the field. "We don't have much to brag about on our team which is in the building process," one Boston veteran said as he witnessed the Bucs at play, "but this Pittsburgh outfit takes the cake, with or without the icing, for being the weakest I've ever seen."[49]

The team certainly would have benefited from a full roster of players. Not only had the club been outclassed on the field, they were also outnumbered. On July 2, Rickey sent out pitcher Joe Muin and Erv Dusak for reassignment to the minor leagues. The transaction set the Pittsburgh roster at twenty-one, four short of the limit allowed.

Bill Meyer was being forced to manage an already pathetic team with his hands tied. Throughout the month of July continuing through the first week of August, Meyer was left with an eight-man pitching staff. The starters were Dickson, Pollet, Friend, Woody Main, and Cal Hogue, which left only three men in the bullpen: Wilks, Harry Fisher, and Paul La Palme.

As would be expected, Rickey's decision to not use the entire allotment of twenty-five players drew barbs from the press. Al Abrams wrote a series of articles in the *Post-Gazette* titled, "Is Rickey Doomed to Failure with Bucs?" Much, if not all, of the blame for the Pirate's woeful performance must be laid at the feet of Rickey, Abrams opined: "(1) The many bad deals he made with the Pirates when he was with the Brooklyn Dodgers have held back the Pittsburgh club's progress. (2) His insistence on the use of Class C and Class D rookies long before they were ready for major league competition. (3) His refusal, or inability, to bring up players from Hollywood and New Orleans farms when the Pirates were down to 17 physically fit players during the past two weeks."

Hoping to soothe his rapidly deteriorating relations with Pittsburgh sportswriters, Rickey invited the city's scribes to a luncheon at the Duquesne Club, "to talk things over."[50] Chilly Doyle wrote in his *Sun-Telegraph* column that "Branch's party was intended to slow down the indignant press."

While the three-hour August 6 gathering was deemed a success by Doyle, Rickey still evaded the press' demand for solid answers to their questions. "In his delightful double talk style," Doyle wrote, "Branch skirted beautifully from the main line to a nearby siding when asked why Wilkinsburgh's (Pa.) Paul Smith and Oakland's (Pa.) Frank Thomas, who has twenty-five homers, were not with the main line team. He gave a fascinating discourse on unusual events on the New Orleans Pelicans, but nobody had been told why these good hitters are not with the parent club that needs hitting."

Doyle certainly had a valid argument. Hollywood's roster was chock full of ex–Bucs — more than a dozen, all told. Still, Rickey refused to recall any player from the Stars that could undoubtedly help the big league club. No explanation was forthcoming from Rickey on the issue until after he finally added some warm bodies to the roster.

On August 8, the Bucs recalled pitchers Jim Waugh and Ron Necciai, outfielder Lee Walls, and infielder Brandy Davis. "It's regrettable that the reduction in the roster hurt the team's chances recently," Rickey said, in a classic understatement.

The general manager had just returned from a prolonged Canadian fishing vacation, which also brought criticism from the press who were wondering why he was taking a holiday in the middle of the season. "I didn't see the papers during the nine days I was away, but I understand there was some criticism. The moves (in July) were made with the approval of manager Meyer, and, with the exception of a pinch hitter on occasion, we didn't expect it to hurt so much."

"This is force feeding on our part," he confessed. "I would like to give all the young playing at Forbes Field right now another year in the minors, but we are just trying to hurry the improvement here. If we were a good team, I wouldn't be doing this. But the Pittsburgh club is not a good team, and I am not saying this to exonerate myself. Right now

I hope that by August 1 of 1953 the Pittsburgh team will be making a stronger showing and causing some comment about its ability ... things just haven't turned out as we anticipated."[51]

On August 9 Ron Necciai, one of the newest Bucs, made his major league debut. Upon viewing Necciai in action in the 1951 spring training camp, Rickey was grandiloquent in his appraisal. "I've seen a lot of baseball in my time," Branch reminded listeners. "There have been only two young pitchers I was certain were destined for greatness, simply because they had the meanest fast ball a batter can face. One of those boys was Dizzy Dean. The other is Ron Necciai ... and Necciai is harder to hit."

The native of Monongahela fulfilled his promise, at the minor-league level at least, when he made baseball history on May 15 after he struck out twenty-seven batters in one contest. Necciai, pitching for the Bristol Twins of the Class D Appalachian League, allowed only one ball to be batted into fair territory. That ball was a ground out to the Bristol shortstop. The "twenty-eighth" out of the game came when the catcher dropped a called third strike and the batter safely reached first base.

The twenty year old didn't fair nearly as well in his first big-league game. Necciai was roughed up by the Cubs, allowing five runs in the very first inning and giving up a total of seven runs in six innings as the Bucs fell to Chicago 9–5.

The "force feeding" program had reached new heights on August 20. That afternoon the Pirates' starting lineup in their game against the Phillies had an average age of twenty-three years. The only Bucs on the field who had been in the majors prior to 1952 were Kiner and Garagiola.

The Mahatma was receiving some support in the press, for the time being. Jack Hernon took the opposite position of his colleague at the *Post-Gazette*. "Rickey could easily have gone along with a seventh place club this season by keeping the players who had tried before and failed, and were better than the group of Rickeydinks now in action," Hernon argued.

"Until the time when the current Rickeydinks arrive, there will be much wailing and weeping, and Rickey will have many sleepless nights, but the Mahatma is on the right track. But, oh, the suffering."[52]

The suffering continued ad nauseam as the club crawled to the finish line. It was a season that, in baseball's terms, would be comparable to the flaming demise of the *Hindenburg*, or the sinking of the *Lusitania*.

The blame for Pittsburgh's sad state of affairs was laid at the feet of the Mahatma and not Bill Meyer, who was seen in most quarters as an innocent bystander at a terrible auto accident. Front office personnel throughout the National League were questioning Rickey's sagacity. "I can't understand some of his projects," one puzzled executive stated. "You have to question his judgment on some young ballplayers he has put on the field this year. I have seen the Pirates play quite a few games in the East this year and some of these boys will never make the major leagues. He has also had a couple of chances to make deals, but always asks too much in return."[53]

Always the good soldier, Bill Meyer continued to impart the company line all summer. But as the season came to a close, the defeatism that surrounded his ballteam became too much to bear. "I've had enough," Meyer told a reporter on September 27, after he announced his resignation. "I just couldn't stand losing with this team any longer."

Meyer's decision became public knowledge prior to the start of the contest between the Bucs and the Reds at Cincinnati's Crosley Field. "These kids we have now just can't do it," he continued. "If there was a foreseeable future to the club, I wouldn't mind sticking it out. Everyone likes to manage a winning ball club, but this one is hopeless."

Meyer had proven, given the semblance of a major league team to work with, he was a competent field general. The 1948 season was a fine example of his capabilities. Armed with a club of has-beens and castoffs, Meyer kept his Bucs in the pennant race until September, an effort that earned him Manager of the Year for that season.

Meyer's resignation came out of frustration, not only with the ability of the men playing under him, but with the dictates put forth by the front office which did not allow him to field the best players at the club's disposal. When asked by a reporter why veterans George Metkovich and Gus Bell were languishing on the bench when they surely could have helped the club more than the major league impostors that were continually taking the field for the Pirates, Meyer was curt and to the point. "We decided early in the season to go with the kids," Meyer answered. *"There's nothing I can do about it."*[54]

An agreement Rickey made with New Orleans also hampered any chance Meyer had of fielding a passable big league club. The Pelicans were promised by Rickey that the Pirates would not call up any player from New Orleans, so as to not disrupt their pennant chances. A similar agreement was made between the Pirate general manager and Bob Cobb of the Hollywood Stars. The crux of these arrangements was that the Bucs had to reach to the lower levels to bring up warm bodies, however woefully inexperienced that help was.

Meyer walked away from a team that was inept in every phase of the game, as the statistics bear out: lowest team batting average (.231), least runs scored (515), least hits (1,201), least doubles (181), least triples (30), least home runs (92), most home runs allowed (133), worst fielding percentage (.970), most errors committed (182). The team's longest winning streak was two games. The Pirates were officially eliminated from the pennant race on August 6.

The Pirates' woes were not confined to the playing field. The club's financial state was becoming progressively worse.

Attendance for the 1952 season was the lowest since 1945. The turnstile count of 686,670 was 297,000 less than 1951. With a budget set that anticipated attendance to reach one million, the team's losses were set at $800,000, which included deficits incurred at the minor league level and bonus payments. "We won't take a loss at Hollywood," Rickey Jr. reported. " [We'll] probably come out even there. And New Orleans will make enough to offset the losses at say, Charleston and Waco. But the others will be losing operations... It is becoming a big problem with major leagues. The clubs just can't go on losing money. They have to tighten up somewhere and chances are the minor leagues will suffer."[55]

The *Post-Gazette* reported in September that the club was having difficulty meeting their monthly payroll. The rumors were not unsubstantiated; however, the team was able to meet their obligations to their personnel thanks in part to another infusion of cash from Galbreath and Johnson. The organization had dodged a bullet, but an embarrassing financial disaster remained on the horizon unless the club found much-needed funds.

Nothing could squelch Rickey's creative spirit. Despite the Pirates' troubles, Rickey made significant contributions to the sport, such as a new style of hat unveiled at Forbes Field on September 12. The "hats," a precursor to batting helmets, were made of plastic and had a band of foam around the hat band to protect the wearer from pitched balls. Jack Hernon cracked that the Bucs looked like "polo players" in their new head gear.

The New Orleans club had been experimenting with the hats, and results were positive. Pelican Dale Long was hit in the head by a pitched ball and simply trotted down to first base after collecting his helmet.

The origin of the helmet could be traced to Bob Davian, a native of Pittsburgh, who first approached Rickey with a hat which had a transparent beak that would better help outfielders catch fly balls in the sunshine. Davian's innovation, the transparent beak, could be flipped down over the eyes, thus replacing the need for sunglasses. Rickey was not enamored with this invention. Instead, the two men devised the plastic protective hat.

Previously, players wore a skull cap for protection at the plate, but the new helmet offered not only more safety, but was a much lighter alternative. The batting helmet would not be Rickey's only enduring contribution to baseball in terms of equipment. Prior to his Pittsburgh endeavor, Rickey introduced a number of significant items to the game, among them:

The pitching machine — Rickey believed this machine to be invaluable. The pitching machine could throw to a batter's weakness, save on pitchers' arms, give confidence to batters, and helped hitters practice bunting much better than live pitching could.

The baseball tee — The tee was similar in concept to a tee that a golfer would use. The batting tee was made of hard rubber and stood several feet off the ground in a stationary position. The tee allowed batters to work on their weaknesses. Rickey believed that it was especially effective for "over striders."

The sliding pit — A simple idea that was developed by Rickey to help players develop their sliding skills.

The electronic umpire — A machine which measured not only balls and strikes, but also the speed at which the pitch arrived at the plate.

Rickey, in his infatuation with anything that *might* help players in their development, introduced a few not-so-successful gimmicks. One such novelty was the "cricket cradle" which he brought to San Bernardino in the spring of 1951. Made of wood, the apparatus was built in the shape of a cradle and was used in England by cricket players to warm up prior to a match.

The cradle created something of a "pepper" effect, sans the batter. Up to six players could participate in a session at one time. This contraption did not catch on as the players found they preferred to play a game of good old-fashioned pepper instead.

One of Mr. Rickey's more offbeat ideas was put into use in Denver during the 1952 season, where the Pirates had a working agreement. The players on Denver's Bears had a strike zone sewn on their uniforms ...

the shoulder to the knees consisted of a different color fabric than the rest of the uniform. These uniforms were, of course, not used during league games, but were saved for practice to help Denver pitchers.

Along the same lines as the peculiar Denver uniforms, during the spring of 1952 Rickey had a strike zone painted on a canvas drop for Pirate pitchers to throw at, again with the intention of honing the hurlers' skills.

Rickey also considered the development of batter's skills. One such device was a "strike zone" for his hitters which was, in essence, an electronic eye. When a ball was thrown in the strike zone, it would light up, letting the batter know the delivery was good enough to hit. In his neverending quest to elevate his ballplayers, Rickey advanced the game as a whole. His passion to improve baseball in any manner would remain with him until his death.

Though critics would argue whether Rickey's many transactions were just change for change's sake, the Mahatma's desire to refine the Pirate roster never ceased. An increasingly prevalent component of Rickey's deal was the inclusion of cash in exchange for Pittsburgh players.

On August 18 the Pirates sold George Strickland and Ted Wilks to the Cleveland Indians. Technically, on December 3 Clyde McCullough was "traded" to the Chicago Cubs. In return for McCullough the Bucs received the wanting Dick Manville, and cash.

As the World Series came to a close in New York City, three Pirate beat writers asked Rickey if it would be safe to take their vacations. Branch assured the scribes that there were no deals pending. "We have nothing in mind," Rickey said. "Go on vacation and enjoy yourselves."[56]

Just three days later the Pirates consummated their biggest deal of the year when Rickey sent his "headache," Gus Bell, to the Cincinnati Reds for Joe Rossi, Cal Abrams, and Gail Henley.

"Between our talks about Bell while the Reds were in Pittsburgh for the first time this year and the telephone conversation by which our deal for him was closed, I must have talked to Rickey about Bell at least forty times and was turned down in my attempt to get him each time," Gabe Paul, the Reds general manager related.

Finally, at the World Series, Paul was able to put together an offer that piqued Rickey's interest. The key man was Henley, whom Paul obtained from the Giants for the express purpose of redirecting him to the Pirates in exchange for Bell. As for Bell's problems with the Bucs, Paul

Galbreath, Benjamin Fairless (a member of the club's board of directors), and Fred Haney.

saw little chance of a recurrence. "I'm sure we'll have no trouble on that score while he is with the Reds," Paul pledged. "We encourage our married men to have their families with them while the team is training in Florida."[57]

Bell himself didn't seem disheartened by the trade. "I couldn't seem to do anything to please Mr. Rickey," he said following the deal. "The more I hustled, the more he'd get me for something. Why, he'd find things wrong with me that I never knew existed. He used to say I didn't run in from the field fast enough at the end of an inning. Can you imagine that?"[58]

Two-and-a-half months passed before Rickey finally settled on Meyer's replacement. On December 11 Fred Haney was introduced to the Pittsburgh media.

"Frankly we tried to get a playing manager and when we failed, Fred Haney was ready to step on," Rickey said, in what could hardly be seen as a ringing endorsement. Haney, late of the Hollywood Stars, was at one time refused a job in the Brooklyn system by Rickey because he heard that Fred "took a drink with his players."

The official explanation for the procrastination in naming Meyer's successor was ascribed to Haney's poor health. Rickey reportedly didn't want "to burden him with a job that is understandably tough." In reality, one of the reasons for the delay was the fact that Rickey was trying to pry Pee Wee Reese away from the Dodgers in the hopes of making him the Bucs' player/manager. Walter O'Malley relished the opportunity to deny his request and so the job fell to Haney.

At the same press conference where Haney was introduced to the Pittsburgh writers, Rickey was asked, "What would you want for Kiner in a trade?"

The Pirate vice president measured his response, "I'd want a catcher, an outfielder, a shortstop, a first baseman, and a pitcher." Came the reply:

"That's what you're asking," another writer chimed in, "Do you really think you could get it?"

"No," Rickey frankly admitted. "But I can't be ruled off for trying. Now that I have a manager, I'm in a trading mood."[59]

Nine days after bringing Haney on board, Rickey celebrated his seventieth birthday. His associates with the Pirates threw a combination Christmas/birthday party for him at Forbes Field. In attendance at the gathering was Les Biederman who sat with the Mahatma and listened to the old, but still vibrant, man touch on many subjects.

Branch Jr. between his parents celebrating the Mahatma's seventieth birthday.

"Work never hurt anybody. But punching a time clock is all out of kilter. It's too bad in our economic system that we have to regulate our lives with a clock. If I had worked in a job all these years starting at nine and quitting at five, I would have looked forward to retirement at sixty-five. There would be too much monotony. I want to die working. I come from a long line of people who lived a long life. My mother was seventy-five, my father was eighty-six, and my grandparents eighty-five."

The pace Rickey maintained in 1952, especially in light of the blight that occurred on Forbes Field's playing surface, was a marvel. It was estimated that he traveled 150,000 miles during the year while existing on five or six hours of sleep a night, though he was known to grab a fifteen minute catnap here and there throughout the day.

Rickey would certainly not dwell on the failure of the 1952 season; there was too much left to accomplish. "Worry is simply thinking the same thing over and over again, thinking in cycles and not being able to do anything about it," he theorized. "In baseball, however, there's always some alternative, something new, something fresh, something different."[60]

4. Wait Until Those Cubans Get a Load of This Pirate Act

Following through on a threat he had made on numerous occasions since going to Pittsburgh, Rickey found a new spring training home for the Pirates. The decision to abandon San Bernardino for Havana was made in June 1952. "The change shouldn't be taken as a denunciation of California," Rickey insisted. "The accommodations for the Pirates at San Bernardino were excellent. The people were fine, but in the three years I tried the west coast, the weather was awful."[1]

In addition to the two years in California with the Bucs, Rickey trained in California with the 1924 Cardinals. "The two seasons with the Pirates have been terrible," he complained. "Nineteen fifty-one was better than last spring, but the decision to move was brought about by the loss of time. You take players to spring training to condition there, but there is no chance when it rains so much."

The Cuban Sports Commission, which sponsored the Pirates' stay in Havana, assured Rickey that the club would have first-class facilities. The news of Pittsburgh's relocation was met with the typical jocularity that seemed to follow this sad-sack group. A wisecrack put forth by one opposing player summed up league-wide mockery, "Wait until those Cubans get a load of the Pirates. It might start another revolution."

The Pacific Coast League was again a topical matter. The league had been granted the open classification status they had sought in 1952. This modification in standing, which the PCL believed would lead to it becoming a third major league, would only accelerate its decline, Rickey believed.

"By 1954 the Coast League won't be a good B League," Rickey claimed. "They are going to force all the strength into the International, American Association, Texas League, and Southern Association."[2]

"What major-league club would send a player to the Coast League when they know there is no chance of buying that player back?" he asked, before quickly adding, "A player can be brought back, but only if the seven other clubs in the [Pacific Coast] league waive on such a man. From now on the Pacific Coast League is entirely on its own. They have to decide to recruit their own talent. They haven't been able to compete with the major leagues in signing young players in the past, and there is no reason to believe they will do so in the future.

"We no longer have a working agreement with the Hollywood club. Certainly the Pittsburgh club will send them talent, but only those players who are no longer of value to us. I am not going to send any players to Hollywood who might be of help to the Pirates in the future."

The new circumstances left Pittsburgh with a void in their farm system. The organization no longer had an affiliate above Double A, a dilemma Rickey was striving to remedy.

As a result of the new classification for the Coast League, and thanks to the worsening condition of the organization's financial situation, the Pirates became the only major league team without a paid scout on the West Coast. Former Pirate scout Bob Clements would head up the Hollywood staff and he took with him Don Lindberg and Bob Fontaine. A fourth Pittsburgh scout, Howie Haak, was reassigned to the Midwest. Peculiarly, Rickey wasn't concerned that he would not have a scout located in one of the country's most lucrative territories for baseball talent. "Hollywood will cultivate its own players since the no option [rule] was put into effect by the Pacific Coast League," he explained. "We no longer have a working agreement, but retain part ownership of the Stars. We can still buy any player on their roster. Hollywood is setting up its own farm system around that area and, with the Coast League trying to become a third major league, the Stars are getting a good start in that direction."[3]

Instead of the Pirates discovering and producing their own players, Hollywood would do the detective work, sign, develop, and then sell the finished product to the Pirates. This arrangement helped the Pirates in their retrenchment program, first by avoiding the bonus market, and also by allowing the Stars to take over the salaries of Clements, Lindberg, and Fontaine.

The Armed Services continued to hamper Rickey's rebuilding plans. While Danny O'Connell was being discharged from the Army in February, pitchers Ronnie Kline and Ron Necciai, along with infielders Tony Bartirome and Dick Groat, were called to duty.

The highlight of Rickey's time spent in Cuba was an afternoon of fishing off the coast of the small island. On the ninth of March, Branch hooked three fifty-pound tarpons. The following afternoon was spent in bed recovering from the expedition. It would be the only day off for the Mahatma all spring.

He studied his players daily, offering tips of instruction and encouragement. Rickey was determined not to see a repeat of the previous season's absurdities, some of which he had already witnessed in Havana. He took a pen in hand and jotted down some criticisms and introspection on his third training camp. "Why at my age should I be satisfied with such perfect mediocrity?" Branch wrote. "I would rather stagger into the storms of an unknown sea, free and unfettered, than I would be to be weighted down to the bottom of a convenient swimming pool.

"Simply because a man has an astronomy book in his hands is no conclusive reason for insisting that he cannot throw a baseball; not run fast; or catch a sign, or not loaf going to third and turning the bag with nonchalance only to be thrown out at homeplate as [Pete] Castiglione was last night. A book on astronomy might have helped him for he was star-gazing with sub-lime ignorance of what he owes in effort to a winning club.

"When you know a man is mediocre, why fool around with him when you don't know if the other fellow may have greatness close to him? It should be common duty to find out about the unknowns and if we are able to say now that there are no unknowns then why not ship them out now? What good are they doing for us and what further good are we doing for them? We are simply creating justified discontents and I have experienced these knockers after they have joined our organization clubs."[4]

A highly publicized contract squabble with Ralph Kiner would overshadow all other happenings in Pirate camp. The otherwise bland training period was enlivened by the animus displayed between the Mahatma and the left fielder. The two ego-burdened men butted heads much to the delight of the sports editors of the three Pittsburgh dailies. With the Pirates coming off their worst season ever and Kiner's production suffering a drop-off, Rickey, with the backing of ownership, believed it was an opportune time to stare down Pittsburgh's idol without abiding terrible feedback from the paying public.

Ralph McPherran Kiner made an immediate and forceful impression in his very first spring training he played wearing a Pittsburgh Pirate uniform. During that grand debut in the spring of 1941, the eighteen-year-old Kiner belted two home runs against the Chicago White Sox. Ralph made another, not nearly so pleasing, impression that same spring when he first garnered the label which his detractors would continually harp upon — prima donna.

Frankie Frisch was managing the Bucs that last season before America's entry into World War II, and one lazy spring afternoon the "Fordham Flash" ordered his charges to run a number of laps around the ballfield. Instead of following his skipper's command, Kiner opted to take to the dugout where he had a seat.

Frisch, in short time, took notice of the rookie lounging on the bench and charged at his young slugger. "What the hell is the idea of loafing?" Frisch barked.

"I've only got one pair of shoes," Kiner reasoned. "I know you're going to farm me out, and they'll have to last all season where I'm going."[5]

The wisecracking rookie spent that season and the following in the minor leagues before joining the Navy and the war effort. Kiner came out of the service in December 1945 and surprised most everyone by making the Pirate roster for the 1946 campaign. He was an immediate sensation on the big league level where he captured the National League home run title with twenty-three.

There would be no "sophomore slump" for the young man from Alhambra, California, who quickly earned the nickname "Mr. Slug." Kiner set the baseball world on its ear in 1947 by making a celebrated run at Babe Ruth's fabled home run mark of sixty when he smashed fifty-one round trippers. The prodigious home run hitter captured the second of what would become seven consecutive league home run titles, an unprecedented feat.

Kiner vowed that his accomplishments wouldn't affect his work ethic. "I'm not going to get fat-headed over my 1947 success, because two years from now I could be back in the bushes," Kiner said modestly. "But I know I've got the power to clear those fences."[6]

He understood from the start that perks came in conjunction with swatting home runs. "They don't shake your hand for hitting singles," he was known to say, and Kiner certainly wasn't shy about cashing in on the residuals offered as reward.

"Mr. Slug" was never known for an eye-popping batting average. He lumbered around the base paths and couldn't be accused of turning heads with defensive gems, yet Pittsburghers were smitten with Kiner. In 1947, spurred on by his assault on Ruth's home run mark, some 1,280,000 Pirate fans clicked through the turnstiles at Forbes Field. Over the course of the previous sixty-one seasons the Pittsburgh organization had never before reached the million milestone in attendance. Amazingly this feat would be duplicated the next three seasons, thanks solely to Ralph Kiner.

He became the darling of not only the typical Buc fan, but also countless squealing teenage girls. These fans, more often reserved for the

Crosby and Kiner, "the Crooner and the Slugger."

like of Frankie Sinatra than for a baseball player, made Kiner uncomfortable. "Those bobbysoxers that hang around the ball park in ambush are worse than the wolves at Hollywood and Vine,"[7] he moaned.

All the adulation resulted in dollar signs, as Ralph Kiner immersed himself in commercial ventures like no other athlete since Babe Ruth enjoyed his heyday. Kiner's status in the baseball world, and the city of Pittsburgh in particular, allowed the slugger the opportunity to sell his name. During the season he found himself busied with a television program dubbed *The Ralph Kiner Show*. He also covered the World Series for the Pittsburgh *Press* and a local radio station, WJAS. Ralph's column in the *Press* was named "Kiner's Liner's." Products on which he lent his name had to be "top quality," and "wholesome" to boot. Ralph's endorsements included a health bread, a breakfast food, a brand of milk, and razor blades. Whiskey and beer were out, but ironically cigarettes were not.

"This business of hitting home runs is swell and enjoyable, but it also brings about a lot of annoyances," Kiner complained following the 1947 season. "I never knew how many agents there were in this world until that last flurry of home runs. At least 60,000, or so it seemed that many, want to manage my business affairs and make me a lot of money from testimonials, endorsements, magazine articles, movies and such."[8]

Members of the Pittsburgh media celebrated Kiner's "extravagant" lifestyle. The scribes enviously wrote of Kiner's "four-bit perfecto," "expensive clothes," and a green Buick sedan he purchased, which, "can't possibly be more than five feet shorter than the U.S.S. *Iowa*."[9]

Kiner, with his $65,000 salary, which was tied with Stan Musial as the highest in the game, was the toast of Pittsburgh when Branch Rickey signed on with the Pirates. At that time, Kiner was as indigenous to Pittsburgh as its numerous bridges or the smokestacks rising from the city's countless steel mills. Still, upon the naming of Rickey as the Bucs' general manager, Kiner knew that his days in the black-and-gold flannel of the Pirates were numbered.

It was a well known fact that Rickey teams were almost invariably void of high-salaried players, and of men who were on the downside of their careers. Rickey's long-time philosophy that it was "better to trade a player a year too soon, than a year too late" seemed to indicate that Kiner would be packing his bags in short order. Rickey, though, dispelled all rumors that Kiner was on the trading block, while acknowledging "Mr. Slug's" vital place on the Pittsburgh roster. Still, the

Mahatma wasn't nearly so enamored with Ralph's playing ability as he was his propensity of planting the behinds of Pittsburghers into Forbes Field's cramped seats.

However, Rickey quickly grew weary of what he perceived to be Kiner's prima donna act. Their baseball relationship was barely a year old when Rickey began laying the ground work to justify trading Kiner. Rickey, though it's doubtless that he needed the reinforcement, had an ally. Manager Bill Meyer, too, was displeased with his star player.

The Pirate brain trust believed that Kiner had one set of rules and his teammates another. Meyer complained of this special treatment and told Rickey how he had tried to convince his previous general manager that "the Kiner problem" needed to be addressed.

"I told Roy Hamey two years ago that he (Hamey) was ruining the club by the way he was handling Ralph, giving him special privileges on reporting, traveling as he pleased, etc.," the manager said.

According to Meyer, Hamey's reply was a simple shrug of the shoulders, followed with an unyielding, "Well, I know, but he puts them in the park."[10]

Rickey laid out his numerous complaints concerning Kiner in a letter to John Galbreath dated March 21, 1952. Fifteen pages in length, the "Personal and Confidential" memo concisely rambles along on a wide array of subjects, all of which condemn Kiner in some personal or professional fashion.

"Bill [Meyer] felt that he could hardly bring other men in line and it had gotten to the place where in 1950 his players took many little advantages; there was very little team spirit and he himself went to pot along with everything else," Rickey wrote. "He [Meyer] doesn't at all blame Ralph for his own dereliction ... but ... it was very hard to get a bunch of men to devote themselves to a common task on a job when the star of the club was not a part of the program, and particularly this was so when, according to Bill, so many of the players felt that Ralph was not at all a star. The players' opinion in this respect is shared by Bill. Indeed, I am inclined to go along with his judgment. If it were not for the single thing, home run hitting, Ralph would be unable to be a member of any major league club. He cannot say this outside and never has. Neither can I say it out loud."[11]

Kiner embodied everything in a ballplayer that Rickey abhorred. Few would dispute the contention that Ralph was a one dimensional player, but he also had indisputable star power the likes of which had rarely been seen since Babe Ruth was swatting long balls at the height of his powers. Virtually no ballplayer could withstand comparison to Ruth, who was perhaps the greatest player to ever grace a ballfield; still Rickey spewed out a damning indictment in verse contrasting the two men:

> Babe Ruth could run. Our man cannot.
> Ruth could throw. Our man cannot.
> Ruth could steal a base. Our man cannot.
> Ruth was a good fielder. Our man is not.
> Ruth could hit with power to all fields. Our man cannot.
> Ruth never requested a diminutive field to fit him. Our man does.[12]

Rickey's complaints about his star player were numerous and wide ranging. High on the list was Kiner's request that the retention of Greenberg Gardens be guaranteed in his contract. The Gardens, a fence constructed inside the left field wall thirty feet closer to home plate, had been in place since 1947, erected in the hopes that the home team might gather some advantage from their two right-handed power hitters, Kiner and Hank Greenberg. Greenberg, who played with the Bucs for that single season, found himself immortalized, in a sense, by the ugly edifice thanks to Francis Rooney.

Rooney, the maître d' of the Forbes Field press room, casually asked writer Al Abrams, "What do you think of 'Greenberg Gardens'?" Abrams then used the sobriquet in the *Post-Gazette* the following day. Thus Greenberg Gardens was born.

Rickey hated Greenberg Gardens if for no other reason than Kiner wanted to keep it, but he was sure to indicate his displeasure more eloquently to Galbreath.

"There is an esthetic value to Forbes Field of which we are justly proud. The artificial enclosure mars it. It is wrong in purpose and the only justification finds itself in the reason for increasing income by creating a home run hitter, and it's conceivable that under a given set of circumstances park alterations could be properly considered. In any event, it would be preferable to insolvency if indeed that were the alternative.

"Not only do players have rights, but the club itself has rights, and surely one of them is to determine and adopt conditions and measurements and policies in general which in the opinion of the club conduces to better attendance, park attractiveness, and public comfort, and surely no one player should be consulted very much when it comes to consideration of matters affecting the club as a whole.

"The fact that one player is even willing to advance his own interest at the expense of other players on the club itself disqualifies him as having in mind team spirit. Victory in games is subordinate to the record he keeps on his own cuff. That is not generally considered to be good."[13]

Was Rickey overstating Kiner's selfishness? After all weren't other right-handed hitting Pirates also benefiting from the shortened fence? Rickey turned this argument on its head. Weren't the park conditions unfavorable to his left-handed hitters? Or, conversely, weren't his pitchers giving up more home runs to opponents and thus inflating their own personal statistics? In all likelihood he disliked the Gardens on its own merit. However, the audacity of a *player* trying to dictate the dimension of a ballfield tickled the Mahatma's ire to no end. To Rickey, this request of Kiner's was just more fuel to his argument that their left fielder was motivated solely by his own self-interest:

"To the extent that any player requires or seeks special conditions for his own sake as against the other players, or as against victory, or against attendance receipts or against public appeal is saying 'to hell with other players and receipts and the pennant and everything else. All that counts with me is my home run record and the club must put in writing the physical boundaries of the park as I dictate.' This idea simply had to be in his head when he made the request to you."

Rickey's complaints extended beyond the playing field. His letter to Galbreath occasionally reads as a petty diatribe which is based in purely personal animus.

"[Kiner] is tied up too closely, I think, with another person who shares a so-called bachelor apartment in Pittsburgh paying $175.00 per month, two bedrooms. The friend is well known for promiscuous domestic infidelity."

What the aforementioned has to do with Kiner, or his on-the-field capabilities, is not laid out in Rickey's correspondence with Galbreath. The impression is left that the letter was written with the intention of besmirching Pittsburgh's left fielder, by any and all means, in order to convince the Pirate owner that Rickey would be justified in dealing away the Bucs' number one gate attraction.

The fact that Kiner had ample opportunity to increase his income outside the white lines also didn't sit well with Rickey. "He has, in my judgment, entirely too many commercial interests even for the sake of those interests themselves," the big-hearted Mahatma commented, concerned with the well-being of his endorsements. "Baseball must interfere with the attention he should be giving to these other interests, broadcasting, television, personal appearances, name identification for gain."

Rickey conveyed the absurd notion that Kiner's success in his off-the-field ventures would eventually, if they hadn't already, make Ralph something akin to a leper in the Pirate clubhouse. "In establishing extravagant standards for himself, he does in fact establish extravagant standards for everybody, and it doesn't matter whether he seeks to do so or not," Rickey wrote.

"He is now on an extremely extravagant scale of living for himself. His home life, both as to place and manner, and indeed including associates are not possibly consistent with the life of any other player," Rickey continued, on a roll, and his high horse.

"Now, I don't object to that at all except, that, in order to point out that the carrying of these methods and practices over into his baseball relationships which has to do with other baseball players, is definitely bad, very bad."

Indeed, Kiner was bad for team morale in essentially every aspect except the thunderous clouts that sprang from his bat, or so it seemed upon reading Rickey's diagnosis of the situation. Certainly Kiner's position as National League Player Representative didn't dispel any negative feelings Rickey possessed toward Ralph. "That [Kiner's role as player representative] in itself is bad for Pittsburgh, and again this in turn has a tendency to affect and probably does, his playing ability."

Particularly irksome to Rickey was Kiner's meddling with his beloved DeLand school. During the fall of 1951, Rickey was riding an emotional high as he soaked in the success of his latest innovation when Kiner brought the instructional school to the attention of the executive council. "We don't expect any action on this year's school," Kiner told Les Biderman, "but we feel we can protect ourselves in the future. Because if Mr. Rickey's school shows results, other teams might practice it in the years to come and the players under major-league contracts should be paid as they would be during the regular season."[14]

"Ralph gave us some bad publicity...," Rickey complained to Galbreath. "He came out with the statement that these players should be paid a salary for the time they were in DeLand... It was purely an invitational affair. The boys were told in writing, in effect, that if it was inconvenient or expensive or an interference with school or job, they would not be expected to come and under no circumstances would their absence be permitted to affect the most friendly relationships with the club. Ralph's was a very unfair and unjust attack."[15]

Rickey's correspondence with Galbreath is a wondrous piece of baseball literature. Galbreath, like much of Pittsburgh, was easily swayed by Kiner's charming personality and his intoxicating power while wielding a bat. Over the course of fifteen double-spaced pages, Rickey's argument, though at times trivial, was persuasive enough to convince Galbreath that putting the star player on the market was in the club's best interest.

The prospect of trading a fan favorite didn't discourage Rickey; it was an experience he had encountered previously. While in St. Louis, he dealt Rogers Hornsby, perhaps the greatest right-handed hitter of all time in addition to being a favorite among Cardinal rooters, to the Giants for Frankie Frisch.

Several years later, in 1938, Rickey sent pitching immortal, and baseball's greatest Depression-era gate attraction, Dizzy Dean, to the Chicago Cubs. Later still, while at the helm of the Dodgers, he dealt the "Peepul's Cheerce," Dixie Walker, to the Pirates. "I learned from those deals that you have to go slow in disposing of an idol," Rickey said. "Now I have a real dilemma here in the Kiner case. I have a duty to perform for the fans and the stockholders in the Pittsburgh club in the shortest possible time.

"The Pirates have lost money the last two seasons and cannot afford to risk a further reduction at the gate," he expanded. "If we trade Kiner, will a substantial number of fans stay away from Forbes Field? If they do, will they come back if the players who replace him improve the club? Those are the thoughts that I must give serious consideration. I hope I shall be able to make the proper decision. It is mine to make, and I am the man who will have to rise or fall with it."[16]

Armed with the tacit approval of Galbreath, Rickey began working the phones in earnest, hoping to pawn his star player off on some gullible general manager.

No one could accuse Rickey of lack of effort, but one year later Kiner was still on his club and the nuisance of number four had grown in status. Several trade offers had come across Rickey's desk, but no satisfactory deal could be reached. As 1952 turned to 1953, Ralph had retained his title as the undisputed star of a pitiful team, but the King of Swat would have to negotiate a new contract with his number one nemesis. John Galbreath had washed his hands clean of performing in any capacity during the contract talks.

"The signing of Kiner has been turned over to Mr. Rickey as it should be," the Pirate owner announced. "He has complete control and it is just part of the front office routine, along with signing other players."[17]

This statement was certainly an ominous sign for "Mr. Slug" — trading places with his good friend and fan was his archrival. Ralph had little doubt that the negotiations would be acrimonious. Writers covering the Bucs were speculating in print that the Pirates were looking to cut Kiner the maximum allowed — twenty-five percent of his 1952 salary.

"Ordinarily a player who hits .244 is given a decrease in salary," Rickey told reporters. "Maybe it's different in Ralph's case, but I wouldn't say for sure."[18]

"Three things determine the salary of players," Rickey explained in a letter to Galbreath. "First, the ability of the club to pay. Second, the ability of the player to earn. Third, comparative salaries paid to players of like age, ability, and experience. The third of these is the most important because, in addition to affecting the amount of salary, it affects team morale. The reason that pennant winning clubs have difficulty in repeating is due very often and largely to the disparity in salaries paid to players on the same team. The Pittsburgh club is surely in [a] vulnerable spot in this respect."[19]

In the dead of a typically frigid Pittsburgh winter, Kiner's contract debate was the hot topic in town. Mrs. Ethel Rees articulated the feelings of many fans when she told the *Post-Gazette* that she supported her favorite player. "So he [Kiner] had a bad year," Reese reasoned. "So did Rickey, judging from the team he put on the field. I go to Forbes Field to see Kiner. There hasn't been much else to see."[20]

Branch Jr. initiated the bargaining discussions when he flew to California and met with Kiner. The Twig returned home quickly though, as the two men reached an impasse shortly after salutations were exchanged.

"They presented me a proposition for a twenty-five percent cut," Kiner reported. "The ballclub has always been very good to me and I'll go along on a salary cut this year, but not twenty-five percent."[21]

Two weeks later, on February 13, Rickey flew to Hollywood hoping to make headway where his son could not. Ralph Kiner was more worldly and refined than most of the naïve young men Rickey typically convinced to meet his terms, and after sitting down with his adversary found the going no better than what his boy had encountered. Perhaps in an attempt to apply pressure to Ralph, for the first time, Rickey publicly acknowledged that he would be willing to deal Kiner.

"If enough is offered, the answer could be yes, *with the approval of Kiner*. There isn't a player on the team more productive than Kiner," Rickey mouthed. "It's simply a question of how much his production is worth, and we'll settle that soon. Over a seven year span, Kiner has hit more home runs than Babe Ruth did in a similar period. Ralph has always been a team man. I don't think there is any serious concern in the front office over his attitude."[22]

This soothing, politically correct statement was in diametrical contradiction to the observations made throughout Rickey's communication with Galbreath the previous year. Yet the Mahatma was able to keep a straight face and convince the public that he truly hated the prospect of dealing his beloved slugger. Unless, of course, he was left with no option.

Privately, before departing California, Rickey made sure that Kiner understood exactly where he stood in reference to the Pirate fortunes. "We finished in last place with you," he forewarned the star in a thinly veiled threat. "We can finish last without you."

The newspapers were chock-full of reports detailing Kiner's contract request, and some of the most vociferous readers of the daily sports pages were Kiner's teammates. "Looks to me like Kiner is taking good care of himself, and not thinking of the rest of the club," one Buc griped.

Murry Dickson was put off by the rumors that Kiner wanted the retention of Greenberg Gardens guaranteed in his contract. "The Gardens cost me eight to ten victories last season when ordinary fly balls which could have been caught, dropped into the bullpen," Dickson complained.

Another Pirate took Kiner's home run total of 1952, thirty-seven, and subtracted the number of blasts that landed in the Gardens, nine. "That leaves only twenty-eight," he smirked, "rather ordinary class of home run hitter."

Kiner was barraged with criticism even from former allies. Tom Johnson, a man Kiner considered a good friend, complained that Kiner was always the last player to arrive at the ballyard and pulled up to the park in an expensive automobile and "stepped out, the picture of nonchalance."[23]

To this charge, Kiner replied, "How can anyone look nonchalant stepping out of an automobile?"

Johnson also accused Kiner of being the first to go home following a game. He plead guilty to this allegation. "Sure I try to get out of Forbes Field as early as possible, when there are still police around," came the feeble admission. "Some of those Pittsburgh fans take this game of baseball seriously and after I've had a bad day at the plate, I feel I need some police protection."

The deluge of bad press forced Kiner into a defensive mode. "It would surprise you if you were to hear some of the things I've been called," he said during a March 15 telephone conversation with the *Post-Gazette*. "Never in my baseball career, and I can't recall it ever happening to me in my life, had anyone sincerely questioned my honesty."[24]

His anger stemmed from Rickey freely discussing the progress, and lack thereof, in contract negotiations. Branch had no qualms discussing specific requests made by Kiner, which the old man knew would put Ralph in a bad light. "The reporting date, the physical structure of Forbes Field, where or when I play in exhibitions, none of those so called issues is causing the delay in my signing a contract for 1953," Kiner insisted.

In previous contracts Ralph had been granted many perks, in addition to the vast salary he culled. One such special privilege allowed Ralph to travel by plane instead of by train with his teammates at times when Kiner had another business commitment, or when the outfielder was suffering from hay fever during the final stages of the season.

This concession had begun to cause some disruption in the club toward the end of the 1952 campaign. Pirate players grew weary of arriving at their destination after a long trip only to find a well rested Kiner there to greet them. Some peeved Bucs went so far as to ask that he remain in his room so they wouldn't be confronted with the advantages given the star player. Kiner saw nothing out of the ordinary in his desire to fly. After all, *he* paid for the air travel, not the ballclub. He continued to insist that these perks had nothing to do with the hesitation in reaching an agreement.

"The only delay in my accepting Pirate terms is salary," he proclaimed. "And I maintain I'm within my legal rights to hold out because of salary difference. Other players have done it, but never has any player had his character questioned or taken the verbal beating I've been subjected to. I've been threatened because I am exercising my right under baseball law. In almost any other business a man who is dissatisfied with his salary could quit and take another job. In baseball you can't do this. You are the property of a club until traded or sold."[25]

Rickey was fully aware of baseball's by-laws. He had been using them to his advantage for several decades. If Ralph Kiner wanted to play professional baseball in 1953, it would have to be with the Pittsburgh Pirates. However, unless Rickey was able to ink Kiner's signature on a contract he would be unable to deal him to another club. A favorable ending to negotiations for the Pirates would not only help the financially strapped team, but also make it more conducive to trade the home run champ.

Spring training had begun in Havana on March 1, and Rickey had ventured south to study his ballclub. Though preoccupied with the players already in the fold, Rickey still continued the contract talks long distance. A flurry of messages between the Mahatma in Cuba and Kiner in California ended with Kiner's telegram to Rickey on the morning of March 16.

"I accept the terms of your telegram and will report as soon as transportation is available. I am anxious to get to spring training and am in good condition. I hope that I can, in some way, help the team get into the first division and I hope to be with Pittsburgh the rest of my career."[26]

The drawn-out negotiations had left an already strained relationship irreparable. Rickey was feeling his oats; he got the best of Kiner and he wanted there to be no mistake about the outcome. "Kiner played a clever game of delay in reporting," he said, conceding little else. "The only thing he won was a late reporting date, otherwise the terms were that of the club. No player is big enough to dictate how he will travel, when he will play or tell any club what the dimensions of any ballpark will be."

Kiner, in his communication accepting the terms offered, extended an olive branch to Rickey, but the bitterness of the drawn-out negotiations stayed with him. "He was impossible," Kiner said of Rickey years later. "He was a hypocrite. He would use any means to sign a ballplayer for as little as he could get him. He was a mastermind, a brilliant man, but certainly no friend to the ballplayer."[27]

With his tail tucked firmly between his legs, Kiner packed his bags and headed to Havana.

Kiner's arrival in Havana created a bigger stir in a few moments than all his teammates combined had in the previous four weeks of camp. As Kiner appeared at Gran Stadium for the first time, the

exhibition game in progress was largely ignored by the 350 fans in attendance. The sparse crowd instead surrounded the Pirates star, and as the
whole of Cuba had conspicuously done all spring, disregarded the rest
of the Pittsburgh squad.

Cubans couldn't care less, fellow National Leaguers used them for
comic asides, and the pundits believed the chore put in front of Fred
Haney was impossible. Still, the new Pirate manager put a positive spin
on his seemingly desperate situation, "The task doesn't appear hopeless
or impossible to me or I wouldn't have taken the job," Haney firmly
stated. "Every year there's a team that finishes eighth and almost invariably that team moves out the next year. In the case of the Pirates, several things can change the outlook. The kids who were here last season
should benefit by the year's experience both physically and mentally.
The one season should enable them to loosen up in 1953. The difference
between being loosened up and being tightened up is the difference
between a good man and a poor man."[28]

The gung-ho leader of the Bucs was forced to reevaluate his original assessment after spending some quality time with his new club. "For
a few brief weeks the Pirates looked like a million bucks," Haney said.
"Then I took a second look. The players, with the exception of a few veterans, were callow kids with Grade A milk still fresh on their lips. A
blustery boy talked all the time to conceal his nervousness. A timid
boy sweated ice whenever he stepped on the diamond. A mamma's boy
couldn't sleep in strange beds. They all wanted to be big leaguers, and
were to wear Pirate uniforms that year and the next. Then I realized that
I was not so much a big-league manager as the head technician in a lab-
oratory in which experiments were being made not on guinea pigs but
on human beings."[29]

What the Pirates hoped would be a lucrative and equally fulfilling
relationship with their spring hosts was anything but. The Pittsburgh
players observed in Havana were the most "disgruntled group of players" Al Abrams had ever seen. "They are openly hostile about their living conditions," the Post Gazette columnist reported.

One Buc grumbled, "It's no way to even treat a last place club."

The complaint list put forth by the players was long and centered
around their living facilities and the cuisine. The Cuban Sports Commission discovered belatedly that few of their country men wanted to
witness the Pirates in action, and the Bucs certainly weren't attracting
tourists to the island nation. Three weeks into training camp the com-

mission decided the Pirates weren't even worth the electric bill they ran up in their night games. They demanded the remaining contests on the exhibition schedule be played in the daylight ... with no admission charged. Since the Cuban government was picking up the tab on all the Pirate's expenses, the club couldn't quibble with the mandate.

The smallest paid attendance at a night game was 300. The largest was 3,968. March 31 was the lowest point of the spring when an intra-squad game drew only 16, including two park policemen and the driver of the Pittsburgh team bus. The Bucs cost the commission an estimated $60,000, thus it came as no surprise when the Pirates and the Cuban Government mutually agreed to release each other from the remaining two years of their three-year agreement.[30]

The "Grandstand Managers," a Pirate booster club, threw a luncheon for the Bucs at the Sheraton Hotel in Pittsburgh to kick off the new season. A female fan spoke up from the audience: "Mr. Haney," she asked, "how did the Cuban fiasco and the Ralph Kiner controversy affect the morale of the ballclub?"

"I don't believe it was a fiasco," Haney answered. "It was a training camp which the players won't forget for a long while. We had splendid weather and the training facilities were good. I believe if you ask any of the players they will say they enjoyed themselves. We came out of training in splendid condition physically."

Haney then addressed the second part of the query. "I only know this: After Ralph signed his contract there was no harder worker on the club."[31]

The odds makers in Reno didn't concern themselves with any controversy that may have been disruptive to the Pittsburgh ballclub. The odds that the Pirates would capture the National League flag were set at 200–1. Fred Haney had much more faith in his boys than the gambling experts in Nevada.

"I firmly believe," the Pittsburgh manager claimed with what was an unintentional oblique compliment, "that after watching the team through spring training we are not going to finish last again. I want the ballclub to have the same confidence in themselves as I have in their ability."

As usual, the Mahatma saw his Pirates through rose-tinted glasses. "Without intention to permit jocular implications, I state unhesitatingly that the Pittsburgh club is on its way up, and without retrogression, toward a National League pennant."

If exorbitant hyperbole could capture a championship, Pittsburgh would clinch the pennant by July 1. Unfortunately, profuse verbiage had yet to propel a lackluster ballteam to victory, but such certainties didn't stop Rickey from pouring forth his propaganda.

"We have the foundation to give Pittsburgh a winner," Rickey said glowingly of the Pirates future.[32] Branch was speaking to a small gathering of reporters in John Galbreath's downtown Pittsburgh office. While puffing on his ever-present cigar, Rickey prattled on for two hours, touching on a dozen points that underlined his enthusiasm. High on Rickey's list was the arrival of the O'Brien twins, Eddie and Johnny. The Seattle, Washington, natives admitted that it was Bing Crosby's influence that helped sway the identical twins to sign with the Pittsburgh organization. The O'Brien brothers, of whom one writer asked, "Can you two tell each other apart?" were "the finest young prospects" Rickey had seen in several years. "They can't miss, I'll wager that," the Mahatma guaranteed.

He was also ecstatic with the abilities of outfielder Paul Smith. "He'll hit .300 or better," Rickey anticipated.[33]

The growing pains of 1952 would, without a doubt, pay off for the Pirates. If not in 1953, then certainly soon after, came the message from Rickey. But the Mahatma's constant promises of a brighter tomorrow were beginning to fall on deaf ears, though he never failed to gather an audience.

"I saw one thing [that] only emphasizes my job here in Pittsburgh," Rickey told the assembled radio and print media at his weekly press conference. "That was the way the fans turned out when the club had the five game winning streak. I thought to myself, 'Let's not act like a man that is seventy-one, I have to believe I am forty again and work that much harder to bring them a winning club.' They showed they haven't quit on our endeavor."[34]

The revitalized Rickey was referring to a modest win streak the Pirates had in May. The string of victories spurred Pittsburgh fans to flock to the Oakland district to enjoy, however brief the moment, the sensation of victory for the home team. Branch was forced to cut the luncheon with the press short. He apologized to the writers, but he had an appointment he must keep with Wid Mathews, the Cubs general manager.

"I don't know what Wid has in mind," Rickey told the newsmen. "We have met on several occasions and talked about many things."

At 12:12 the following afternoon what Mathews had in mind was made clear. The Pirates had completed the biggest trade in the history of the franchise. Slightly an hour before the Bucs' June 4 contest with the Cubs, Branch Rickey announced that Ralph Kiner, Joe Garagiola, George Metkovich, and Howie Pollet had been sent to Chicago in exchange for Preston Ward, Bob Addis, Bob Schultz, Toby Atwell, Gene Hermanski, and George Greese. In addition to the six players, Pittsburgh was to receive an estimated $100,000. The players involved in the swap hurriedly dashed to the opposite clubhouse and switched uniforms.

Along with the trade announcement, Rickey let it be known that Greenberg Gardens would be torn down prior to the June 6 contest against Cincinnati. It wouldn't have surprised those who were aware of Rickey's chilled relationship with Kiner if the Mahatma would have delayed the Pirate-Cub contest so the garish fence could be removed before Kiner's first at bat as an opponent in Forbes Field. Regardless, Rickey was made aware after the trade that to tear down the Gardens before the end of the season, he must have the approval of the seven other teams in the senior circuit.

Having stated both publicly and privately that he "didn't believe in building artificial barriers to suit any individual," one is left to ponder the reasons behind Rickey's restraint in not ordering the Gardens be torn down during any of the three previous off-seasons of his tenure as the Pirate general manager.

If Murry Dickson had his way, Rickey wouldn't have to wait for league approval. "I might be out there tonight with a block and tackle to take the Gardens out of there," Dickson joked.

The key man in the ten-player deal wasn't surprised at the news of the transaction. "The trade didn't come as a complete shock to me," Kiner said after the 6–1 Pirate victory. "I figured it would happen from the day Branch Rickey came here. I guess I'm not his type player."[35]

As Ralph took the field wearing the road gray Chicago uniform with the number 29 stitched on the back, the Pittsburgh faithful gave their hero a round of applause which was rousing, considering the paltry number of patrons present. Kiner was appreciative of the fans he had gained during his days in the home whites. "I'm sorry to leave Pittsburgh," he admitted, "which has been my home for some many years, and I'm sorry to leave so many fine friends here. The fans have treated me well."

The deal quickly sliced the Pirate payroll of some $122,000. In addition to Kiner's $75,000 salary, Pollet made $20,000, Garagiola $15,000, and Metkovich $12,000. The total of the six salaries taken on were under $50,000. Add in the $100,000 cash received in the deal, and the financially strapped Bucs certainly came out of the trade in good shape fiscally, if not in actuality.

Following the deal only Murry Dickson, Bob Friend, and Danny O'Connell remained from the 1951 club Rickey inherited. O'Connell wasn't on the active roster in 1951 as he served in the Army, but he was Pittsburgh property. The turnover in personnel was sweeping. Perhaps not coincidentally, the June 14 deal with the Cubs sent the Pirates' team representative, Pollet, and National League representative Kiner, to Chicago. Kiner's pro-active role as league representative was a constant thorn in the side of Rickey.

Rickey's vision of a vast network of minor league teams affiliated with a major league club radically changed professional baseball. Prior to 1921, when Branch developed the farm system for the St. Louis Cardinals, big league teams purchased players from independently owned minor league teams. Cash-deprived clubs like the Cardinals could not financially compete in the bidding process for the best minor league talent, and were thus left to fill their rosters with leftover bush-leaguers.

"Starting the Cardinal farm system was no sudden stroke of genius," Rickey modestly explained. "It was a case of necessity being the mother of invention. We lived a precarious existence. Other clubs would outbid us; they had the money, and the superior scouting system. We had to take the leavings or nothing at all."[36]

The innovation was an unqualified success for the Redbirds. The St. Louis farm system became a pipeline of talent for the Cardinals, and the club was able to sell off excess players for much needed capital. Rickey couldn't have imagined his plan working better. From 1920, when St. Louis bought Jesse Haines from Cincinnati, until 1945, the organization purchased no players. The unmediated result of the farm system was nine National League titles for the Cardinals through 1946.

"We knew our own material; we had followed it for several years," Branch explained. "We brought it along to each level. That justified a larger scouting staff, which meant more players were signed and put into the proper area of competition. We controlled the institution and discipline, and we had a much better idea of a player's major league ability than if we had gone blindly into the open market."[37]

Rickey's farm system wasn't without its detractors. Cynics would come to call Branch's plan, "Rickey's plantation." The connotation being

the players in the St. Louis system were little more than slaves
to the big league club.

"I was a number to Branch
Rickey," former Cardinal farm-
hand Lou Kahn said. "He ran
baseball *factories,* and he
screwed his players every way
but right side up."[38]

Baseball's first commis-
sioner, Judge Kenesaw Mountain Landis, disliked not only
the farm system, but also the
man who originated the concept. The Judge would often
refer to Branch as "that sancti-
monious so and so." Rickey's
practice of "quality through
quantity" drew the attention of
Landis. The commissioner's
dislike for the farm system and
his aversion for Branch led him
to curtail the Cardinals' ever-
expanding organization. The
judge's campaign culminated
with the Cedar Rapids decision

Branch Jr. surveying the minor league rosters.

in which he "freed" ninety-one Cardinal farmhands. The justification
behind the decision was Landis's staunch belief that Rickey was guilty of
collusion.

According to the judge's ruling, Branch and the Cardinals had
attempted to obtain "complete control of the lower classification clubs
through secret understandings." Landis was also aghast to learn that the
Cardinals controlled all clubs in the Nebraska State League, thereby
making every player in the league a St. Louis prospect.

Rickey, and his grand scheme of developing his own players, survived the judge's jurisprudence. Following the Cardinals' great success,
other major league clubs followed suit, but no team ever attempted to
build the wide-ranging system that Rickey constructed in St. Louis. Even
after every other organization replicated Branch's farm system, Rickey

remained fiercely protective of his brainchild, and staunchly defended any criticism that may have been directed at the institution.

The popularity of the minor leagues had been on the wane in the wake of the Korean conflict. In previous war time settings the number of minor leagues and attendance dropped significantly. The Korean affair proved to be no different. Those who were predisposed to bury the minor league system used the current decline to sound the death knell of the farm system. The number of leagues in the minors had dropped from a peak of fifty-nine in 1949 to thirty-eight for the 1953 season.

Branch Rickey saw no need to worry about the state of the minor leagues. Relaxing in his Forbes Field office, Rickey leaned back in a swivel chair and discussed the problems confronting organized ball. "I'm not alarmed at what I see in the future for the minor leagues," he said, all the while chewing on an oversized black cigar. "Don't forget that the Pirates are in the minor league business with their farm club and I am vitally interested.

"The only trouble is that the minors, like the majors, geared their expenditures to the tremendous increase in attendance which followed the ending of World War II. Now they must realize that, even though it is undeclared, we are now in World War III and every business, including baseball, must tighten the hatches.

"Expenses in the minor leagues, where income has not kept pace with outlay, must be paired down. Office expenses, hotel bills, travel costs, player limits, must all be cut. It is a fundamental precept that you can't pay out what doesn't come in. And this relates to player's salaries as well as everything else."[39]

James T. Gallagher, the business manager of the Chicago Cubs, entered into a debate with Rickey in the pages of *The Sporting News*. The matter of discourse was the viability of the minor leagues.

"You read that this club controls three hundred players, that club controls two hundred," Gallagher complained. "A couple of years ago I read that, under Branch Rickey, the Brooklyn club had control over as many as six hundred players. That sort of thing is murderous to the game. No club needs to control over even the forty players it is permitted to carry on its reserve list, because it never can play more than twenty-five of them between May 15 and September 1."

Gallagher's solution went against the very premise instituted by Rickey when he originated the farm system. "The first thing we have to do is leave each major league club on its own," Gallagher suggested.

"Take away from each club its working agreements, its right to take players off, its self-owned affiliates."

Rickey's response to the Chicago executive was one of condescending indignation. "Baseball would stop overnight if we had no farm system," he emphatically stated. "Where would the players come from?

"In baseball, disaster can be avoided by income meeting expenses. If the farm system was needed years ago out of necessity, it is surely needed now. I say the farm system is a necessity. It saved the game once.

"Like our democracy, the farm system is not perfect, but it's the best thing we've got. No, I am reminded of another parallel. It would be wonderful if all the families in the world could have children in this way, but they can't, so they adopt them. We sustain our own pride and happiness and bring happiness and well being to the fortunate children. It's much like that with the minor leagues. It would be ideal if they could support themselves and prosper, but they can't, and so we [the majors] came to their aid and comfort."

James Gallagher's recommendation was taken as a personal affront by Rickey. "Gallagher now wants to put baseball back in the hands of the millionaires," Branch complained. "Sure, money can buy, but we learned through 'blood, sweat, and tears,' how to accomplish results with good judgment."

Gallagher also offered forth in his interview with *The Sporting News* that, "fewer worthwhile players are coming up than ever before."

This lament sparked a boisterous retort from Rickey. "We're producing more players today than ever before in the history of the game... If the war were to stop tomorrow and the players return, we'd have more players than ever before. The minor leagues couldn't afford to go out and dig up players. If you remove working agreements, you simply wouldn't have minor-league teams. Kill the farms and you have no minors. You wouldn't want to sign budding prospects without a place to develop them."

Rickey went so far as to say that without the farm system, six years following the introduction of the first black player to the major leagues, baseball would not yet be integrated. "Do you think for one minute we could have brought Jackie Robinson right into the majors without a previous trial in the minors?" he asked. "We learned at Montreal that Robinson had the stuff and the temperament, and his way to the majors was made smoother by his term in the minors."

Even in the current time of hardship, the Mahatma argued, the game would persevere. "Some [minor league] owners cry, 'But if we cut salaries, if we offer a boy less than he can get working in a gas station, we will lose him.'

"American boys are no different from what they were thirty years ago. You can't tell me that the attitude, the ambitions, the courage and fortitude of our youngsters have deteriorated in less than two generations. I am dealing with boys day after day and I can't see any difference. In fact, as I think, I believe that the present youngster has more ambition than his predecessors."

The advent and growth of various youth leagues — the Babe Ruth League, Little League, American Junior Legion Leagues — were serving as incubators for professional baseball.

"Do you know that there were more than 300,000 boys under twelve years of age playing in organized Little Leagues last year?" Rickey inquired of his interviewer, Dan Daniel. "And within two years, there will be at least 500,000. They are learning the game, [and] their love for it will become an integral part of their lives, their whole beings."

These leagues, Rickey contended, would serve not only baseball, but society as a whole, by curbing juvenile delinquency. "Idle time on their hands is dangerous time," he preached. "They do not think, they act. Playing baseball is filling this time in the finest possible way, and Organized ball is going to reap a harvest it did not sow. In a few years there will be so many boys playing, or wanting to play baseball, that teams will start up all over."

The wise and obstinate Mahatma summarized his two-hour dialogue with a judicious prediction, "Baseball faces its Golden Age."[40]

The Pittsburgh Pirates were still longing for any indication that their "Golden Age" was somewhere on the horizon, but the organization was showing no outward signs of revitalization. Once again, despite Fred Haney's protestations prior to the season, the Pirates finished in eighth place in an eight-team league. Even with an improvement of eight games over the 1952 win total, the Bucs still finished a whopping fifty-five games behind the Brooklyn Dodgers.

Rickey didn't let the depressing truth of the National League standings deter him in his pursuit of players that would, in time, turn those standings on their head. Signing kids fresh out of high school was still the main source for stocking the Pirate farm system, but beginning in 1953 Rickey began to delve deeper into the college ranks in search of talent. A spate of collegiate signings caused some writers to dub the club

Kings of futility, the 1952 Pittsburgh Pirates.

"Rickey U." After Branch brought in Jack Shepard of Stanford and Pete Naton from Holy Cross, the number of ex–college players signed by Pirate scouts in 1953 was six.

The reasons for Rickey looking to the college ranks for help were simple, with four years of ball already under his belt, the college boy was obviously more advanced than a kid straight out of high school. Members of the Pittsburgh press were questioning why Rickey had altered his program for stocking the farm system and the major-league club. "I know Mr. Rickey hasn't changed his program. The scouts have no different instructions from 1951," Clyde Sukeforth said. "It just happens that we have found more prospects this summer. Back in '51, when Mr. Rickey took over in Pittsburgh, we covered all the college tournaments, just as we have this year. But the talent didn't measure up to the boys we signed this season."[41]

Sukeforth should be taken at his word. The Pirates had been scouring the land in search of ballplayers anywhere and everywhere. Rickey ordered his scouts to seek out help, not only on the sandlots of middle America, but in prisons where inmates played on rock infested infields.

Army and Navy teams were looked at as well as black colleges. The unorthodox scouting techniques yielded little in terms of major league prospects, but did render insight on how resolute Rickey was in his desire to turn around the moribund Pittsburgh franchise.

Rickey's efforts were producing little more than copious criticism from the press. Les Biederman, a beat writer for the Pittsburgh *Press* and a correspondent for *The Sporting News*, in particular was biting in his analysis of the Rickey regime. Following several dispatches in *The Sporting News* in which Biederman questioned Rickey's baseball acumen, he was relieved of his duties at "Baseball's Bible."

J. G. Spink, publisher of *The Sporting News*, wrote to Biederman and explained the reason behind his dismissal. "Your letters [columns] reflected a sour attitude towards the Pirates for some time and particularly Rickey, which I felt were just not consistent with the news policy of a baseball paper that tries to be objective.

"Now you know we have never hesitated to criticize anyone in baseball, including Rickey, when we felt such criticism was justified, but we have never kept heaping criticism and abuse just because we, or any of our correspondents, happens to dislike a particular individual."[42]

Using his columns as evidence, it doesn't seem as if Biederman was pinpointing abuse on Rickey. Rather, he was simply reporting a reasonably accurate portrayal of Pirate family happenings. Of particular annoyance to the Mahatma was Biederman's report that, "The lineup that took the field for the Pirates on June 6 against the Reds at Forbes Field probably presented the lowest paid nine men on a big league team in recent years. Not one player is believed to be earning more than $9,000 a season."

Biederman also informed readers that following the Kiner deal Rickey appeared on a local Pittsburgh television show and explained why the trade was made. The scribe then pointed out that the show following Rickey's appearance was called, "Now I'll Tell You One." Hardly libelous, but offensive nonetheless, to Spink ... and Rickey.

Branch addressed the affair in a letter to Galbreath: "I have been around newspapermen all my life, and I have had plenty of criticism on my judgment on how to build ball clubs and a lot of other things, but Les Biederman has caused me for the first time ever to go past the writer himself with any kind of protest. Very definitely I am not in front of any kind of compromise with this man as long as he shows malice and distrust and makes personal accusations. I have no use for him and I will have nothing whatever to do with him and I will tell him just that, and my action will be in accordance with that position. There are two kinds of writers. Biederman represents one kind and a man like Arthur Daley represents the other."[43]

Why did Rickey burden himself with the writings of a correspondent? There is no doubt, despite Spink's denials, that Rickey used his influence to have Biederman removed from his post at *The Sporting News*. But the Mahatma had no such pull with the editors at the Pittsburgh *Press*, and Biederman continued to have a forum for revealing the facts as he perceived them. By having his antagonist removed from *The Sporting News*, however, Rickey was able to quell a critic with a national platform.

Several weeks following the Biederman furor, Rickey answered questions posed to him by George Kieseda, who asked Branch about newspaper criticism of his various decisions. "I've got to risk that," the Mahatma answered without a hint of irony. "I can't please everybody. You rise or fall on the best judgment you have of your team. If you wait until the public knows the players are no good you're too late. You must anticipate. You must have made a mistake, in which case the fans have a right to criticize. I don't expect any encomiums at the moment, I'd have to search pretty hard myself to find something nice to say about myself."[44]

Rickey could, and did, find reasons to pat himself on the back. When queried about charges in print that he was making trades solely based on monetary reasons, Rickey's bushy eyebrows furrowed. "That's a joke!" he howled. "If they [his critics] will consider age and experience, I believe they'll find I pay the highest salaries in baseball. I have no trouble signing players. I have happy players. I'm liberal on salaries."[45]

However generous Branch was when bequeathing salaries to his subordinates was certainly debatable. In Pittsburgh, more so than any stop since his days with the St. Louis Browns, Rickey had reason for being tight with his owner's money. As the 1953 season wound to a close, the Pittsburgh Pirates, in all practicality, were insolvent.

Player salaries represented only one third of the expenses incurred by the Pirate baseball club. The team was also responsible for numerous incidentals. First-class train fares, along with transportation between the hotel and ballpark, were the burden of the team. The Pirates were also accountable for hotel rooms and meals. Jim Herron estimated the expenses over the course of seventy-seven away games, hotels, meals, transportation, et cetera, came to approximately $70,000.

Additional expenses: $48 per uniform, with five complete uniforms needed for each player. The price of one dozen baseballs averaged $20. Herron estimated the total number of baseballs needed for the Bucs and all their farm clubs in the organization to be in the neighborhood of 1,000. The team would also have to purchase between 1,000 and 1,200 bats at a cost of $2.50. Even materials as minute as a set of bases were expenditures the ballteam was required to meet. Six sets of bases, which certainly weren't tattered due to overuse by the Bucs, cost the Pirates $40 a set.

Maintaining the playing surface of Forbes Field was the responsibility of a grounds crew of two dozen men. These men were employed year round and their wages were an estimated $60,000 to $65,000. Sodding the outfield, foul territories, and the infield ranged between $15,000 and $25,000 a year.

Those expenses were the tip of the proverbial iceberg. Pirate payroll expenses since the McKinney takeover were as follows:

1947	$300,000
1948	$300,000
1949	$325,000
1950	$460,806
1951	$300,000
1952	$400,000

The continual financial concerns that had burdened the ownership group had begun to fatigue the Pirate president. "I have my hands in several businesses," John Galbreath said, "most of them much bigger than baseball, but none has ever given me the worry and headaches I get out of being a big league club owner."

Galbreath's partner, Tom Johnson, also had become dismayed with the condition of the Pittsburgh franchise. "It's not much fun anymore," Johnson admitted. "When we first started out it was a lot of fun, especially the big year we had in 1948. But now, I don't know. Even my close friends kid the devil out of me about the Pirates."[46]

The inept performance between the white lines had taken much of the steam from their sails. These men were privy to information that neither the fans nor the press had access to. The sorry plight of the club on the playing field was, perhaps, matched only by the terrible financial condition in which the organization had found itself.

An August 30, 1953, memorandum from Jim Herron detailed for Rickey the bleak economic state of the team. "Our immediate cash position is very critical," the Pirate treasurer warned. Herron then listed twenty-one debts that would come due over the course of the ensuing two weeks:

 1. Accounts payable to be paid immediately, including
    Rickey's pay check $39,000
 2. August Admission taxes 28,300
 3. August withholding and Social Security taxes 18,400
 4. Insurance premiums for Pittsburgh and New Orleans 24,500
 5. Park employee payroll due September 5 9,900
 6. Maintenance crew payroll due September 2 6,200
 7. New Orleans owned accounts payable, including taxes 22,300
 8. Waco owed accounts payable, including taxes 5,600
 9. Brunswick owed accounts payable, including taxes 3,900
10. New Orleans player payroll due September 7 5,000
11. New Orleans park payroll due September 5 3,500
12. New Orleans semi-monthly payroll due September 15 1,300
13. Brunswick player, park, and office payroll due
    September 15 3,200
14. Waco player, park, and office payroll due September 15 3,500
15. Pittsburgh payroll on September 15 43,500
16. Bonuses due players due September 15 10,000
17. Owe Fond duLac for players due September 10 5,200
18. Forbes Field income tax due September 15 900
19. Forbes Field dividend due September 15 4,000
20. Scout expenses 2,100
21. Bank loan interest 5,000

$245,000

The Pirates had $32,000 cash on hand, and Herron's estimation of the team's income during this period was $62,000, leaving the club $151,300 shy of their obligations.

A similar letter was sent from Herron on October 7. "If our cash condition becomes publicly known, it might result in considerable embarrassment to Mr. Galbreath, Mr. Johnson, and yourself. I am greatly concerned about such a development since our creditors are numerous and widespread, both as to the type of business and geographic location.

The failure to make free agent bonus payments when due could prove a handicap to our future scouting if it becomes known."[47]

Instead of traveling to New York for the Subway Series between the Dodgers and Yankees, Rickey flew to Billings, Montana, for a hunting expedition. Joining him in "Big Sky Country" was Bob Cobb. Prior to heading back east, Rickey was presented with a live owl by the Billings Mustangs as they declared him, "one of the wisest men in the game." The honorariums continued when Branch went back home to Stockdale, Ohio. On October 19 he was honored by the communities of Stockdale and Lucasville. Rickey visited his birthplace and addressed the student body at Valley High School in Lucasville. Following his trip home, he flew to Cleveland, where he was celebrated as one of the fifty famous sons and daughters of Ohio. And on the October 20, Rickey appeared on Bob Hope's national television show. All the events in Cleveland were part of an Ohio sesquicentennial celebration.

Exactly one week after Branch's homecoming, his sixty-five-year-old brother Frank died in Portsmouth, Ohio, of a heart attack. Frank had played professional ball in 1910 with Galveston and Chillicothe. He later joined the Cardinals scouting department in 1926, and stayed with the Redbirds until 1943 when he went to the Giants. He rejoined his brother in Brooklyn in 1946 and followed him to Pittsburgh.

Branch returned home again to bury his brother.

5. The Sun
Will Be Rising

Nothing Rickey would ever accomplish in his life would better emulate his vision of the American Dream than his gift to baseball: the signing of Jackie Robinson. For his part in breaking baseball's color line Rickey was labeled by some as a modern-day Abraham Lincoln. Though Branch steadfastly refused to place himself in the same pantheon as the sixteenth President of the United States, the comparisons must have pleased the self-admitted admirer of Lincoln.

The decision to introduce Robinson into organized baseball was made with much deliberation over the span of several years. Under the guise of aspiring to stock a feigned Negro League team called the Brooklyn Brown Dodgers, Rickey had his scouts seek out a man who not only had the physical talent to play in the major leagues, but also the proper makeup to bear the mental anguish the first black was sure to endure.

Jack Roosevelt Robinson was qualified on all counts, but Rickey didn't make his determination until he personally interviewed the twenty-six year old in the fall of 1945. The Mahatma squared off with Robinson in his Montague Street office — a confrontation designed to test Jackie's mettle.

"Have you got the guts to play the game no matter what happens?" Rickey asked Robinson. "That's what I want to know."

Jackie, without hesitation, responded, "I think I can play the game, Mr. Rickey."

The Mahatma knew there would be more to this expedition than the ball game on the field. Robinson's experiences would be unique, and Branch wanted to make certain Jackie knew the going would be tempestuous. "So I'm an opposing player, and we're in the heat of a crucial game," Rickey gave as an example. "I slap the ball out into the field and I'm rounding first and I charge into second and we have a close play and I collide with you. As we untangle I lunge toward you," Rickey, who was pacing the floor of his office as he talked, suddenly lunged toward Robinson, "and I shout, 'Get out of my way, you dirty black son of a bitch!' What do you do?"

Jackie, who was silently stunned by Rickey's demonstration, knew the proper reply, but before he could respond another barrage followed.

"You're playing shortstop and I came down from first, stealing, flying in with my spikes high, and I cut you in the leg. As the blood trickles down your shin I grin at you and say, 'Now how do you like that, nigger boy?' What do you do?"

Robinson was a man brimming with self pride and never let such language pass without retribution. "Mr. Rickey," he asked, "do you want a ballplayer who's afraid to fight back?"

It was exactly the question Rickey was hoping to provoke. "I want a ballplayer with guts enough not to fight back," he answered with a flourish.

"Remember what I said, Jackie. This is one battle we can't *fight* our way through. No army, no owners, no umpires, virtually nobody on our side. This is a battle in which you'll have to swallow an awful lot of pride and count on base hits and stolen bases to do the job. That's what'll do it, Jackie. Nothing else."[1]

Robinson's debut in the minor leagues came in 1946, and the following spring he became the first black to play major-league baseball in the twentieth century. Jackie's play on the field, and his conduct off, were exemplary. Had Rickey made no other contribution to the game of baseball other than that of Jackie Robinson, his place in its history would be secure. Though Robinson suffered through many of the indignities that Rickey expected, "the great experiment" was an irrefutable success. In baseball, as in many other enterprises, the competition mimics proven success. Still, in the bigoted world of organized baseball, change came ever-so-slowly.

Rickey's courage for his part in the integration of baseball is seldom questioned, but the motivations behind his bravery are sometimes debated. The cynical believed that Rickey's incentive for desegregating the game was not entirely puritan. Some critics felt the entire scheme was concocted by Branch purely for financial gain. These detractors believed Rickey envisioned Ebbets Field full of black fans flocking to see their hero.

Commentators also quibbled with the fact that Rickey harvested talent cultivated in the Negro Leagues. Rickey would rarely, if ever, reimburse the owners for players that he plucked from the rosters of black baseball's teams. "Mr. Rickey didn't even answer our letters when we wrote him about [Don] Newcombe, let alone give us anything," Effa Manley, co-owner of the Newark Eagles, said. "He knew we were in no position to challenge him. The fans never would have forgiven us."[2]

Ricky justified this "raping" of the Negro Leagues. They were, he said, "a front for a monopolistic game, controlled by booking agents in Chicago, Philadelphia, and New York."[3]

"They [the Negro Leagues] are the poorest excuse for the word league and by comparison with organized baseball, which they understandably try to copy. They are not leagues at all. I failed to find a single player under contract, and learned that players of all teams become free agents at the end of each season."

Rickey's opinion of the Negro Leagues was undoubtedly self-serving. His total disregard for the affairs and well-being of the Negro Leagues is reprehensible. His detractors, though, overlooked the verity that his actions concerning the Negro Leagues, however deplorable, were greatly outweighed by his resolve to tear down the color barrier in organized baseball.

The seeds of integrating baseball were sown in Rickey's mind as early as 1904 when he was a twenty-three-year-old manager at Ohio Wesleyan University. The tale of Tommy Thompson, the sole black on OWU's squad, forced Rickey to confront the reality of the America he inhabited and the lofty ideals that the country he so cherished was founded upon. The truths that all men were created equal was not readily apparent in a land where its government and people imposed varying forms of apartheid throughout its boundaries.

On a trip to South Bend, Indiana, where Ohio Wesleyan was slated to play Notre Dame University, Thompson was refused lodging at the Oliver Hotel solely because of the color of his skin. An outraged Rickey demanded the hotel relent with the threat of moving his entire team. Against the wishes of the boarding house manager, a compromise of sorts was met. A cot was provided, and Thompson was to stay in Rickey's room.

It was in the sanctuary of his young manager's room that the events of the day sunk in, and Thompson broke down. The image of his disheartened player remained with Rickey for decades. "Tears welled in the large staring eyes," Rickey recalled. "They spilled down his black face and splashed to the floor. Then his shoulders heaved convulsively, and he rubbed one great hand over the other with all the power of his body muttering, 'black skin ... black skin. If I could only make 'em white.' He kept rubbing and rubbing as though he would remove the blackness by sheer friction."

Rickey continued, "Whatever mark that incident left on the Black boy, it was no more indelible than the impressions made on me. For forty years I've had recurrent visions of him wiping away his skin."[4]

The Inn's attempt to turn away Thompson was Rickey's firsthand introduction to racism, and the vision of the young black man furiously trying to rid himself of his God-given skin color also made a marked impression on him. It was a memory he would hearken back to frequently after he moved to desegregate baseball.

"The Negro in America was legally, but never morally free. I thought; if the right man with control of himself could be found...,"[5] Rickey liked to impress upon all who would listen. Whenever he conjured up the tale of young Tommy Thompson for entranced audiences, even if the story was slightly exaggerated, he was sure to sway some minds to his side.

Despite the proven success of the few clubs that had followed Rickey's lead and integrated, the majority of baseball in late 1950 remained lily white. The Pittsburgh Pirates inherited by Branch Rickey were one of eleven major league teams that remained segregated, a fact wrought with irony. Not only did Rickey have a virtual monopoly on black players in Brooklyn, but Pittsburgh was a city steeped in black baseball history. Two of the finest clubs in the storied Negro Leagues called the Steel City home — the Pittsburgh Crawfords and the Homestead Grays.

In 1938, long before Rickey gave serious consideration to the prospects of integrating baseball, Ches Washington, a writer for the Pittsburgh *Courier,* sent a telegram to then Pirate manager Pie Traynor recommending several players who surely would have helped push the Bucs closer to a National League championship. The telegram reads:

KNOW YOUR CLUB NEEDS PLAYERS — STOP. HAVE
ANSWERS TO YOUR PRAYERS HERE IN PITTSBURGH — STOP.
JOSH GIBSON CATCHER 1B B. LEONARD AND RAY BROWN
PITCHER OF THE HOMESTEAD GRAYS AND S. PAIGE
PITCHER COOL PAPA BELL OF PITTSBURGH CRAWFORDS
ALL AVAILABLE AT REASONABLE FIGURES — STOP. WOULD
MAKE PIRATES FORMIDABLE PENNANT CONTENDERS —
STOP. WHAT IS YOUR ATTITUDE? WIRE ANSWER.[6]

There would be no response. On the subject of integrating the
National Pastime, the sound emanating from Traynor mirrored that of
the rest of organized baseball ... deafening silence. The Pirates would not
acknowledge Washington's proposal. Even in the aftermath of Jackie
Robinson's dynamic arrival in Brooklyn, the club wouldn't make any
attempt to desegregate under Frank McKinney.

William Benswanger, however, on several occasions did voice his
displeasure with baseball's then unwritten ban on blacks. Unfortunately
Benswanger did not have the fortitude to be the individual that would
take the gallant first step. And, by the time Rickey did just that, Benswanger had sold his interest in the Pirates.

Shortly after signing on with the Bucs, Rickey made his intention
of integrating the Pirates known to Branch Jr. "I think that we will take
all good colored players regardless of background, or age, or salaries.
Everything hinges on ability," [7] Branch wrote in a memo to the Twig.

Progress toward desegregating the Pirates, however minimal it was,
came during Rickey's very first spring when Ed "Sante Fe" Morris became
the first black to ever work out with the club. The six-foot-three pitcher
had spent several seasons tooling around the sandlots of southern California dominating semi-pro batters. Morris, who picked up his sobriquet in honor of his travels along the well known railway line, had at one
time pitched for the Kansas City Monarchs of the Negro American
League. Though "Sante Fe" left San Bernardino without a contract,
Rickey did sign a twenty-one-year-old Mexican named Felipe Montemayor. Felipe, an outfielder, worked out with the Bucs for one week
before being assigned to New Orleans.

Though the Pirates counted a dozen Negro players on their various
farm teams in the summer of 1952, none, other than Montemayor, was
a viable major league prospect. With great irony, Rickey, the great pur-
veyor of baseball's integration, couldn't find a black player with enough
talent to join the worst team in the game. The organization's financial

plight, and the ensuing cut-back in scouting, was a significant contrib-
utor to Branch's failure to land a qualified black for Pittsburgh. Still the
failure to desegregate the Pirates by the end of 1953 couldn't be totally
blamed on monetary concerns. The question bears asking: had Rickey
lost some of the passion he felt for the cause of integration? Certainly, if
he felt that strongly about the cause, a black player *could* have been found
adequate enough to play for the pitiful Pirates.

Joe Brown, a minor league executive for the Pirates during Rickey's
regime disagreed with such an assessment. "I don't think it took him so
long to bring a Black to Pittsburgh," Brown stated. "There's no sense
integrating with players who weren't good enough. You've got to get
your hands on good players ... acquiring contracts, signing players, buying them, trading for them, that are good enough to help you."[8]*

As Rickey's third season with Pittsburgh wound to a close, the
Chicago Cubs became the eighth major league team to integrate, leaving eight other clubs with all-white rosters. Slightly more than a month
after the Cubs added Ernie Banks and Gene Baker to their roster, twenty-
four-year-old Curtis Benjamin Roberts became the property of the Pittsburgh Pirates.

Roberts entered professional baseball directly upon graduating from
McClymonds High School in Oakland, California. At age eighteen he
then joined the Kansas City Monarchs where he played under the tutelage of Buck O'Neil and alongside such notables as Satchel Paige, Hilton
Smith, Elston Howard, and Ernie Banks.

In a scene reminiscent of Rickey's encounter with Robinson some
eight years prior, Roberts and his wife Christine were called into the
general manager's Forbes Field office. "I want to know every bill you've
got," Rickey demanded, "I want to know how you and your wife get
along. I want to know every worry that you've got, because it's going to
be rough."

Rickey then explained to the couple that he had chosen Roberts to
break the color barrier in Pittsburgh because he possessed a demeanor
similar to Robinson's. "You'll have to be patient with people," he lectured. "If you hear something from the stands or from any players, you'll
have to let it go. Since you are the first Black Pittsburgh Pirate, you

*Pirates scout Howie Haak did find a player talented enough to help the Pirates — Ernie
Banks. Haak discovered Banks while Ernie was playing with the Kansas City Monarchs. "I
bought him for $1,000 down, $5,500 in thirty days." Unfortunately the cash needed for the
purchase was not approved, and the future Hall of Famer slipped away from the Bucs.

are going to go through these things. You can't let your temper flare up."

Roberts well understood the significance of the venture he was conscripted to undertake. As spring training drew near, his apprehension grew. Christine Roberts painted a picture of her husband worriedly pacing through their home, anticipating what may await him. "Not knowing what was to come ... he was like a caged lion," Mrs. Roberts remembered. "I couldn't do anything to calm him down. He paced, and drank coffee."[9]

"There will be criticisms, much of which cannot be answered and much of which indeed may be justified," Branch Rickey wrote with three full seasons at the helm of the Pirates behind him. "I am by no means perfect. I am not a baseball God. I have never pretended to be so. I do not claim perfection. Far from it. But I am not God damned, and I never will be. No series of articles from writers anywhere can divert me of the job at hand, or dull the edge of my courage to do the things I think ought to be done to bring a great team to this town. Cicero had his Catline, Abraham Lincoln had his Vallandigham, and even ordinary individuals like myself can have detractors who have tangent modifications. Let the records of the future take care of such, and without comment from any now or late."[10]

The trilogy of dismal campaigns stirred up a frenzy of anti-Rickey sentiment in Pittsburgh. His soothing divinations were finally met with recriminations in the press. The men of the fourth estate had put the Mahatma's feet to the fire. But even the most adamant naysayers in print couldn't dampen Rickey's desire to build a Pittsburgh contender. The biggest deterrent to Branch's grand scheme continued to be the red ink in Jim Herron's ledger.

Still, Rickey continued to insist that the economic constraints he was facing wouldn't forestall the inevitable about-face which was within his grasp. Pittsburgh would begin to benefit from his concentrated efforts of building a reputable and prolific farm system, Branch claimed, perhaps as soon as the upcoming season. Rickey held persuasive evidence to back his roseate rhetoric. When developing his great Cardinal teams, Branch undertook a survey which he hoped would determine the length of time it took a player to mature into a "major-leaguer."

"As I recall," Rickey said, "the survey covered the period from 1925 to 1935, or thereabouts. The survey covered ten years and related only to the Cardinal organization."

The initial order of business for Rickey was the determination of what would constitute a regular "major-league player." "I selected the definition arbitrarily," he explained. Rickey's denotation was to include all pitchers who had worked two hundred innings in the major leagues. Other players were rated as "regulars" if they had been on the roster of a major league team for two years.

"The survey showed something in excess of 3.5 years minor league service before a boy could qualify as a regular in the majors. It was a very accurate report, even showing the exact number of days players spent in the minors."[11]

Several years after Rickey's study, the New York Yankees did a similar five-year survey. Using the same criteria as Rickey, the Yankees determined the approximate time spent in the minors for a regular major-league player was four-and-a-half years.

"As applied to the present situation in Pittsburgh, the survey keeps me from being too pessimistic about our club," Rickey said. Since taking over at Forbes Field, Rickey had added roughly 450 players whose names were not in the organization previously. At the start of 1954, approximately sixty were retired, ineligible, suspended, or on the restricted lists. The armed forces claimed 170 of the remaining 390. Left in the farm system were about 220 active players signed by Rickey and his subordinates.

"It is not in the books, surely, for me to expect a more rapid development than I had, say, in St. Louis for example. There are obvious reasons for understanding a greater rate of progress in St. Louis than we had in Pittsburgh. One sufficient reason is the fact that in those days we had far less competition in the free agency field. We were alone in the farm system.

"Pittsburgh spent more money in the year 1951 in securing the contracts of free agents than St. Louis spent in any five consecutive years, during my 25 years there. Of course, our Pittsburgh club ran out of ready cash to keep up the spending orgy that is inevitably involved in the old bonus contracts.

"With further reference to my remark that the record doesn't support to date, any sort of discouraging pessimism, I am prompted to add that until the time comes when these boys have had at least four, and more likely four-and-a-half years, we can not rationally expect the club to arrive as a serious competitor. That would mean it would indicate a good team.

"I remember last spring when Mrs. Rickey and I were coming up the driveway to our home and she called attention to a luxurious rose bush on our yard fence, saying the roses were going to bloom in the next few days. The whole bush was a healthy green, about all of it, just green. At a distance not a single bud was discernible. We got out of the car and went up to the bush and found not less than one hundred buds, more than that. Just a few days later, we again came up the same driveway and upon turning into the yard, there was hardly any green in site on the bush. It was a vivid color.

"The making of a ball club from nothing into something is not too unlike that rose bush. I think I have the right to believe that these youngsters will bloom, perhaps rather suddenly. It is a matter of timing and possibly we will arrive at a better team if players who cannot reasonably be part of a future great team are disposed of at such times as to enable us to raise the proceeds for deals for example to bring about seasonable fruition.

"Nature controls the rose bush and the buds unfold very certainly at a given period in the spring time. I am not a master of development. But all of us in the Pittsburgh organization are doing the best we can to do a job in developing a team along the same lines as the garden illustration."[12]

Thirty-four rookies reported to Shamrock Village in Ft. Pierce, the third spring training home in as many years for the Pirates. The newcomers were being put through the paces by Rickey and a number of his assistants, including Clyde Sukeforth, Fred Haney, Bill Meyer, Howie Haak, Rex Bowen, and Sam Narron. Rickey, as in previous camps, regaled the rookies with a lecture, explaining to the youngsters what he expected from them, followed by a list of regulations. There would be a 7:00 A.M. wake-up call and a midnight curfew. But it was item number four that was emphasized by the Mahatma more than any other.

"This is a training camp in the best sense of the word, and the use of alcoholic beverages is strictly prohibited on or off the premises," he demanded. "Roughhouse tactics will not be tolerated and players will be expected to conform to rules and regulations established by the field managers on the strength of long experience."

Rickey concluded his address to his men whom he hoped would pull the club out of the cellar. "We are developing players who can help produce pennants in Pittsburgh. All of us have a common goal. Baseball is a serious business. Give it all you got."[13]

On March 1 a full squad of Pirates and Pirate hopefuls had just finished their morning meal at the Flamingo Hotel when Haney and Rickey approached a podium to address their men. "First of all, dress and act like a major leaguer," the manager directed his players. "We represent a great city, our owners are big business men, our actions and dress on and off the field must reflect credit to them. Get up at nine. Breakfast well, for no food is to be eaten in the clubhouse except between games of a doubleheader. Shave in your motel room, if you want to, but you don't have to. We're not T. V. actors; we're ballplayers. Report at ten-thirty for day games. Until the game is over, do nothing but think, talk, and play baseball. The blonde in Box 101 may cost you a two-bagger. The loss of the two-bagger may cost us a game."

"I want you fellows to know our aim before we get to work out on the ball field," Haney said, "and it isn't last place. In this camp we have the potential of a first division club and pennant winner of the future."[14]

The enthusiasm which had continually flowed from the lips of his boss had obviously rubbed off on Haney. When he finished his address the manager handed the floor over to Rickey. "I want to correct something," the Mahatma began with his familiar mantra. "Our goal is first place and nothing else. In three departments we have pennant winning players. In my opinion there are five departments of a ball club: pitching, catching, infield, outfield, and first base. I am satisfied that we have pennant producing players at three of them, and possibly a fourth, pitching."

Rickey's pollyannaish view of his team's abilities came to a crashing halt when he discussed the outfield. In his evaluation of Pittsburgh's fly chasers, the Pirate general manager believed he stopped shy of having a club full of "pennant winning players."

It was unlikely, despite Rickey's assurance that three, if not four, departments on the team contained men talented enough to propel the Bucs into the position of chasing a flag in 1954. "I have not said in the past, nor will I say now, we will not finish last again," Rickey emphasized. "But the sun is rising in my estimation ... I don't want defeatism in your minds."[15]

Andy Cohen reveled in observing three of his "boys" attempting to make the Pirates' Opening Day roster. Cohen, the manager of the Denver Bears, was equally proud of the trio—Curt Roberts, Jack Theis, and Nellie King—but took a particular interest in Roberts. "I just hope they stick with Robbie," Cohen said. "He will have some trouble with the pitching in the big leagues for awhile, but he'll be able to handle it well enough eventually."

Cohen's keen interest in Roberts began when he scouted and signed Roberts in Mexico. The two men then spent three years together in Denver. "He isn't a smart alec, but is more on the quiet side," Cohen said. "I noticed here that he was more or less holding himself back. You know how he might react, being the first Negro player on the Pittsburgh club. He doesn't want to make the wrong impression. You'll never have to worry about him along those lines. He is a good boy."[16]

Cohen's words were euphemistic in the world of the 1950s. What the Denver manager was implying was that Roberts would "know his place." Roberts's "place," during spring training, would be the "colored" section of Ft. Pierce, where he, along with the two other Blacks in camp, Sam Jethroe and Lino Donoso, were forced to stay. The remainder of the Buc squad was housed in newly refurbished facilities, a world away from their black teammates.

Roberts had a tremendous spring. In addition to solidifying his reputation for terrific glove work around the second base, he also batted .395 in Florida. Donoso, unlike Roberts, wouldn't be among the players chosen to begin the season with the Pirates. Jethroe would make the club, but following just two regular season appearances, he was released.

Fred Haney took note of his players' reactions when the not-so-lucky men were told they wouldn't be beginning the season in Pittsburgh. "None of them took the news very well," Haney observed. "I don't blame them. No one likes to leave the big leagues."

The most prominent casualty was former bonus baby Paul Pettit. Pettit was the talk of the baseball world when he signed with the Pirates on January 31, 1950. Fourteen of the sixteen clubs in the major leagues bid for Pettit's services, but Pittsburgh's overwhelming offer of $100,000 won out for the youngster's services.

"There hasn't been a school boy pitcher around like this for a long, long time," Rickey, then in Brooklyn, said shortly after the signing. "He's the [Bob] Feller type definitely, and maybe by this time next year a lot of people will be sorry they didn't offer $200,000."[17] Rickey's decree indicated that his proclivity for hyperbole didn't begin when he transferred to Pittsburgh. His statement also was contradictory to his avowal of the bonus rules that he had actively campaigned against in Pittsburgh.

Pettit's major league career never approached the prognostications for greatness that preceded his professional signing. His single victory

Branch, manager Fred Haney, and traveling secretary Bob Rice.

in the National League came on May 1, 1953, against Cincinnati. The Pirates, upon releasing Pettit, assigned his contract to Hollywood of the Pacific Coast League. The Coast League spent just one year as an open classification team. League officials decided to renew working agreements with major league teams, the only stipulation being that the teams would not accept more than five players per major-league club on option from affiliates in the major leagues.

The plan implemented by the PCL in 1953 backfired terribly as attendance dropped off drastically when the major league teams assigned their better players to lower classified minor league teams. The Pirates used their relationship with New Orleans to great effect in 1953, when the Pelicans were given the quality Buc farmhands. The Bucs were pleased with the PCL decision; however, with another year under their belts several Pirate farmhands were finally ready for the more talent-laden Triple A Coast League.

Beginning in 1954, the Pirates would be the first team to make all their regular season trips by air. This decision established another in the long line of baseball firsts that could be directly attributed to Rickey. He, along with Galbreath and Haney, gave the go-ahead for the change in transportation from rail to air in late January. Following the alteration it took six weeks for traveling secretary Bob Rice to coordinate the details, and on March 24 Capital Airlines sent three representatives to Ft. Pierce to finalize arrangements. The club would travel in a fifty seat aircraft. Management took out the maximum insurance allowed with the airline, $3,000,000, and also took out an additional $2,000,000 with Lloyd's of London for the players' families.

Haney was pleased with the new mode of transportation his team would be utilizing. "Practically all the Coast League teams go by air," Haney said, "and have found planes great time savers."[18] He also added that his former club, the Stars, had been commuting by air for sixteen years.

Pittsburgh would now be within a two-hour average of every National League city by air. The longest trip the Bucs would make in the season, New York to St. Louis, would take three-and-a-half hours by air in comparison to twenty-one by train. The only trips that wouldn't be handled by Capital Airlines were the short jaunts between Chicago-Milwaukee, and New York–Philadelphia. The commute between these cities would still be made by rail.

"The main idea of going by air is to have the players sleep in a hotel bed or their own bed every night, which Milwaukee did often last season and with considerable success," Bob Rice said. "The night and day changes in the schedule from one city to the next make it really rough on the players, rushing off a train to play. Rest is all important, and don't forget too, the players could be with their families one night longer before making a trip, and return a day sooner."[19]

In an editorial, *The Sporting News* endorsed Rickey's latest initiative. "While other clubs were making occasional jaunts by air and their officials were still wondering whether all season plane travel would be feasible, The Mahatma, in characteristically vigorous fashion, stepped forward to take the leadership. It is Rickey's custom to act while others talk. In many instances, he has not even reached the talking stage among the game's traditionally conservative leaders."[20]

The group of men that had gathered in Ft. Pierce was absent two veterans who were traded in the off-season. On December 28, Danny O'Connell was dealt to the Braves in exchange for Sid Gordon, Max Sukront, Sam Jethroe, Larry Lassalle, Fred Waters, Curtis Raydon, and cash. Slightly more than two weeks later Murry Dickson was sent to the Phillies for Andy Hanson, Jack Lohnke, and cash.

The O'Connell transaction was typical of the deals that Rickey had been fashioning in Pittsburgh. Throughout his tenure with the Bucs, Branch had been choosing quantity over quality, with a substantial pinch of much-needed cash included. The ages of the players acquired from the Braves dispelled Rickey's oft repeated vow of building through youth. The key men in the deal, Gordon and Sukront were thirty-six and thirty-two, respectively. Jethroe, at thirty-two, was a shadow of the player who had won the 1950 Rookie of the Year Award. Of the remaining three men, only Raydon ever took the field as a major-leaguer, and his career was ever-so-brief.

On March 12, during an exhibition contest in Bradenton against the Braves, Rickey revealed how the O'Connell trade could have been distinctly altered. Rickey sat in the Bradenton stands with Jack Heron, admiring a rail-thin rookie in Milwaukee's camp. The youngster, Henry Aaron, was touted by Rickey as one of the "most outstanding prospects" in all of baseball. The Pirate general manager then confided that he could have obtained Aaron for Danny O'Connell "straight up."[21]

It would have been impossible for Rickey to foretell that the young Henry Aaron he spoke of would become the most prolific home run hitter of all time. However, if Branch truly believed Aaron to be one of the best prospects in the game there is no defending the trade that was accomplished. It had become increasingly obvious that the incentive in Rickey's dealings wasn't acquiring talent that would help the Bucs achieve his goal of first place. The monetary concerns had become much more than coincidental; they had become a necessity. This was a fact Rickey could never admit publicly. The desolate condition of the franchise found Branch seeking reassurance and understanding from his most ardent supporter, John Galbreath.

"I can not help having the feeling that you have lost the ardor for, and the expectation of, an early winning team in Pittsburgh," Rickey wrote Galbreath. "Your interest has not, however, lessened for you have continuously supported the club with substantial loans. As you must very well know, I regret exceedingly whatever contributing part I have played in your disappointments.

"The early expenditures of unusual sums for new players were made with a misunderstanding on my part, whether justified or not, that it was my urgent job to make a winning team as quickly as possible... We are now grossly in debt and an entirely different program, viz, we are to make ends meet, financially, in any event without borrowing anymore money from anybody anywhere. It is my understanding that this is the present policy. This is said upon the assumption that a further loan of $100,000 by yourself and Tom will be made shortly. This change of policy has already meant the marketing of players, largely for cash and it will continue to mean just that if the club should find itself unexpectedly in need of finances.

"Your faith in me, which was indeed very real at one time and indeed has been continuously steadfast has, undoubtedly and understandingly so, been sorely tried. I have not lost one bit of faith in myself or the boys about me, although I have been much perturbed and much embarrassed by the lack of funds. Even if we find it necessary to make cash sales of players contracts, I do not now believe that such sales can do more than retard the development and full realization of a winning team in Pittsburgh. We are on our way."[22]

Rickey took to his job in Pittsburgh with inordinate zeal. His knowledge of the game, and his dexterity in communicating his vision for the Pirates, easily won Galbreath's confidence. However, three years of continual failure on the diamond and the desolate state of the club's financial condition saw the Pirate owner become morose concerning his team. Rickey's aim in writing his letter to Galbreath was to offer justification, and clarification, of his actions thus far as Pittsburgh's general manager. His intent was met, and as an added enticement he helped soothe Galbreath's mounting frustrations with his correspondence.

Galbreath expressed his guarded optimism with Al Abrams. The two men conversed while watching a number of Galbreath's thoroughbreds run at Gulfstream Park. Contributing to the Pirate owner's positive disposition was the success of his horses, as several ponies from his Darby Dan stables crossed the finish line first. "I wish the Pirates would do as well," Galbreath chuckled. "We're beginning to see the light at last. I don't mind telling you I was very much discouraged for a long period, but I believe we're finally on the right road."

Galbreath informed Abrams that the city wouldn't be embarrassed by their Buccos' performance during the upcoming campaign. "Respectability," he declared, "is something the Pittsburgh club will have this year. I admit we didn't have it the past two seasons, but I'm certain now we won't be ashamed of the ball club we'll field for 1954."[23]

The individual whose scheme brought Branch to Pittsburgh, despite his momentary disillusionment, remained the Mahatma's staunchest champion in the Pirate hierarchy. Tom Johnson, never a proponent of Rickey's guile, was increasingly dissatisfied with the general manager's performance.

"It didn't take me very long to become dissatisfied with Rickey," Johnson confided. "I would sit down with and listen to my friends that put him on a pedestal and I couldn't understand how they could be taken in. He never had me."[24]

Johnson's animosity was not one-sided. Though he was a co-owner of the club, and technically Rickey's superior, Johnson was by-passed by the general manager. Instead Rickey reported to Galbreath, who was recognized as the predominant owner of the team. Much of Rickey's distaste for Johnson grew, for the most part, from Johnson's refusal to bow down to the Mahatma. In addition, Johnson's occasional sampling of an adult beverage was an act which was not met with approval by the tee-totaling Rickey.

"At parties I would take a drink with the writers," Johnson admitted, "and I think he thought I drank too much. Rickey had sort of a sneering attitude toward people that would take a drink. I think he felt people who took a drink weren't on the same moral or ethical plain as he. Rickey was such a moral sepulcher. He believed that he was a far better man than some one who took a drink."[25]

Using an adjective he'd learned from a grandchild at Christmas, when the child opened a gift and exclaimed, "I'm gladder than anyone," Rickey told the writers at the Grandstand Manager's Club in the William Penn Hotel on April 26. "I'm gladder about the present mechanical approach to a good ball club than ever before."

Rickey then introduced each player on the club to the gathered media. "Be a little modest, boys. Stand long enough for these people to see you. You're not afraid out there on the ballfield for two or three hours." Every member of the Bucs was identified by Rickey to the assembled press corps. He took the time to say something about each player.

"The tallest man in Pittsburgh, he's 6 foot 8 inches, or 8 foot 6 inches, Nelson King. He is quite a comedian, but also has something above the neck. This boy is quite a character, but can also pitch."

Of the first black to don a Pirate jersey, Rickey chuckled when he said, "This boy will be a fine help if he ever gets in shape."

In reference to Gail Henley, "This chap ran into the right field wall and was injured. He wasn't thinking about the price of the catch. This boy went pell-mell into the wall, not thinking of an injury. It shows the desire of the club and I understand he commented while lying on the ground that he should have made the catch. I'm happy about that."

"The representative of the players, Bob Friend, ... potentially is one of the great pitchers in the game. He will reach there one of these days and I am fondly waiting for it."[26]

Branch was named the head of a committee whose purpose was to restructure the major-league draft. At a July 12 meeting held in Cleveland just prior to the All-Star game, the nine-man committee proposed an amendment to the Major-Minor League rules. The change that the group hoped to implement was that three players could be drafted from any individual minor-league club Class A or higher. Previously only a single player could be drafted from any club.

The amendment was a vital change for the individual player. Hitherto, many players would languish in the minor league, but the new rule would remedy that situation to a great extent. The old policy "would permit the 'haves' to hoard material and exclude the 'have nots,'" one member of the committee explained.

"This change, when adopted, will indirectly reduce the cost of free agency contracts and will have a direct tendency to equalize the opportunities of weaker clubs to get players, and will directly affect the power of money alone to control the playing strength of wealthy clubs,"[27] Rickey elucidated.

This rule change would benefit baseball as a whole, and not coincidentally the Pittsburgh organization specifically. "I had to meet the lack of funds by increasing the opportunity to make a team without funds and this effort [will] have obvious and direct purposes in that direction."

Correspondingly, over the course of the All-Star break, the players' representatives formally organized into the Major League Player's Association. The players denied the Association would become a union. Regardless of that assurance, management was troubled that their employees had become organized.

Baseball owners had long before adopted the philosophy of Henry Ward Beecher, a Brooklyn preacher of the late 1800s: "God has intended the great to be great and the little to be little... The man who can not live on bread and water is not fit to live." Players had few rights in the 1950s. They could play under the conditions dictated by the owners, or they could opt to stay home and procure a "real" vocation. That the players would organize and attempt to bargain for better working conditions rankled management, not excluding Rickey.

The newly formed Association made several proposals to the owners. The players asked that spring training not start prior to March 1 and that no exhibition game begin before March 10. Another request was that the restrictions on the number of players allowed to participate in the winter leagues be lifted. The current rules allowed no more than three men from each team's roster, in addition to two rookies, to play in Latin America in the off-season. "The choice to play should be up to the individual player," the representatives argued, "not up to the organization."

Some owners wanted to not just limit the number of players participating in the winter leagues, but prohibit the practice altogether. Rickey believed winter ball, in moderation, was a good thing. "We must continue our good neighbor policy toward our Latin American brothers, and it would harm that policy to keep our major leaguers from playing winter ball," Rickey stated. "The game is a big factor in manufacturing good relations with our South American, Caribbean, and Mexican friends.

"I am a great believer in the theory that there are just so many pitches in a pitcher's arm, and so many hits in a hitter's bat. If they squander them during the winter, they will not be there for the regular season. I have had some unfortunate experiences which I would rather not enlarge upon."[28]

Rickey saw little need for the Player's Association. His skewed view of the player's well-being certainly wasn't helped by the prominence of Ralph Kiner in the Association. Branch righteously believed the players were well taken care of by ownership. And while there may have been a need of representation on such minor issues as meal money and the like, the relationship between management and labor need not be adversarial. His actual predication was best summed up by Brooklyn Dodger Chuck Connors. "There are two things Mr. Rickey loves," Connors said. "One is players, and the other is money. But for some reason he never lets them get together."[29]

At the age of seventy-two Rickey was still demonstrating a fertile baseball mind. In the August 2 issue of *Life* magazine he revealed a complicated formula that he claimed was the vital factor which determined winning and losing. Rickey asked Allan Roth, the Dodgers' statistician, to help compile the data for his project. The duo concluded that by taking runs scored per game by major league clubs over an entire season and measuring them against opponents, some type of pattern could be concluded.

Statistics were assembled for individual seasons over the previous two decades. The numbers so overwhelmed Roth and Rickey that the two men took their figures to the Institute of Advanced Study located in Princeton, New Jersey.

Rickey determined from the analysis that three basic components for offense were on base average, extra base power, and the percentage of men who reached base and eventually scored. The numbers indicated that the vital pitching stats were hits and walks allowed. "After examining all the evidence," Rickey explained, "I was forced to admit that strikeouts contributed nothing more to the end result than pop fouls caught by the catcher. After all, they were just another means of getting men out. In view of this we valued the strikeouts at one-eighth of the other three more vital factors."

Rickey intended on utilizing this formula into making Pittsburgh a pennant contender.

The formula reads as follows:

$$\text{Offense} \quad \frac{H + BB + HP}{AB + BB + HP} + \frac{3[TB-H]}{4AB} + \frac{R}{H + BB + HP}$$

$$\text{Defense} \quad \frac{H}{AB} + \frac{BB + HB}{AB + BB + HB} + \frac{ER}{H + BB + HB} - \frac{SO}{8(AB+BB+HB)} - F = G$$

For those with a degree in mathematics, Ricky's data were fascinating. Others wondered why the old man was not directly addressing the concerns of the Pittsburgh ballclub. Complicated mathematical formulas do not win pennants ... players do, and the average fan saw little use in the information. The same week that the *Life* article came out Rickey was out of the country on vacation. Taking a holiday in the middle of the baseball season drew the ire of Al Abrams.

"While Pittsburgh fans burn, Rickey fiddles with his fishing rod on a Canadian vacation.... I guess we wouldn't care much either if we were paid $100,000 a year plus expenses."[30]

That wouldn't be the only barb coming from Abrams. Beginning on July 28, the *Post-Gazette* published a six-part examination of the Pirate organization. Authored by Abrams, the series was titled, "The Truth About the Pirates." The initial installment gave the public its first glimpse at the financial condition of the Pittsburgh Athletic Club. The team's indebtedness ran to an "uncomfortable" $1,409,000 according to Abrams, which he broke down in the following manner:

> First mortgage bonds $134,000
> Note Payable to bank $490,000
> Demand note held by Johnson, Galbreath $535,000
> Offered convertible debentures $250,000

Abrams, without citing any sources for his information, estimated that the ownership group had lost roughly $1,850,000. "Financially we've taken a beating," Galbreath admitted to the *Post-Gazette* in an interview conducted for the series. "I'll continue to put up the necessary money until we find out how we stand in 1955. If I thought the sale of the club would remedy the situation, I'd sell in a hurry, but I'm determined to hang on as long as I can. I've never quit on an undertaking while it was down."

Abrams asked the Pirate owner if 1955 would be Rickey's "make or break" year. "We can do little else, but go along with the man," Galbreath answered with what was seemingly a half-hearted endorsement. "We realized in 1950 that our policies weren't getting us anywhere [so] we went out and got the number one man in baseball ... Mr. Rickey."

He continued, "I admit I don't know a thing about the operations of a team, and Tom [Johnson], here will tell you the same thing, that's why Rickey was hired. We believed then, as we believe now, that he will eventually get us out of this mess. We're most unhappy over results so far, but I have the utmost faith in Rickey. When he tells me our farm clubs are ready to produce, I must believe him. When he tells me we will soon have players of championship quality in pitching, catching, and infield departments, I must believe him."[31]

For his third segment of the series, Abrams went to Rickey himself for some answers. "I made the mistake of being too optimistic when I came to Pittsburgh," Branch acknowledged. "No more of that. But, I can assure you it won't be long." He then made a sweeping motion with his arm in the direction of a blackboard on the wall of his office. The board consisted of every roster of each Pirate farm team. "There lies the future of the Pittsburgh Pirates!" Rickey exclaimed. "We're getting more players from the service than are going in. Our farms are beginning to produce the way I thought they would. The young players we have today are even better than those I had in St. Louis and Brooklyn."

Abrams was a veteran of Rickey's proclamations. The writer dutifully recorded the Mahatma's propaganda before launching another pointed question: "Did Rickey regret any player trade that he had made in Pittsburgh?"

"My only regret is that I could have received much more value in return for Gus Bell had I wanted." The Bell trade was easily the biggest blunder of Rickey's Pirate career. Bell, since his trade to Cincinnati, had flourished. Still Rickey was not about to admit the deal was an error. "As far as trading Bell, I'm not sure it was a mistake. He was a .240 hitter in Pittsburgh. He is a .340 hitter in Cincinnati because of his mental approach, and a handy right field fence. When I made that deal I believed, and I believe now, that Bell would not have been the player in Pittsburgh that he might have been elsewhere. He had no adventure, he has none now."[32]

"The Kiner deal was a tempest in a tea pot," Rickey said, switching gears. "I've never regretted it for a minute. Neither do I apologize for any other trade, or sale, I've made here. The majority of clubs need money to operate. I've made deals where the Pirates benefited in a monetary way, but we've never gotten the worst of them."

The interview concluded with Abrams asking whether Rickey was displeased with the results to that point. "Certainly I'm disappointed, but I feel we're far ahead of schedule on our plan."[33]

Rickey's continuous optimistic deliberations were groundless as far as the public was concerned. The content of Pittsburgh's minor league system was of little concern to the average Pirate fan. The paying customer was tired of the repeated promises of a brighter tomorrow when their Buccos showed virtually no improvement at the major league level. The support for Rickey's five-year plan had all but evaporated both in the press and in the public.

Following Abrams' particularly critical look at the Pirate organization, Rickey pleaded his case to the almost always sympathetic *Sporting News*. "There's something more than hope in this organization," Rickey told the St. Louis–based publication. "There is faith … out of which come some facts, some knowledge, and some results. My men have faith."[34]

In a memorandum, he commented: "There is so much truth in criticism that it makes unpleasant reading. I can't afford to take the time to review the contents of all these things. I need all my time and energy to do the job." The distinction between an excuse and an explanation is precarious, and Rickey found himself toeing the thin line repeatedly.

"We were hurt [by the Korean conflict] more perhaps than the other clubs, because we were building with young players and they were the ones needed in the service." At the war's peak, 174 players in the Pittsburgh system were in the armed services; by August of 1954 the number had been reduced to 120.

"It should be noted that as of November 1, 1953, the boys coming out of the service back to our active list will finally equal the number going in," Rickey said. "This means considerable to the Pittsburgh organization because the men we have contributed to the armed services were vital to us at the time and we could have used them. There is scarcely another club in either major league that needed these players as much as Pittsburgh."[35]

"We no longer can use that as an alibi. From here on these boys will be coming out as fast as they'll be going in.

"We have some disappointments here in Pittsburgh," Rickey put forth. "It took me a whole year to find out we didn't have the nucleus for a winning club. I don't say we didn't have good players. But we just didn't have the nucleus. Many of our hopes and expectations and estimates of ability were too high. Some of the players we had and some that we acquired were not what I thought they were."

Rickey stared off blankly, lost in thought, for a moment. For an instant he let down his guard and the optimism vanished, ever-so-briefly, "Maybe the old man has slipped."

"The long hours are getting a little rough on me," Branch confessed. His work days remained long, and he continued to travel extensively. "I'm not getting any younger, but my health is fine," Rickey said in the dog days of August. "I have pushed a lot of work along to Branch Jr. and Harold Roettger. No longer is everything concerning the organization funneled through me."

The Twig was concerned with the workload his father had been assuming. "Dad works awfully hard at his job," the younger Rickey said. "Generally twelve to fourteen hours a day. Another year or two at this pace, plus all the worries he has had might be damaging to his health."

His pledge to slow down didn't refrain Rickey from traveling to Louisiana for a visit with the minor league Pelicans. While entering New Orleans Stadium, Branch suffered a fainting spell. His collapse was caused by Ménière's disease, a form of vertigo. "My doctor tells me that I might have a dozen attacks in one day and then perhaps never have another. I suffered a series of eight attacks in three years and then never had another for a stretch of five years. But about four or five years ago the symptoms returned.

"They tell me that Ménière's syndrome is not fatal, but when you have an attack you sometimes wish it was. It leaves you nauseated and weak. You black out temporarily. Oddly, you are immune if you are totally deaf, it only hits those who are losing their hearing."

Branch had suffered several attacks caused by Ménière's between 1950 and 1954, but these incidents were not publicly known. The occurrence in New Orleans, severe as it was, wasn't going to hasten Rickey's departure from the Pirate front office. It was his intention to serve his contractually agreed-upon five years. "This decision was made four years ago when I came to Pittsburgh," Rickey said. "My contract expires at that time, and it was my decision to retire after next season."[36] The increasingly infirm Branch refused to accelerate his own retirement. If the thought had entered his mind, it was quickly dismissed. Rickey wasn't about to use his illness as an excuse to bail out on his, thus far, failed Pittsburgh venture.

Another last place season was playing out at Forbes Field as Rickey was recovering from the attack of Ménière's. The third consecutive eighth place finish was the catalyst for a confidential note penned by Rickey to his son. The sensitive nature of the letter centered on the general manager's discontent with Fred Haney.

"You know how concerned I have been about the management of our team," Branch wrote. "Never in my life have I been faced with greater reluctance on personal grounds to change an employee. One can have, and does have a sort of affection for Fred regardless of all considerations of capacity, effort, and circumstances. He is kindly, thoughtful, and cooperative, and anxious to do well and spares no personal effort. He does his level best."

A more resolute and unflagging endorsement of a man's character would be difficult to find. However, in Rickey's estimation, Haney wasn't the man needed for the job in Pittsburgh. "We are still confronted here in Pittsburgh, with the developing of young players, a greater preponderance of young players in this coming year than ever before. The job is a teaching job. It needs assignments in detail, individual, and team, for specific kinds of work under skilled and experienced instruction. We have none of that and have had none of it after spring training for the past two years. I don't believe Fred, or anyone of his age is physically able to meet the demands of our managerial job. It takes a younger man. There is nothing but worry in front of Fred for another year and I am thoroughly convinced that the combination beginning with myself, and ending with the bat boy, is not now so set up that we can rationally expect to improve greatly next year."

Perhaps Haney wasn't the only person getting too old for the task confronting the Pittsburgh power structure. "We must make a change, and it may be that the further change of myself a year from now would lend further strength to the administration of the club."

Another fault with Haney, according to Rickey, was the manager's lack of input away from on-field managing. A shortcoming he shared with Bill Meyer. "In the four years I have been here in Pittsburgh, I have yet to have either Fred or Bill manufacture or think up any deal anywhere. Bill would tell me that so-and-so could not help us in his opinion, and he would follow through personally, or outline negotiations in a player deal. I think Fred would do the same thing but even less likely to originate personnel changes than Bill."

Branch with his arm around Bobby Bragan.

Rickey had a candidate in mind to replace Haney, Bobby Bragan, then the skipper of the Hollywood Stars. Bragan, who had played for the Mahatma in Brooklyn, was a self-proclaimed "Rickey man." Despite being a personal favorite of the old man, and the first choice for replacing Haney, Rickey was apprehensive about bringing Bragan to Pittsburgh.

"Bragan has his faults," Branch communicated to his son. "In the first place, his very manner on the field is antagonistic to umpires.... I believe his extreme slowness and positiveness in movement lends itself to public disapproval.

"The hazard in bringing Bragan to Pittsburgh lies, as I see it at the present time, in the direction of his self-conceit he doesn't sense. Beyond question, he is sound enough in general field tactics.... But he doesn't know very much about the skills of individual positions or play, and he is fairly unacquainted with the techniques of instruction, either in a lecture room or on the field. I can give him twenty-five questions in the field of correct technique in baseball and I will be surprised if he makes sixty percent of perfect answers. There is much for that boy to learn."

Rickey concluded, "I can not think of anybody but Bragan. I can find more faults with and have more doubts about every other person I can think of than I do about Bragan. Clay Hopper will be sorely disappointed not to have been given favorable consideration. I must not let anyone's personal disappointment affect our choice."[37]

Bragan's well publicized incidents of umpire baiting, both in Hollywood and at his other managerial post in the Texas League, left Rickey wary of hiring his former catcher. On October 13, four weeks after he wrote his thoughts on Haney and Bragan, Rickey decided to maintain status quo after all. His procrastination belied the faith he publicly proclaimed to have in Haney. For his part, the manager was unaware of Rickey's discontent and he dutifully went about this job, which in the off-season consisted of very little outside of answering an occasional telephone inquiry from a probing reporter.

The men in the Pirate front office were not engaged in the same inactivity. Once again Rickey missed the Fall Classic and the Giants four-game sweep of the Indians as he and Branch Jr. were holed up in their Forbes Field offices planning for a winter of trade activity. The Pittsburgh brain trust busied themselves with preparations for the upcoming major-league draft, in which the Bucs would have the first pick overall.

The 1954 major-league draft was held on November 22 at the Hotel Commodore in New York City. The Pirates, because of their last place finish in the just-completed campaign, were granted the first pick overall. At precisely 11:00 A.M. Charles Seegar, the Secretary Treasurer of baseball, instructed Pittsburgh to make their choice. The decree had scarcely been out of Seegar's mouth when Branch Rickey Jr., the Pirate representative at the draft, sprang to his feet and announced, "Pittsburgh selects Roberto Clemente of the Montreal Royals."

Clemente, a twenty-year-old native of Puerto Rico, had played the 1954 season with the Brooklyn Dodger affiliate in Montreal where he batted .257. His mediocre average didn't portray his full potential, and a number of teams were vying for his services.

"Clemente was number one on the lists of four or five major-league teams," the Twig told reporters. "We've had several men scout him. Clyde Sukeforth did a thorough job on him. We know he can field, run, and throw. He has power for sure. He didn't hit for average in Montreal, but we're hoping he'll do it for us."[38]

Sukeforth stumbled upon Clemente by chance. Rickey had instructed his trusted scout to follow the Royal club with the dictate of evaluating a pitcher named Joe Black.

"We're sending you to Richmond to see Montreal beginning tomorrow night. You've got to stay until Joe Black pitches," Rickey told Sukeforth.

"I get there just in time to see the Montreal club take the field for fielding practice," the scout later recalled. "I notice in right field they had a colored boy with a great arm. I hadn't been there three minutes and I saw him throw a couple of times, and that was that.

"About the seventh inning Max Macon, the Montreal manager, put in a pinch-hitter to hit. He sent up this right fielder, this Black boy with the good arm, up to hit. He hit a sharp, routine ground ball to the shortstop, and would you know it, it was a very close play at first base.

"I said, 'There's talent there. There's two things he can do super.'"[39]

Roberto Clemente in the shadow of the Cathedral of Learning. (Author's collection.)

The talented young man in question was Clemente. Because of the bonus rule in effect at the time, any player signed for $4,000 or more had to be retained by the parent club or else be subjected to the major league draft. Roberto, because of the $10,000 bonus he received from the Dodgers, would be eligible for the post-season draft. The Brooklyn front office understood if Clemente's talent were known he would surely be taken by another club come November. In the hope that Clemente might possibly be passed over in the draft if their competitors remained ignorant of the Puerto Rican wunderkind, the Dodgers asked Max Macon to "hide" Clemente.

"I stayed and saw five games and Joe didn't get to pitch and I didn't see hardly anymore of Clemente," Sukeforth said. "But I wrote Mr. Rickey and I told him, 'Joe Black hasn't pitched. I haven't seen him pitch, and he's not ready to pitch. He's working himself into condition.' Before I signed the letter I wrote, 'I haven't seen Joe Black, but I have seen your draft pick.' And I put in a report on Clemente."

Rickey respected Sukeforth's opinion immensely, but if Clemente was so exceptional, he wondered why the Pirates hadn't heard of the prodigy. The Pirate general manager dispatched another of his loyal lieutenants, Howie Haak, to take a look at this Clemente.

What Haak witnessed when he caught up with Montreal in Rochester confirmed Sukeforth's enthusiasm. "I saw Clemente get two triples and a double, and when Rochester removed their left-handed pitcher, Clemente was taken out for a pinch hitter. I then realized the Dodgers were trying to hide Clemente."

The naïve Puerto Rican, though, didn't understand why his playing time was unreasonably sporadic. His frustration had reached a crescendo when he was removed from the game in Rochester. Clemente headed to his hotel room with the intention of packing his belongings and going back to Puerto Rico. Haak, upon hearing of Clemente's tantrum, followed him to the hotel where the scout explained that by leaving the team he would be playing into the Dodgers' hands. "If you desert the Royals, Brooklyn will put you on the suspended list," Haak told Clemente. "You would then be ineligible for the draft. If you just bide your time with Montreal, I promise you you'll be a Pittsburgh Pirate next season."[40]

Clemente heeded Haak's prudent advice and finished the season with the Royals. The final decision on who the Pirates would choose with their pick was made shortly before the draft at a conference held at Rickey's Fox Chapel farm.

Rickey called the meeting to order, "We have the first draft choice as you know. Who are we going to draft?"

Several of Rickey's men spoke up. One scout wanted to select a player in the Southern League. Another preferred a prospect on the Coast. Rickey then looked at Sukeforth, "Clyde, what would your choice be?"

"Clemente is definitely our man," Sukeforth replied.

Haak was next in line and his response to Rickey's query was in agreement with Sukeforth. With his two top scouts in agreement, the decision was an easy one for Rickey. Roberto Clemente would become a Pittsburgh Pirate.

"I had a good line on this boy," Branch told reporters following the

Treasurer Jim Herron

draft. "Two different members of the scouting staff observed his play. On the reports, I would have paid more than the $4,000 it cost the club. I would have paid $10,000. Or even $30,000 for him. But for $30,000 I would have gone out myself and checked on him."[41]

The acquisition of Clemente was a rare ray of light in the Pirate front office. Though Jim Herron, had the option been available, would have chosen a sack of gold instead of the right fielder.

"I do not know how much longer I can hold off our creditors," Herron began a November 10 correspondence with what was now becoming a familiar refrain. "Every day we receive letters and telephone calls requesting payment and, quite frankly, I am running out of excuses."

Three months had passed since the last financial crisis, and the club treasurer was still buried in restitution requests. On August 17 Galbreath and Johnson gave the team another much-needed infusion of cash. "There is no secret that we have been putting up cash to carry this program, and we will continue to do so to see it through," Galbreath vowed. "I personally have never taken a dime from the club, either in early profits, or for any expense. This city and its people have been good to me, and I want to see them win. It's been a helluva worry, but I'm not going to quit now."[42]

The team's treasurer felt no relief, though, from the August influx of funds. "What can I tell Dale Long?" Herron asked in his November 10 letter. "He has written in twice for the return transportation which he is entitled to under his contract. We owe a total of $3,180.41 to players for return transportation at the end of the season.

"What can I tell Capital Airlines about the $10,451.59 we owe to them for transportation furnished as far back as August 12?

"What can I tell Spalding about their statement for $1,347.50 covering baseballs we received September 9?

"We cannot meet our November 15 payroll unless we get $4,000 before that date."

Frustration seeped from Herron's typewritten page. His was a thankless job, and in Pittsburgh the position required experience in the art of nagging which he had acquired in spades. "I am concerned about our season sale for 1955, not so much about the acceptance by the public as by the fact that most of my time is spent juggling, and I mean juggling, our working capital, and I have not had the time to plan and organize the sale [of the next year's season tickets]," Herron illustrated. "Please understand that I am not complaining about my position with the company (I still have a little hair), but thought that you should know a little about the frustration and pressure I have been under the last month."

Following Herron's plea, the ownership group added another quarter million to the team's kitty. In addition to that contribution, the club received another $250,000 from the sale of the New Orleans Pelicans. The Pirates appeared to be solvent for the first time since early in the Rickey regime. "Two or three people wanted to corner me," Galbreath remarked, "and commented they wanted to talk about Frank Thomas. I said I wasn't interested and they replied they had some cash to offer. I told them, 'We crossed that bridge a long time ago.'"[43]

Rickey could, at last, run the team without his hands being financially handcuffed.

6. I Am Not Down and Out

Rickey habitually sang the praises of his players. More often than not, the Mahatma's kind words were impulsive and out of focus. In Roberto Clemente, Branch finally had a man whose talents he could trumpet and not be alone in his opinion.

Herman Franks, who was managing Clemente in the Puerto Rican winter leagues, in a letter to Rickey wrote that Clemente was "the best player in the league except for Willie Mays."[1]

This was not the first, nor would it be the last time, that young Clemente was favorably compared to Mays. Branch, though, perhaps because of his over eagerness to heap praise in the past on unproven players, restrained his enthusiasm for Clemente.

"We can't go overboard on what we've heard," Rickey said. "It might be hard on the boy if he gets a lot of rave notices. The people might expect too much of him. I've had so many good reports on this boy, I'm anxious to get a look at him myself."[2]

Branch would have the opportunity to view Clemente firsthand when he traveled to the Caribbean. On the afternoon of January 25, Rickey sat in the bleachers and witnessed Clemente's Santurce club battle Ponce. After the contest Branch filed a scouting report on the club's number-one draft choice:

> I have been told very often from sources about his running speed. His running form is bad, definitely bad, and based upon what

145

I saw tonight, he has only a bit above average major league running speed. He has a beautiful throwing arm. He throws the ball down and it really goes places. However, he runs with the ball every time he makes a throw and that's bad.

He has no adventure whatsoever on the bases, takes a comparatively small lead, and doesn't have in mind, apparently, getting a break. I can imagine that he has never stolen a base in his life with his skill or his cleverness. I can guess that if it was done it was because he was pushed off.

His form at the plate is perfect. The bat is out and in good position to give him power. There is not the slightest hitch or movement in his hands or arms and the big end of the bat is completely quiet when the ball leaves the pitcher's hand. His sweep is level, very level. His stride is short and his stance is good to start with and he finishes good with his body. I know of no reason why he should not become a very fine hitter. I would not class him, however, as even a prospective home run hitter.

I do not believe he can possibly do a major league club any good in 1955. It is just too bad that he could not have his first year in a Class B or C league and then this year he might have profited greatly with a second year as a regular say in Class A.

In 1956 he can be sent out on option by Pittsburgh only by first securing waivers, and waivers likely cannot be secured. So we are stuck with him, stuck indeed, until such a time as he can really help a major league club. —

The most disappointing feature about Clemente is his lack of adventure, of chance taking. He had at least two chances tonight to make a good play. He simply waited for the bounce. I hope he looks better to me tomorrow night when Santurce plays San Juan, the final game of the regular season and the city championship of San Juan is at stake. Perhaps this boy will put out in that game.[3]

The two-week sojourn, which took Rickey to Havana and Puerto Rico, lifted Branch's spirits noticeably. While in the Caribbean, the Mahatma scouted twenty Pittsburgh farmhands including Dick Hall, Ronnie Kline, and the Freese brothers — Gene and George. Following his return to Pennsylvania, though, Clemente was the name on the lips of Pittsburgh beat writers.

"The boy is a great prospect," Branch said, answering the scribes' repeated inquiries. "But you must remember he is only twenty years old. He is a big boy who can run, throw, and hit... He has never been put to a test in competition. He needs a lot of polish but God gave him all the necessities of becoming an outstanding ballplayer."[4]

The annual chore of inking each player to a contract was at hand, and Branch, as usual, saw no reason to expect any holdouts.

"We always expect some arguments and that's why we don't put stock in the first figures we offer," Branch explained, while exposing his negotiating ploy of "low balling" his players. The initial contracts, Rickey revealed, "are merely filled in, according to baseball law until I can sit down and talk face to face with the players."

"I've already jotted some names for raises. But there aren't likely to be any cuts for fellows on whom we were counting to remain with the Pirates. I don't expect to have any trouble."[5]

Much thought and effort was expelled by the Bucco front office into the mediation of player contracts. Branch Jr., who had by 1955 been given the task of handling contracts, oddly preferred that a player's spouse sit in during negotiating sessions.

"We want the wives to discuss salaries with their husbands because a happy family man is a better player," the Twig said. "But sometimes it doesn't work out that way. The wife usually tries to fit the player's salary into the family budget. The player may be the father of thirteen and naturally he'll need a lot of money to take care of everybody. But unfortunately, he doesn't have the ability as a player to command a salary in keeping with a family that size. The ball club must conduct negotiations on the ability of the player plus the ability of the club to pay.

"One player always referred to his wife at contract time and we always had an ordeal. She was really the boss. We had to talk to her with her husband sitting silently by. This fellow was a pitcher and a good one. He had great potential but never was able to capitalize on it. She warned him one time if he took a cut in salary, she'd leave him.

"Well, he drifted out of baseball and I understand he and his wife are now divorced."[6]

The elder Rickey once sent out a contract to a player which contained a raise, but there were stipulations attached to the agreement. Branch informed the wayward player that they would meet in training camp and discuss the conditions.

Rickey had heard through the grapevine that the young man's off-the-field habits were lacking in character, and he was hoping to come to an understanding with the player. The player in question though, brought his better half to training camp and she sat in on the contract discussions.

"Naturally I wouldn't bring up the delicate subject of his off the field behavior, so we just forgot all about it," Rickey remembered. "I wonder if he's still trying to figure out what I wanted to talk to him about."[7]

The Rickeys wouldn't experience any engaging anecdotes whilst negotiating 1955 contracts. The Mahatma's early assessment of a compliant contract season was in line. Clemente quickly signed on February 7, though as a rookie he had virtually no leverage. Dick Groat, after completing his two-year stint in the Army Engineers, left Fort Belvoir, Virginia, and anxiously agreed to terms. Groat and Clemente, along with all but one of their teammates, were under contract by the third week of February.

The lone holdout, Frank Thomas, was hoping to gather $25,000 in 1955, appreciatively more than the $13,000 he gathered for his 1954 efforts. Thomas had a solid campaign in 1954, belting twenty-three home runs, and driving in ninety-eight runs, with a batting average of .298. Frank, who grew up in the shadow of Forbes Field, fancied himself the second coming of Ralph Kiner. Rickey, however, viewed the situation differently. "It may be a blessing if Thomas doesn't show up here," Rickey said from the Bucs' new training site in Ft. Myers. "We need outfielders and Thomas' absence will create a wonderful opportunity for somebody else.

"We're far apart on what he's asking and what we want to give. Salaries are based on abilities, length of service, and drawing power. Ralph Kiner was paid because he was an attraction at the gate but Thomas hasn't yet shown that he can draw the fans."[8]

Thomas's holdout was long and quarrelsome. Branch Jr. stepped aside and allowed his father to handle the difficult talks with Thomas. Frank fell in line two weeks into training camp after accepting an offer that gave him a slight increase over his 1954 contract.

"It's much easier playing with a contender," a forlorn Thomas moaned to a Gotham city scribe shortly after arriving in Ft. Myers. "A fellow is supposed to be relaxed playing baseball, and how can you relax when you lose everyday ... a player gets his spirit down when he loses so frequently."

Les Biederman could sympathize with the Pirate outfielder's complaint that "it's hell to play with a last place club. ... It sure is. And it's just tough writing about a last place team too."[9]

Contrary to Thomas, Groat was anxious to come to terms. "We had no argument," the Twig said of the fifteen minute negotiating session. "He was given a substantial raise over his 1952 salary, which was close to his asking price. You don't have any trouble signing a player like Dick."

"All I can say is that I'm very happy about the situation," a beaming Groat told reporters. "I just hope that I can play better ball than I did my first year up, and I think I can. I've kept in good condition playing baseball and basketball during the two years I have been in the Army, and I should be improved."[10]

While in the service, Dick participated in a number of games with the Ft. Wayne Pistons of the National Basketball Association. One condition of Groat's Pirate contract forbade Dick from playing basketball professionally. The Rickeys were concerned that the health of their versatile shortstop would be compromised if they allowed Dick to pursue basketball in the off-season.

Manager Haney immediately penciled Groat in as his starting shortstop. "In my own mind, I have Gene Freese and Curt Roberts (at second)," Haney forecast. "Dick Groat at short and possibly Sid Gordon at third because of his power."

Haney was excited about seeing the much-ballyhooed Puerto Rican in Ft. Myers. "Everything I've heard on the West Coast this winter about Roberto Clemente is favorable. Willie Mays told me he is a good ballplayer and so did Tom Sheehan, the Giant scout. Sheehan said that the kid might be a year away though.

"Our main objective this season is to get out of last place. But if the other clubs improve as much as we do, we might still be on the treadmill. We were better off in 1954 than the previous season, but so were seven other teams."[11]

The analysis put forth by Rickey was similar in tone to Haney's evaluation. "Last spring we were encouraged," Branch told several members of the press. "We thought we had the kind of material that would come to be a winner when the players grow up in their skills.

"But," Rickey added pessimistically, "we are not set in the outfield, at first or third base. My catching is pennant winning, and I am nearer to the pitching we are striving for than ever before." No, all was not doom and gloom, Rickey insisted... "I have the pitching to carry me eventually to the pennant."[12]

Branch, in his annual address to the players, was less ornate and more biting with his commentary. "We're now challenged to find out where we stand, and where we're going," Rickey told his men. "Last spring we had encouragement. We thought we had the kind of material that could come to be a winner when the players grew up in their skills, when they matured. We thought we had the stuff to win a pennant eventually.

"In all fairness, I can't repeat that today," Branch bluntly told his charges. "I don't think this organization now has the players who can win a pennant.

"Maybe I'm not as good as I was and that's why I lean so much on the men around me. We must pool our efforts, our resources, for the common good. There's not a player in this room who doesn't want to win. He doesn't want to be identified with a cellar team, or a team in the second division. I'm tired of losing, tired of the emotions of defeat. I've become short tempered, irritable, not because of ill health but because of defeats. I'm not here to finish third or fourth. I'm here to win.

"I'm not going to be satisfied with mediocrity. I don't want to seem discouraged, but I'm just giving you the facts. If you have a personal problem, try to solve it yourself. Don't delegate your problem to a third person."[13]

Rickey's elocution was given on the diamond of the Pirates' new spring home, which just a few short months earlier was little more than a cow pasture. Ft. Myers lured the Bucs to their fourth spring home in as many years when they promised the organization that the city would construct a covered grandstand that would seat 3,000 fans. The gulf coast Florida town followed through with its promise. A ballpark was constructed, and within its confines were beautiful expansive clubhouses which were built for the players' comfort.

Though the ballclub was exceedingly pleased with their modernistic surroundings, the team was beset with a housing quandary. "We will be using three hotels," Bob Rice, the Pirates' traveling secretary reported. "The Morgan, the Bradford, and the Franklin Arms. The first group will live in the Morgan, while the main club will be housed in the Bradford, which will be the [team] headquarters. The overflow, those who can't be accommodated in the Bradford, will live in the Franklin Arms."

Rice conveniently disregarded a small group of players on the squad ... the black members of the team. Because of segregation laws prevalent in Jim Crow Florida, Curt Roberts, Roman Mejias, Roberto Clemente, Felipe Montemayor, and Lino Donoso, were forced to live apart from their white teammates.

Regardless of where his players laid their heads, Fred Haney was pleased with what he had seen during the opening weeks of training camp. "It certainly is the best gang I've had in three seasons," the Pirate skipper declared, "and I know it's better than Bill Meyer's last club. That was the one that had what you fellows refer to as the midget infield."[14]

Rickey concurred with his manager's roseate prognosis. "When this club explodes favorably, as it can, it will not be a jump simply out of last place. It will be a progressive jump and flight will not be concerned with any particular stopping place. This development — pitching wise — is not too far away, and could conceivably come this year."[15]

Haney's cheery outlook quickly turned sour as Branch's boys continued to suffer from altophobia. Just six games into the season, the Pirates were without a victory and already seven-and-a-half games behind the league-leading Dodgers. The winless drought did not conclude until the ninth contest of the year, when the Bucs thrashed the Phillies 6–1. The Pirate clubhouse took on the appearance of a championship celebration following the administration of the final out. Back-slapping players were whooping it up for the benefit of pleading photographers who were anxious to document the rare occasion of a Pirate victory.

Prior to the April 24 contest with Philadelphia, Haney lectured his players and challenged their pride. "We've got to win," he demanded of the men. "We're going back to Pittsburgh for a long home stand and we're going to play in front of empty stands unless you win. Empty stands mean less paychecks, and you're just taking money right out of your pockets. Now go out there and play like you can. You can do it."

The Corsairs could do it, as they proved that afternoon, but the Bucs remained kings of futility. The losses continued to mount subsequent to the Pirates' victory over the Phillies, and Branch, rather than pour all his efforts vainly into the last place Bucs, continued to extend his faculties to issues larger than the Pittsburgh organization. These ever increasing forays into the individual dynamics of the game eased the misery he incurred from watching his Buccos perform.

One problem, the swelling amounts of cash paid out as bonuses to prospects, was particularly alarming to Rickey, particularly in light of the Pirates' financial state.

"In my opinion, the bonus rule has ruined the game," Rickey ruefully protested to *The Sporting News.*

"Why a bonus?" Branch rhetorically asked. "Why a bonus for a boy to learn his profession? A boy goes to medical school for eight years to study to become a doctor. Why, in the old days a boy who wanted to become an attorney paid for the privilege of working in a lawyer's office. Sometimes we're forced to the wrong things through competition and unfortunately baseball legislation permits this bad practice."

Rickey's rant continued, "It's a tragic event that this bonus had to come into baseball. Most of the owners in the game today are highly successful men in other fields, and they certainly wouldn't apply these methods to their own businesses. It's high time we put our house in order. It's up to us who run the game for the owners to do something about it… We in baseball all agree that the patient is sick, but we can't agree on a cure. My idea may be revolutionary, but I would gladly accept a rule making every player who signs a contract with a minor-league team subject to the unrestricted draft. If a major-league team wishes to continue to pay bonuses, then this team would be forced to abide by the present bonus regulation making the team retain him on the roster for two years. This is penalty enough, I feel this would eliminate the big bonuses and keep the game alive for rich and poor alike."[16]

Rickey's concern for the "poor" clubs was not in evidence while he resided in Brooklyn. Equalizing the playing field for the less fortunate franchises was not high on his agenda during his Dodger tenure. However, in Branch's defense, he surely couldn't have had the knowledge that teams such as Pittsburgh were in such poor condition financially, and thus unable to compete on a level playing field. "Baseball salaries," Branch clarified, "are controlled by three factors: The ability of the club to pay, the ability of the player to earn the salary, and the comparative salaries paid to players of like age and ability and experience.

"Salaries have gone all out of proper proportions and there are plenty of teams unable to realize a reasonable profit on their investments. There just isn't a margin of safety for a bad season at the gate anymore. We in baseball must come down to earth and help save the game and ourselves."

Three different major-league teams relocated in the previous three seasons, the Boston Braves shifted to Milwaukee prior to the 1953 season, the St. Louis Browns went on to Baltimore, where they became the Orioles before the 1954 campaign, and the Philadelphia Athletics moved to Kansas City for the 1955 season. The landscape of big-league baseball was drastically changing, both fiscally and geographically. There were now just two cities with multiple teams, New York and Chicago. The franchise movement over the previous three years theoretically strengthened six franchises, as the remaining clubs in St. Louis, Boston, and

Philadelphia also benefited from the relocations. Thus the gap between the wealthy clubs and their destitute brethren was even wider. The Pirates, despite John Galbreath's proclamations that he would not sell to anyone, remained a candidate throughout the game's rumor mills to relocate, most likely on the West Coast.

Rickey's close friend Bob Cobb was openly inviting the major leagues to the coast — San Francisco and Los Angeles. "The doors are wide open, and we'll give them blessing and support," Cobb announced. He didn't, however, believe Wrigley Field, the then home of the Los Angeles Angels, would be satisfactory for the major leagues because of inadequate parking. Cobb, though, believed there was a perfect locale in Los Angeles for a prospective ballyard to be built, an area of the city known as Chavez Ravine.

Each of the three cities that had recently gained a major-league franchise, Baltimore, Kansas City, and Milwaukee, all provided the clubs with a municipal ballpark built with tax payers' money. This practice had received wide publicity, and much criticism. Cobb, despite much opposition, proposed public funding for a new ball park in Los Angeles and put forth a supportive argument.

"Why should the people pay to build a major-league ball park for private interest anymore than they should pay to erect a department store for Macy's," Cobb posed. "They shouldn't," he answered after a brief pause, "but the proposition at Chavez Ravine called for much more than a baseball park. It [will] be an all purpose sports center."

Cobb pointed out that there were 256 acres of land available in Chavez Ravine. The easy accessibility to the freeway made the parcel of land especially appealing to any prospective big-league team. "And we sit here like dopes and refuse to use it,"[17] Cobb moaned.

Rickey wasn't averse to the proposition of the major leagues venturing to points West. On the contrary, he had long been an advocate of such. Infiltration of the coast by the big leagues, though, was sure to continue the disparity of wealth between the clubs, a possibility Branch resolutely opposed.

The bonus, and the relocation of financially struggling clubs, were not the only issues Branch was busying himself with throughout the summer. The advent of television, and the adverse consequences of televising major-league games, deeply concerned the Mahatma.

"Radio had made major-league fans out of minor-league fans," Rickey said. "It created a desire to see something — television is giving it to them. Once a television set has broken them of the ballpark habit, a great many fans will never reacquire it. And if television makes new baseball customers, as some are claiming, why don't Broadway productions televise their shows? The only way you can see a Broadway production is to buy a ticket — and I cannot concede that baseball has, under the oft-used heading of the 'public interest,' any obligation to give it away continuously at only a fraction of its real worth, the only thing it has to sell."[18]

The broadcasting of home games was a common practice among a number of clubs ... a practice that Rickey ardently disagreed with. "I believe that the telecasting of ALL home games, even if confined to one's home territory, is economically unsound. However, each club should be given the right to determine which of its games are telecast.

"All members of a league should participate in the receipts of all games telecast. If it should become advisable in the interests of baseball generally that there should be a network of a major league 'game of the day' once a week throughout the country, for example, then the receipts from such a program should be channeled to the minor leagues for promotional purposes."[19]

The invasion of television and radio into minor-league territories was a disastrous trend, Branch asserted. "It is not good for us to broadcast games to minor-league territories, and thus detract from their gate receipts. This is one of our problems which has beset us as an outgrowth of the changing times. Radio and television are evidence of great progress in our modern civilization and we must be foresighted enough to meet the problem head-on. Baseball is an enduring sport. It has survived wars, depressions, and all oddities of human endeavor and machinery. I am confident we will meet this new menace, if indeed it can be called that, and fall into harmony with it. We haven't yet, but we must.

"I believe that if we do a good selling job, we can convince the government of our right to radio and television curtailment."

Rickey's coolness towards the growth of televised games contrasted his ardor toward radio, and the benefits baseball could gather from the use of that medium. As with every other aspect of the game, Rickey took distinct interest in the broadcasting of content over the airwaves. Branch, without fail, became an authority. (Or at least thought of himself as adroit on any subject he cared to educate himself about.) Following a Pittsburgh-Milwaukee game, Branch offered several prerequisites for radio announcers broadcasting baseball games.

"There should never be a period of silence in any broadcast to exceed five seconds, and not very many as long as that," Rickey advised. "There should be very little horseplay in a broadcast. It is a business proposition. Now and then an anecdote is quite proper and now and then reference to plays in previous games or a historical baseball incident can be properly related or referred to."

Rickey's expertise continued, "Broadcasters should have frequent conversations with club owners or club secretaries and as often as possible with managers. Any broadcaster should have more ideas to talk about than he can properly use, making periods of suspense completely impossible.

"Scores of other games are interesting.

"The most important thing in all this world for a broadcaster is to have in mind *CONSTANTLY*, and I mean *CONSTANTLY*, is to realize that 1,000 people have just turned on their radios at home, or in the office, or in an automobile, and everyone of these thousand hasn't heard a thing about the game, and immediately start asking themselves the question, i.e., who is playing?, what is the score?"[20]

The recommendations offered by Rickey, while written for the benefit of all broadcasters, likely were initiated by the stylings of one announcer specifically, Bob Prince.

For seven years, Prince had been the second man in the Pirate radio booth, taking a back seat to Rosey Rowswell. Following Rowswell's death on February 4, 1955, Prince moved to the number one chair, much to Rickey's chagrin.

In correspondence with John Galbreath concerning Ralph Kiner, Rickey spoke dismissively of Prince. Branch struggled to hide his contempt for the free spirited Prince, even going so far as to criticize the broadcasters' spring training attire. ("A festive pair of Bermuda shorts.") The root of Rickey's distaste for the colorful broadcaster, though, was Prince's close friendship with Ralph Kiner. Branch was annoyed to hear of Prince taking Kiner's side during the duo's contract squabble, and was angered to learn that he criticized the slugger's trade on the air and to anyone he ran into out of the booth. ("Well we got six jock straps for Kiner, and that's all there is to it.")

Branch went so far as to dictate a memo to the Pirate board members critiquing one of Prince's broadcasts. "In almost every broadcast I have ever heard by Prince, he is inclined continuously, to make editorial comment, and comparisons," Rickey wrote. "...In his late broadcasts he has been quite liberal in giving the favorable records of opposing players and in the same broadcast giving unfavorable records of Pittsburgh players.

"When [Prince] talks, he talks plenty, but he has unfortunate stretches of silence until anyone trying to get the game on the dial would think that there was no broadcast, or they had any game... There should not be LONG periods of silence in a broadcast."[21]

Baseball's great renaissance man mired himself in the minutia of a petty feud. If Rickey opened himself for criticism during his Pittsburgh tenure, it would come in his micromanagement of the ballteam. The burden of heading a baseball franchise is enough that a general manager need not concern himself with every utterance of his team's broadcaster.

Following his successful venture in St. Louis, the die was cast, and Branch Rickey became the epitome of what a general manager should be. However, the Branch Rickey that came to Pittsburgh overextended himself and attempted to right all the wrongs of a franchise in disrepair.

"Has Rickey Lost His Touch?" a *Sport* magazine article asked. The impartial answer would be no, he was still the brilliant man that had built the dynasties in St. Louis and Brooklyn, but circumstances and times change. Few critics publicly recognized the financial constraints Rickey endured in Pittsburgh. The farm system was no longer a novelty. Building a franchise into a powerhouse, as he had done with the Cardinals, couldn't be done as easily, not with the stiff competition for young prospects that then existed. Yet, Branch, in the face of continual failure, still preached of pennants waving proudly above Forbes Field.

Haney could offer no excuses for his team's discouraging performance through the first weeks of the season. "It's the little things that are beating us," Haney said to a packed hall at the annual Grandstand Manager's luncheon, held at the William Penn Hotel.

"Sure we lost three or four when other teams overpowered us, but we lost the others by giving them away on our own mistakes."

Traditionally Rickey, as master of ceremonies, would introduce the players at the yearly luncheon. Branch, however, was absent from the 1955 assembly as he extended a visit with Bob Cobb in Hollywood. Instead, Haney did the honors, and introduced his entire club to the audience with the exception of Clemente and Mejias. "These two boys were here, but they wore sports shirts without ties, and went back to their hotel," the skipper offered as an explanation for their absence. "I asked them to remain, told them it wouldn't make any difference, but they said they wouldn't feel right."[22]

The manager broached the problem of communicating with Clemente and Mejias during spring training. The two Latin Americans were struggling in their efforts to become acclimated in a new country and Haney was one of the few men to reach out to the young men. After an exhibition contest during which both rookies ran through the third base coach's stop sign into outs, Haney decided to purchase a Spanish dictionary. Haney held a private meeting with the duo and explained to them the purpose of the third base coach. "All I'm going to learn now is how to say "stop" and "go" to those kids,"[23] Haney told an amused press corps.

Chuck Dressen, manager of the Washington Senators, couldn't have differed more in opinion from Haney. Dressen's Senator club consisted of five Cubans and one Venezuelan. "I want the Cubans to learn English good enough to get the signs and talk some baseball," Dressen said. "They don't seem to have any trouble picking up enough English to order their meals. I can't send over to the United Nations for an interpreter every time I want to give a sign."[24]

Dressen's callous comments were not uncommon for the era. Latino players were expected to adapt to the new culture, with baseball, on the whole, giving little consideration to the difficulties facing the young men as they attempted to become adjusted to their new surroundings. Having no experience with Latin American players in Brooklyn, Rickey, while not espousing repugnant views à la Dressen, made no concerted effort to help accommodate his Latino players, or for that matter the African American players on the Pirate squad.

With spring training winding to a close, the Pirates worked their way north playing a series of exhibition games in various cities along the way. One such contest was scheduled in Birmingham, Alabama, against the Philadelphia Athletics. Because of a city ordinance outlawing blacks and whites from competing together on the same playing field, Mejias, Roberts, and Clemente were not permitted to dress for the game. Instead, the three men sat in the "Negro" section of the stands and watched their teammates perform.

Strangely, unlike his previous efforts when he and Robinson as a pioneering tandem forced baseball to reconsider its self-imposed apartheid, Rickey sat idle. Certainly Branch could not have forced the city of Birmingham to change its Jim Crow laws single-handedly, but the option of refusing to field his team under the segregated conditions was open to him.*

Perhaps comparing the circumstances surrounding Jackie Robinson's debut in major-league baseball with the black players that followed in his immediate footsteps would be unfair, for he faced indignities and slights that the pen struggles to adequately measure. However, throughout the ordeal that Robinson endured, Rickey was staunchly behind his player using all means at his disposal to make Jackie's initial season as comfortable as possible. Robinson's and Rickey's names are firmly and deservedly linked in baseball's enduring history for their respective role in the integration of the game, but their relationship blossomed beyond the mere happenstance of their place in baseball lore. Branch became more than a mentor to Jackie; he was a surrogate father. "Rickey's relationship with Jack became very personal, very intimate," Robinson's wife, Rachel, recalled. "It was paternal — not paternalistic, but paternal. And it gave Jack deep support when he badly needed it."[25]

Mrs. Robinson was present at many meetings between Branch and her husband. "Rickey kept in close contact with us throughout [1945 and 1946] and in 1947, after Jack joined the team in Brooklyn, he would periodically invite us to meet privately with him in his hotel suite. I came to view these visits as quiet strategy sessions.... Jack and Rickey cemented the life long trust and respect they felt for each other in those sessions."[26]

Expecting Rickey to duplicate his relationship with Robinson seven years later with Curt Roberts would be absurd. Still, Rickey could have taken steps to ease the difficulties Roberts encountered during his inaugural season.

For Robinson's benefit, Branch placed Pittsburgh *Courier* writer Wendell Smith on the Brooklyn payroll so that Jackie would have a companion and roommate during Dodger road trips. Smith, long an activist for the integration of the game, helped Robinson through his lonely and brutal rookie season with the friendship he provided.

Following the release of Sam Jethroe two weeks into the 1954 season, Roberts, like Robinson for much of his rookie year, was the sole black on his club. No precautions were taken to quell the egregious indignities and to ease the feeling of isolation felt by Roberts in 1954.

*Which is precisely what happened in 1956 when Rickey's successor, Joe Brown, refused to field a team under the same conditions, and the contest was canceled.

Robinson's circumstance was unquestionably unique; still, Roberts' experience paralleled Jackie's on many levels — Roberts was met with indifference in the clubhouse, and on the road without his family to go home to, he was left to fend for himself. After the final out was administered, he would dine alone, occasionally take in a movie, and then head back to his hotel room. While his existence on the ballclub may have been tolerated on the playing field, the relationship between he and his teammates could be termed cordial at best. Roberts' teammates certainly did not extend a hand of friendship beyond the white lines. He even had to endure racial catcalls in his home park.

"Get that black cat."

"Knock down that coon."

"Nigger!" and other unlettered epithets filtered down from the Forbes Field stands and into Roberts' lonely ears. "Curt would come home upset if he heard something," Christine Roberts remembered. "'Sometimes it just gets to me,' he would tell me, and he would sit and drink coffee and talk. By the end of the night he was fortified, ready to fight another day.

"Curtis was a very patient, thinking man. It's so ironic that when he played in foreign countries, he never had to deal with the abuse and prejudice, but here in his own country, and his home ballpark..."[27]

Beyond his initial words of encouragement to Roberts during their first meeting, Branch offered not a single utterance of support. Fittingly, such a message came from Robinson himself:

> Curtis,
> I hope you understand why I am writing and will accept this letter in the manner I write it. Your job in Pittsburgh is a ticklish one, you must be careful, just as I had to be for awhile.
> I want to wish you the best and hope everything works out. Just don't defeat yourself by giving up.
> My best to your family   Good luck,
>   Jackie Robinson[28]

Roberts finished the 1954 season with a feeble .232 batting average. Though he drew rave notices for his fielding prowess, Rickey wasn't impressed with the weak hitting second sacker. "Roberts," Branch wrote, following the 1954 season, "will hardly make the club [in '55]. Eugene Freese, last year with New Orleans, will take the job easily at second."[29]

Several months after making the preceding observation, Rickey remained critical of Roberts. "If he lives to be a million years of age, he will never hit .250, and it will be a lucky year when he does that. He is the worst fly ball hitter on the ball club — bar everyone,"[30] Branch commented following an exhibition contest between the Bucs and the White Sox.

The cynical could surmise that Rickey's lack of interest in Roberts and his tumultuous first season lay in Roberts's shortcomings on the field. Perhaps Rickey was blind to the struggles facing Roberts. "After all," he may have thought, "it has been *seven* years since Robinson." Or, probably the most likely scenario, Branch had moved on. "The Great Experiment" was an unmitigated success, and Rickey had taken his energies to the next cause.

Clemente and Mejias, as Roberts was before them, were met by their teammates with ambivalence. The young Latinos, though, were fortunate to have Roberts as a mentor. Roberts, who was fluent in Spanish, made the assimilation to the big leagues easier for both Mejias and Clemente. Clemente's successful rookie season, while correctly attributed to his enormous talent, owes, at the very least, a small nod of acknowledgment to the presence and companionship of Roberts and Mejias.

Roberto's rookie campaign began well. He batted safely in thirty-seven of the Bucs' initial forty-four games. But by late May a tired Clemente began to struggle at the plate — a swoon both Roberto and Haney attributed to Clemente's participation in winter ball. The manager relegated the rookie to the bench with an occasional pinch hitting appearance. The demotion lasted throughout the month of June and much of July.

When Clemente returned to the lineup, he enjoyed both a twelve and fourteen game hitting streak. Jack Hernon, among other Pittsburgh writers, was smitten with Clemente's talent. "He has power, speed, arm, instinct, and trigger reaction," Hernon wrote. "He does everything with a natural flourish. There's a dash and color about almost everything he does…"[31]

The scribes were not the only Pirate watchers to take notice of Clemente's exceptional ability. Rickey, recognizing a previously untapped source of talent by Pittsburgh, dispatched his number one scout, Howie Haak, to scour the Caribbean. Branch also increased the club's efforts to seek out prospective black players. Among the fifty-five commissioned scouts on Pittsburgh's payroll, twenty-two were African American coaches of black colleges and high schools. Among the scouts were Edward Robinson of Grambling University, James Haines of Morehouse College, and Thomas Johnson of Howard University.

"We have the coaches of many of the outstanding Negro colleges and universities working for us now," Joe Brown explained. "And we should have a definite edge over our competitors on the good college boys. It is likely, however, that many Negro high school athletics would prefer to enter professional baseball rather than attend college. The implementation of high school coaches, therefore, may enable us to sign boys who might be signed by other clubs immediately following their graduation from high school."[32]

The Pirates' performance on the field continued to frustrate the weary Rickey. "This is a hard thing for me to say, but I don't know if we will be any better in August of '56," Branch glumly said, as the dog days of his fifth Pittsburgh season drug on.

Losing was beginning to take its toll on Branch, but his fighting spirit remained. Leaving his position as general manager with a legacy of four consecutive last place finishes was not what Rickey desired. In late August he began to launch a covert campaign to remain as the Pittsburgh general manager.

Traditionally, since becoming Pirate general manager, Rickey sat with several reporters and evaluated his club's performance for the season. On August 25 the Bucs were in their accustomed position of eighth place, and Branch was left plying for a kernel of hope. "I am to blame for the way the club has performed," Rickey said. "I force fed the youngsters and it failed. But I could not build with men whose day had passed. I must not change my way of doing things. My successor might. *If* I have a successor here, he will have a softer bed in the future. I would like to become an ambassador without portfolio. I am not going to desert the ship."

Rickey's sly maneuvering in the midst of his appraisal, during which he left open the possibility that he may return for yet another season as Pirate general manager, did not go unnoticed by his inquisitors.

Had he and Galbreath discussed the subject of him returning as general manager? Rickey was asked. "Yes," the Mahatma answered without hesitation, "Mr. Galbreath has told me, 'Branch, if you go, I go.' But I believe John meant that in connection with the contract as it stands right now, with the five years as an advisor."[33]

Regardless of what may have been implied in the answer, Galbreath flatly denied the conversation that Rickey recalled ever took place. The Pirate owner was questioned about the meaning of his alleged statement of "Branch, if you go, I go," and he claimed ignorance. "I've had no official talks with Branch Rickey on the subject of whether he remains with us as general manager, or relegates himself to an advisory role as his contract stipulates," Galbreath tersely stated on August 28. "I believe Mr. Rickey would like to remain as general manger another year in an effort to see this thing through, but we've come to no decision."

Galbreath spoke at an impromptu press conference held between games of a Pirate and Braves doubleheader at Forbes Field. The normally reserved Galbreath issued several provocative comments. Rickey, not coincidentally, according to reporters, was absent from the ballyard, as the interview took place on the Sabbath.

"We are obligated under contract for five more years to Rickey, but it doesn't mean we can't make a change if we see that it is the proper thing to do. This is no time to talk of next season," Galbreath insisted. "Let's get this year in first."

The real estate mogul had discovered long ago that baseball ownership wasn't for the faint of heart, but he still had no desire to abandon the undertaking. "We have plenty of problems, not only with the team, but financially. This is a terrible load to carry," Galbreath told the reporters present of two separate offers he had received for the club. "One man contacts me on the average of once a month. But he always gets the same answer, 'No.'

"Just recently a friend of mine approached me and said he thought I might be getting tired of it. This man has enough money to buy the team himself, but he said he represented a California syndicate and they wanted to shift the franchise to the West Coast. I have no interest at all in selling the club to move it out of Pittsburgh. There is nothing wrong with Pittsburgh, it's the ball club we've had here.

"Tom [Johnson] and I are disappointed, but not discouraged. We thought we would be farther along after five years than we are now."[34]

Rickey's position for the next season may have been undetermined, but Fred Haney's role with the club was clarified on the next-to-last day of another disappointing season. Haney had signed a two-year contract following the 1954 campaign. The agreement, however, contained a clause which stipulated the deal could be terminated by either party in writing on, or before, the last day of the season.

On September 23 Branch wrote two separate letters to his manager.

The first note, abrupt and terse in tone, simply reminded Haney of the contract conditions that he had agreed to the previous year, and concluded with, "This letter is notice that the club does not desire to extend the contract."[35] Rickey recognized the impersonal mode in the note, and duly rectified the foible:

> Your contract with the Pittsburgh club provides that it is automatically extended for 1956 unless notice not to extend is given by either party before the end of the present playing season. You and I have recently discussed the various uncertainties confronting our club and I am sure you understand the reason for this notice that the club does not desire to extend your contract.
>
> Our personal relationship has been to me most pleasant, and if indeed, either or both of us shall not be with Pittsburgh next season, I shall always have in mind your loyalty to your job, and to me and to everybody. I firmly believe that the club will come to be a very respectable contender, and when that time comes, it is possible that your effort to bring a successful team to Pittsburgh will be fully appreciated.
>
> Sincerely yours,
> Branch Rickey[36]

Rickey's kind words for his manager were sincere. Branch had a soft spot for him, and would play a significant role in Haney gaining employment with the Milwaukee Braves. Regardless, the relationship between the two men was tempestuous at times during the preceding summer. The rift that had developed between Haney and Rickey began in June, when Branch sent Ben Wade and George Freese to Hollywood for Lino Donoso. As the summer wore on, Haney disagreed with several of Rickey's decisions concerning player personnel. The rancor that had grown between the men did not trigger the ouster of Haney. The conclusion to fire Haney was based on Rickey's belief that his club needed a younger man at the helm.

Haney, angered by the impersonal handling of his termination, bitterly complained to the press that he was fired, "by a messenger boy." But the fifty-seven-year-old Californian was philosophical while accepting his dismissal. "I'm leaving Pittsburgh with a clear conscience. I tried to give one-hundred percent to the club and if my best wasn't good enough, that's it I guess."[37]

If Tom Johnson were to have his way, Rickey would promptly be following Haney out the door. Johnson was resolute in his desire to rid the organization of Rickey. "We ought to be able to get a last place team for a lot less money," Johnson sharply complained to reporters following a meeting between he and Galbreath at the River Club in Pittsburgh.

Speculation in the dailies read that Rickey's days as general manager were certainly coming to an end. On October 19, Rickey ended the meditation. He would, effective November 1, step aside as Pirate general manager.

"I haven't changed my mind," Branch said. "Although it's been written in various ways during the past summer, I am retiring, but you can put quotes around that word. I no longer wanted to punch a clock and intend to see the Pittsburgh club play more games the upcoming season than I have for the last two or three.

"I will be seventy-six years old on December 20, and I think it's about time mother and I started to enjoy life a bit. I have a date on November 4 in Ft. Myers to go fishing with Dr. Joe McClure, and I intend to be waiting at his boat that morning."[38]

Long before Rickey came to Pittsburgh, John Galbreath revered the baseball giant. The pecking order didn't change even after Rickey became Galbreath's employee. The strangeness of the juxtaposed relationship was best exemplified when the owner spoke in reverential tones, even as the most dire circumstances encompassed his club. The Mahatma, at all times, was addressed by Galbreath as "Mr. Rickey."

Tom Johnson, on the other hand, was never one to hold his tongue, publicly or privately, concerning his aversion to Rickey's modus operandi. Johnson's cynicism made no mark on Galbreath, at least he made no inroads with the Pirate president until the summer of 1955.

There is evidence to suggest that Rickey would have returned for at least one more season had Galbreath been receptive to the prospect. Much to Branch's dismay, Galbreath, when given the opportunity at his August 28 press conference, didn't welcome the idea of Rickey returning as general manager.

Galbreath was left with the prospect of allowing the Mahatma back for another year, or losing Tom Johnson as the Pirate vice president. Given the Pirates' dismal performance on the field and at the gate, and taking into consideration Rickey's age, Galbreath chose to discreetly not endorse Branch's return. "I think what he [Rickey] feared most was that Galbreath would fall into my camp, and that is precisely what happened," Tom Johnson explained. "Galbreath wanted to bring him back for one more year, and I said that you might as well kiss it good bye, and count me out."[39]

Following Rickey's announced retirement, Galbreath remained a good soldier and diplomatically spoke of Branch's efforts. "Mr. Rickey did a fine job," he began. "I don't think we need to make any apologies. No man could have done more or tried harder. We are optimistic about the future. This coming year will see the fruits of Mr. Rickey's labor on the playing field. The time is coming when we no longer will be pushed around by other clubs."[40]

At Rickey's October 19 press conference, he suggested that either Joe Brown or the Twig would be suitable choices to replace him as general manager. Galbreath and Johnson quickly decided on the thirty-seven-year-old Brown. "John and I agreed to come up with a general manager as quickly as we could, as soon as we heard of Mr. Rickey's resignation," Tom Johnson told reporters.

"The change in our general managership does not mean that Branch Rickey Jr. will go out," Johnson insisted. "But I will say this, the new general manager is going to be the boss. He will name the new field manager of our baseball club."

"And," Johnson added, "he will be the man who will run the team from the front office."[41]

The man who would run the Pirates described himself as a "Rickey man," but Joe Brown left no doubt that Rickey, no matter his past stature in the game, wouldn't be peddling influence in the Pirate front office. "Experimentation with the Pirates is out the window," Brown told *The Sporting News.* "I understand it was necessary in the past. But from now on we will use players from our higher classification clubs and those with some major league experience.

"There is going to be some talk that I am just a front for Mr. Rickey. That isn't so. I wouldn't take the job under those circumstances. I am not fronting for him. I have my own ideas now, as I did when working for him the past five years. We haven't always agreed on things but have talked them out... I will not be running to him every time I have a problem," Brown explained. "Even if he wanted it that way, I wouldn't do it. I have confidence in my own ability. But I would be pretty small potatoes if I didn't take advantage of his advice when it's needed."[42]

Even though Branch professed to be anxious to get on with fishing and other leisure activities, he would not slip quietly into the world of retirement.

"I will not sit back and be a watcher," Rickey vowed, belying his title of advisor. "My challenge remains here and I am going to lick it. I will remain as an active advisor until I have either done so, or died. I will devote my time to developing and buying players in order to help Pittsburgh. It will be semi-retirement, and you can put quotes around that."[43]

Chester Smith wondered in his Pittsburgh *Press* column if, regardless of the duties Rickey would undertake in retirement, he would be a disruption. "If he dabbles with the farm clubs, he'll be jamming traffic with the farm director," Smith wrote. "If he goes around the country looking at young players and presumably passing judgment on them, he'll be intruding on the field that rightfully belongs to the staff of scouts and their chief. If he confines himself to going to Forbes Field and looking at ball games he will be the most expensive fan the Pirates will ever have had."[44]

Smith's musings turned out to be prophetic. Branch was asked to cancel his anticipated fishing trip with Dr. McClure. Instead of leisurely whiling away the days angling on his friend's boat, Rickey traveled to Mexico and studied prospective Pirates.

The request for his assistance would not continue after his trip to Mexico. Joe Brown was determined to succeed, or fail, on his own, and he respectfully chose not to turn to his mentor for advice. "Semi-retirement" began to resemble retirement more than Rickey would have liked.

As Branch cleared out his Forbes Field desk, a well meaning reporter said to him, "Now you can do nothing, Mr. Rickey."

"Do nothing, young man?" the Mahatma exploded. "You expect me to do nothing? Preposterous. I started out to do nothing for three days once. I never was so tired in all my life. Age in years, young man, is no criterion of a man's usefulness."[45]

Branch complained to Galbreath that the younger Brown never sought his learned advice. Nor did the new Pirate general manager consult Rickey on any front office moves. He wasn't handling player negotiations as was expected, and he was never brought into any trade discussions. "I haven't spoken to Brown, and I get the very strong impression that under no circumstances was I to make any move whatsoever."

The sad truth was that Rickey's title was ceremonial only. The second five years of Branch's contract was a gift to one of baseball's great ambassadors from an admirer and a friend, John Galbreath. Though he gladly continued to collect his paycheck, idleness did not suit Rickey.

As the decade wound to a close, Branch found a project into which he could expend his energies. The Continental Baseball League, Rickey's latest undertaking, would never blossom into the third major league he envisioned it to become. The prospects of such a league backed with money men (and women) such as Lamar Hunt, Joan Payson, and Jack Kent Cooke, was taken seriously by the major leagues. In an effort that successfully short-circuited the Continental League, baseball expanded.

In 1961 the American League expanded by two teams, adding the Los Angeles Angels and Washington Senators. (The original Senators had relocated in Minneapolis and became the Twins.) And, in 1962, the majors brought the National League back to its rightful place, New York City, as the Metropolitans were born. The senior circuit also added Houston to its membership that season.

Rickey's desire to bring a third major league into existence was circumvented by expansion. The Mahatma, however, even at the age of eighty-two was still a pathfinder — a visionary and a force that could not be ignored... A mind that never tired.

On November 1, 1955, Branch dictated a letter to his children. Though Rickey would live another decade and continue to contribute to the National Pastime, the note read as a fitting epitaph for a magnificent career. Rickey's printed words captured his essence, precisely conveying the way he lived his unparalleled life. They breathe of wit, wisdom, and an undying, unfettered, optimism.

> Dear Children,
>
> I am not down and out, — not at all. In fact, I think I am on the spring board of happier days, — everything counted, — more than I have ever been.
>
> ...It is with deep discomfiture that I regret, for mother's sake and perhaps yours, the uncomplimentary articles which must, of course, come to your attention. I am what I am and sufficiently imperfect that I must not complain over much when things are written about me which may in some cases be true or partially true.
>
> Doubtless you have been perplexed by no inside news on my so called "retirement." If I shall be treated with kindly consideration by Joe Brown, then indeed I can be very happy in my new relationship. If not, I shall do exactly what Judge Landis told the old reprobate whom he sentenced to Leavenworth Penitentiary for two years. Under repeated falsetto protests that he "couldn't stand it," the Judge told him, "Well, sir, you do the very best you can."
>
> In any event, I propose to be busy, and with vigor to work within the sphere of my potentials for worthwhile things. Happiness is a byproduct, it surely is. I don't think one can work for it as an objective per se. A very elderly gentleman once said in morning

service in Gray Chapel in my student days that happiness was like a stranger cur dog met up with in an alley. You chase it and it flees from you. You chase it and it ever runs further away. You turn about and it may come close to you, even wishing to be petted, never quite to be caught.

...we are both [Mrs. Rickey] expecting everyone of you at our place this Christmas and I am certainly going to give her a real nice gift of some sort next June 1. 50 years of married life for one woman with a husband such as I is worthy of greater love and consideration than I can manifest by any gift. We two will have a celebration and it will not be complete unless you are close to see it.

Meanwhile, look out for the Pirates. The team has turned the corner.

Appendix:
Branch Rickey's Letters

San Bernardino, California
March 14, 1951

Memorandum of Agreement between M.G.M., represented by Mr. Clarence Brown, Producer-Director, and the Pittsburgh Athletic Company, Inc., Branch Rickey Executive Vice President and General Manager.

M.G.M. wishes to produce a picture, "Angels in the Outfield" or, in any event, a baseball picture. M.G.M. wishes to use Forbes Field and also the name of the Pittsburgh Club, including the word "Pittsburgh" or the nickname of the Club, viz "Pirates," and all the facilities of the Pittsburgh Baseball Club, both inside and outside the park.

The Pittsburgh uniforms and all other equipment, or paraphernalia, incident to the operation of the Base Ball Club, both home and on the road, are to be made available for such use as M.G.M. may desire.

The cast of such paraphernalia, e g., uniform, jackets, baseball bats, etc. is to be paid by M.G.M.

Park help, including clubhouse and field employees, ushers, ticket takers, etc., are likewise to be available if required.

Personal services are to be paid by M.G.M.

The Pittsburgh Base Ball Club agrees there is to be no rental for the use of the park or incidentals, and grants to M.G.M. without compensation the use of all names or nicknames of the Club free of charge. In other words, there is no expectation on the part of the Pittsburgh Base Ball Club for remuneration for its cooperation with M.G.M. on the making of the picture.

It is understood that a technical adviser having to do with the tactics of the game or the technique of play is desirable. The Pittsburgh Club recommends Mr. Harold "Pie" Traynor available to M.G.M. However, consideration for the services of Mr. Traynor will necessarily be made direct by M.G.M.

Thirty-five (35) uniforms, both home and road, are required together with thirty-five (35) jackets. These to be complete with stockings, caps, and belts, and are to be delivered on or before April 1, 1951 to M.G.M. Studios, Culver City, California. Accordingly, the Pittsburgh Club agrees that these uniforms will be delivered on or before that date.

Mr. Bill Meyer is Manager of the Pittsburgh Base Ball Club and the legal clearance is necessary to use freely the title of Manager of the Pittsburgh Club throughout the picture. The release will be required by M.G.M. and the Pittsburgh Club will see to it that Mr. Meyer will give such release.

It is understood that the actual names or nicknames on the Pittsburgh Club will not be used. If, however, such names or nicknames are used, releases must be obtained by M.G.M. Indeed, this same provision must apply to any and all employees of the Pittsburgh Club.

The Pittsburgh Base Ball Club has seen and read a copy of the script of the play as written under date of January 11, 1951, and finds no objection whatsoever to that script. If there are to be substantial changes in the script, it is understood that same will be submitted to the Pittsburgh Base Ball Club for approval.

It is understood that this entire agreement is predicated on the fact that Clarence Brown is going to produce and direct this picture, and that the world premier will be in Pittsburgh.

May 7, 1951

PERSONAL AND CONFIDENTIAL

Mr. John W. Galbreath
42 East Gay Street
Columbus 15, Ohio

Dear John:

On March 8, 1951, I sent you a survey of our players, and I told you at that time, I would later write further observations on the team. Here it is.

McCULLOUGH, Clyde

McCullough is in good condition physically. He is mentally fit. He is opinionated. That is not *necessarily* a fault. Defensively, he has some minor faults. First, frequently he stands four or five inches too far back of the batsman, and, second, he doesn't indicate often enough to the pitcher where he would like to have the ball pitched. He has one major fault. He doesn't always get the mask off when starting after a foul ball until he has located it visibly from his catching position. Then, of course, he is too late on the tight plays. The same fault is in evidence in his breaking from his position to back up plays at first base.

This boy can run faster than I thought he could. For a big man of his build, he is not slow.

McCullough is an extrovert. He can put on a show and likes to do it.

It seems to me he is afraid of a fence.

I believe McCullough is overbearing and perhaps bombastically so. With certain people he is domineering. His tendency is to tear down an individual, and not ever to build him up. It is said by one who is generally considered a conservative and competent observer that he is the most destructive influence on the Pittsburgh club — a morale breaker. Another chap, Rip Sewell, told me that the greatest service I could render the Pittsburgh Club would be to get McCullough off the team for the sake of producing a winning club; that he is a show-off; a pretender — likes him personally, and has never had any difficulties at anytime with him.

Offensively, he has a major fault quite obvious to everybody. He has what is known in the baseball circles as a "hitch" — a decided "hitch." This alone could account for a .250 batting average. Pitchers who offer a problem to batsmen in the field of timing make poor hitters out of men who "hitch." A "hitch," may I explain, is a preliminary and unnecessary movement of the hands or arms, usually the hands, whereby, the batsman is unable to assume the complete back position of the bat in proper time to swing in only one direction after the ball is in flight. Having said this, I can understand that the reader may not understand what I mean.

It would be much easier to demonstrate. In any event, McCullough has this very grievous fault and it is a very difficult habit to change. It is like a brain lesion of a gambler or a drug addict or cigar smoker, or something. McCullough is a power hitter, but not a good hitter. He has doubtful market value.

FITZGERALD, Edward

You must know that I am dictating these observation as I call them without re-reading my previous survey. In fact, I have not re-read it at anytime since the first writing. I recall, however, that I stated in my first letter to you that it seemed to me that he had some of the qualities of a pussy cat, a will-of-the-wisp sort of fellow — no fight. He still strikes me in that manner. However, the common criticism of him, viz, that he could not catch, meaning that he was not a good receiver, is much exaggerated. There is nothing bad in his method of catching that time and practice will not cure. Mechanically, I think, he is satisfactory, although strong criticism still comes to me about his "receiving." He can run and throw, and I see no reason why he will not hit. He has not shown good accuracy in throwing so far this Spring, and he has not given the power stroke in batting that I had hoped to see. He is entirely worthwhile until we find the exceptional catcher we are looking for and need so much. Fitzgerald is a fine gentleman in every way.

It is not true as was generally reported in the papers that I said I would give Fitzgerald $100,000 if he would punch somebody on the nose. That was part of a jocular comment much more extended and even so, it was not accurately reported. Moreover, the comment was made only in the presence of our own officials, and offers me the occasion to remark that we have had several careless leaks from within the family.

REISER, Pete

Without a doubt, a confirmed neurotic. Ability today, and none tomorrow. As volatile as alcohol and seeks an easy and common level as conveniently as any fluid. He can hit and run, and throw passably — as great, indeed, as probably his neuroticism and his wife will permit. I leave your curiosity at this point for oral exposition. He reminds me of the fellow who jumped out of the 20th story window. In the games to date, he has passed the 10th floor and he is all right so far.

DICKSON, Murry

Dickson is a scatterbrain, which may explain a scatter-arm. A pitching staff of ten Dicksons would finish about mid-way in the race. A good club could spot him and find him helpful. His record for the past three years shows that it takes him half the season to get ready to pitch the second half. He has an assortment of a great number of pitches — adjustments of rotation to velocity — varying both the direction and rapidity of rotation to velocity — so much so that he is continuously flabbergasted in making a decision of what pitch to make. He reminds me of the fellow in the army who complained of every job given to him and was unsatisfactory in all of them and finally he was given the job of sorting potatoes. At the end of two days, the sergeant asked him how he liked his new work, and he said, "Terrible, I don't like it all — it almost worries me to death." "What worries you," said the sergeant, and the reply was, "The damn decisions." I will say Dickson reminds me of that chap. He ought to be a really great pitcher. He fields his position splendidly and he can hit.

WERLE, William

Werle is one of our better pitchers. Has the student approach to his job. If he could select and perfect one of Dickson's numerous pitches — just one, added to what he now has, Werle might be in the pennant winning class. He needs an additional "pitch" to make him great.

CHAMBERS, Cliff

He could have been the Illinois democratic politician who supported Lincoln and came to be General McClernand whom Sherman fired. Later, McClernand wrote his "memoirs," and asked Uncle Abe to write the preface and Uncle Abe did write it, and this is what he said. "This is a good book for those who like this kind of book."

CHESNES, Robert

He has gone. Poor fellow. He lost his arm. He couldn't throw. He has been placed on option with Hollywood simply because of the hope that he might recover the use of his arm, and vindicate Pittsburgh's generous purchase of his contract.

FRIEND, Robert

A promising youngster with possibility, if not probability of greatness. Rapid orientation is his great need. "At homeness" does not come to some boys easily. It is my opinion that his acquaintanceship can be hastened, and poise and knowledge be acquired best by keeping him right with the Pittsburgh club — and pitching him a great deal. If he is not pitched, he must 'go out.' He can become what is known as a power pitcher.

LAW, Vernon
    Without question, he figures in all our plans.

LOMBARDI, Victor
    He has lost his fast ball and we have optioned him to Hollywood. There was no money market for him and a successful season in the Pacific Coast League may bring us next fall some cash returns.

PETTIT, Paul
    He could be embryonic neurotic. Complains a great deal. Ailing so frequently — fearful all the time lest, for example, his elbow will get sore "again." Then, both consciously and, of course, sub-consciously, he changes his delivery to accommodate his fear, and thus runs the hazard of positive injury to his shoulder, or, indeed, some place other than the elbow. One day 'he has it.' The next day he doesn't.
    In a test of general intelligence, he would pass easily fine physique and a lot of stuff. Friend and Law, and certain others in the Pittsburgh organization are, it seems to me at the moment, better investments.
    Pettit has one foot in the army.
    I have placed Pettit's original contract, made with one Mr. Stephanie, who was a party, in my judgment, to an insincere arrangement, with Mr. Tom Johnson. Do we owe Pettit's salary for the time if and when he is in the army? Generally speaking, I do not believe in long term contracts, and most surely a nine year contract for an eighteen year old boy is bad. It might be good if Pettit could make a great splurge and reach a profitable market for us.

PIERRO, Bill
    A blatherhead. Typical low grade Brooklynese. Hedonistic. A six footer or more with a paper thin body, a troublesome but transparent head, who can throw a ball harder and with more skills than his 150 pounds entitle him to do. Certain functional organs dominate him to such an extent that his judgment, practices, and consequent habits are

completely subordinated. In other words, he does not put duty or fidelities to his job or to other people first. He does not care enough about success in his work.

For example, he had an engagement to meet two of the coaches in the morning for special work. They were to be on the field in uniform at 8:30 A.M. I was to have charge of this workout, having in mind his acquiring a 'change of speed' pitch. Poesdel and Narron were on the field at 8:30. I was there too. Pierro came at 9:10 A.M. I met him outside the park as I was leaving. Very quietly I told him that his glove and shoes were all wrapped up in the clubhouse and suggested that he pick up these articles and proceed immediately Eastward toward DeLand, Florida, expressing also the hope that some method of transportation might overtake him on his journey; that I would complete the workout in DeLand where I would next see him. He did report to DeLand where I would next see him. He did report to DeLand where some days later I met him and had some appointments with him. He observed each of them promptly. It is possible that Pierro may be one of our very top pitchers, and that too before the present season is finished.

Recently, Pierro became quite ill. Several doctors have attended him and there is a definite diagnosis of encephalitis. He is a poor boy and has always been in debt. His illness, indeed, is most regrettable. With all his off the field faults, he was possibly the most likely twenty game winner on the club. The club has brought his wife on to Pittsburgh where the boy is confined to the Presbyterian Hospital, and he is receiving every possible attention calculated to help him. He has been placed on the Disabled List.

WALSH, James

Still in my book scared to death. No cocksureness about anything. He is a bit different from Newcombe of the Brooklyn club, who, in the middle of a tie score game, permitted the first batsman to single and the next one to single and the next one to single, all of them on the first pitched ball, whereupon Campenella, to a rotund colored catcher of some force, went out to the mound to big Newcombe and said, "Newk, I say, throw de ball hard I say." To which admonition, Newk replied, "What you mean throw de ball hard. How can I throw de ball hard when I can't throw de ball hard." Walsh can throw de ball hard and does. A thrower, not a pitcher.

KOSKI, Bill

A 19 year old, 6'4" right hand pitcher, who frequently keeps one prong of the pivot foot spike in contact with the hard rubber in delivering the ball. A fault which should and could be readily corrected. This can affect control and on a vital pitch — lose a game. This boy has almost no experience, but he already is a great pitching prospect. He can be lost to the army on quick notice. It is one chance in a thousand that a boy out of high school can immediately help a major league club.

Koski is a Crosby product. I am coming to think that this fellow Crosby may be our underpaid scout. He has several children and I intend to propose to the Board some further consideration in his behalf.

BASGALL, Romanus

A good boy, a good fielder. Not enough running speed, and not enough power at the plate. If Strickland should be our shortstop, then Basgall is possibly the best man for second base. But, if we are making our decisions on the basis of 1953 or 1954, then, indeed, Basgall is more than doubtful. Right now, Murtaugh is better, and if neither man is part of the plan for the 1953 or 1954 club, then, of course, Bill will play the man who can help us most in 1951. We will see.

CASTIGLIONE, Pete

It is possible that if Strickland could be moved to second base Castiglione might be our shortstop. I say this without any consultation with our manager. It just seems to me that it might work out that way. Castiglione, this Spring, has been playing third base most of the time, sharing the work in that position with Dillinger. However, Castiglione can play short. He will outrun Rojek and he will outhit him, and he may field acceptably. He has a queer fault, one that I have never observed in any other player. On all ground balls hit to him, he will look at the ball before he throws it. Castiglione is aggressive and unafraid.

DILLENGER, Bob

Continues to hustle. Has had a couple of weeks of shin splints — whatever that is. Unless a miracle in change of effort happens, the best we can hope for is that he will prove to be good enough to reach a valuable player market within a year. It is possible that he will be disposed of as the cut-down date approaches.

LONG, Dale

Build, age, dexterity, and desire justifiably attract the steadfast attention of our manager. Long might eventually alternate with Phillips at first base, this, in event Kiner doesn't 'make good' at first base. Long is a left hand hitter with power. 25 Longs' on any ball club would make an interesting team, and eventually probably hard to beat. The player was drafted from Kansas City, and Kansas City has a "claim" on him. Player should go to New Orleans on one day recall optional assignment for the present season.

DEMPSEY, Cornelius

With one or two exceptions, Dempsey has been unimpressive in all appearances so far. Pittsburgh is now asking waivers the second time, and if received, the player will be returned to San Francisco. If player is claimed, then we must pay an additional $22,500 and take our chances.

Dempsey is thirty years of age. He has poise and sense and character. But, he shows no more independent thinking than a mere youth. He is hybrid, a maverick — an offshoot. This curve ball breaks — the next one doesn't. This fast ball pitch goes where he wants it to go — the next one goes anywhere else. He has no pitching bloodline — no pedigree. A REALLY NICE FELLOW.

FISHER, Harry

Fisher has been optioned to Indianapolis for the season.

MUIR, Joseph

Left hand pitcher. Doesn't have a lot of stuff, but pitches with what he has. Game, cool, and his ability approaches his capacity. We have to keep him whether we like it or not. We need numbers.

QUEEN, Mel

Has surprised everybody. Claims complete recovery and his work indicates a sound arm.

MERSON, John

Has been optioned to Indianapolis for the season.

MURTAUGH, Daniel

Has lost both agility and running speed, as well as power in hitting. If Sewell should be replaced as Manager at New Orleans, Murtaugh would be a good man to take Sewell's place. The only way Murtaugh can help the Pittsburgh club to win the pennant is with his head. At present, we need arms and legs — hopeful that ancestry has conceived them thoughtfully.

COOGAN, Dale
Coogan is with Hollywood on option.

GRUNWALD, Alfred

O'CONNELL, Daniel   (All are in the army.)

MACDONALD, William

PHILLIPS, Jack
Phillips can be carried as a utility man, or, perhaps as a regular on a high class winning team, but he will never carry a strong part in producing one.

ROJEK, Stanley
If it be true that God's universal redeeming grace is proved by the salvation of one soul that was lost, then Rojek is the evidence. The lost lamb has returned to the moral fold. I do not think he should be classed a matrimonial coward. Outside of his physical virility, I doubt if he has much to offer.

SCHENZ, Robert
Full of pep. A bench jockey. A better ball player than his last year's records shows, and a better ball player than most people think he is.

THOMSON, Robert
Whatever I said in my previous report still goes. He is certainly no better. He is a drafted player, and it is likely that on the cut-down date we will let him go on the Rochester claim at $7500.00. However, I hope the St. Louis organization releases its claim.

STRICKLAND, George
During Spring Training he was a 'free swinger'— showed power at the plate. He has tightened up. Strokes defensively. He may come out of it. Otherwise, he is O.K. I would like to see him at second base.

BEARD, Ted

Ted has changed the Manager's mind. Meyer now wants to keep him. He is the best fielding outfielder in the Pittsburgh organization. However, he doesn't seem to be able to do very much at the plate with a curve ball — thrown by anybody.

BELL, David

Can run, throw, and hit with power, but if the game goes long enough, he is likely to lose it. He reminds me of Hermanski. Obtuse, possibly opaque. I am not sure.

KINER, Ralph

This boy has improved as a first baseman very much, but in comparison to a Chase or a Sisler or a Phillips, he has a distance to go.

METKOVICH, George

I am afraid he is a streak player. Good for a time, and then bad for a time. A good team man.

SAFFELL, Tom

Has done very little to date. Not unlikely that he will be sent back to Indianapolis on option for the season.

WESTLAKE, Wally

Most marketable player on the club.

RESTELLI, Dino

I like him. Some people think he is not a good fielder. That may be. Manager Meyer doesn't like him. This boy can run pretty good and in my judgment he can hit, and with power. His arm is not great, but good enough. I would be very much pleased if it so happens that Restelli would be retained as one of our twenty five players throughout the resent season.

Very truly yours,
BR/b

cc — Mr. Thomas Johnson
cc — Mr. Harry "Bing" Crosby
cc — Mr. Benjamin Fairless

October 1, 1951

Mr. W. W. Forster, Editor Pittsburgh Press
Blvd. Of the Allies
Pittsburgh, Pennsylvania

Dear Mr. Forster:
  Starting today and continuing throughout the month of October the Pittsburgh Club will conduct in DeLand, Florida something entirely new in baseball.
  This innovation is a post-season school of development in their efforts to win places for themselves on Pirate teams of years to come.
  The underlying objective of the operation is to advance the day when Pittsburgh again will have a pennant-contending club. In my judgment this month long series of daily instructional work aimed to correct the faults and defects common to young players, and to hasten the development of their natural abilities toward the meeting of major league requirements, will advance, perhaps, by as much as a full year the time these boys will be ready to fill Pirate uniforms and give Pittsburgh a winning team.
  Approximately 70 boys, carefully selected because of their impressive possibilities, will attend the DeLand school which will be under my personal full-time direction. Other instructors will include — Bill Meyer, Manager of the Pittsburgh Club; Fred Haney, Manager of our affiliated club at Hollywood; Danny Murtaugh, recently appointed Manager of our New Orleans Club; George Sisler, Head of our Scouting Activities; Bill Burwell, Consultant to Pittsburgh Organization Managers and many others. Some of the players on Pittsburgh affiliated minor league clubs during the season just concluded. Still others are highly promising youngsters who will enter upon professional careers next season.
  Out of this group and their accelerated development in the DeLand school will come the Pittsburgh Club of the future. This fact combined with the fact that the post-season school is novel, and that a large number of the players participating reside in the Pittsburgh area, makes me wonder if the daily activities at DeLand may not be of sufficient interest to your readers to warrant sending one of your baseball writers to the school to give your paper special coverage, if not for the school's duration then, at least, during the last two weeks of the month when the

World Series is over. I will be pleased to have you send such a writer as guest of our club for whatever period you may wish to send one. Should you desire special art coverage we will be glad to provide a photographer on all services which your representative may desire.

Will you please let me have your reaction to this suggestion at your earliest convenience?

Cordially yours,
Branch Rickey, General Manager

San Bernardino, Cal.
February 26, 1952

PERSONAL

Mr. John W. Galbreath, President
Pittsburgh Baseball Club
Forbes Field
Pittsburgh 13, Pa.

Dear John:

In a conversation with Tom Johnson just before I left, I got the very definite impression that he is, indeed, quite discouraged about baseball, — not only in Pittsburgh, but in general. He seems to have the feeling that there is nothing ahead of us but losses and even if we win we cannot make money; that the market for players is closed because everyone produces his own players and that, therefore, if we produce players in Pittsburgh even more than we want or need, there will be no sales market for the surplus contracts, etc., etc.

There came a time in the conversation where, if I had the money, I would have said to him something as follows. "Tom, feeling as you do about it, don't you think it would be advisable for you to consider the sale of your stock to somebody or other?" Indeed, as I started to say, if I had the money I would have asked his price. I told Tom that I did not believe the market for good players would ever disappear.

Of course there is understandable reason for Tom's discouragement. The year 1951 was a dismal financial showing and our present circumstances are pressing and most unfortunate. I speak of my conversation with Tom because I think you are entitled to know that, in my judgment, he is even less inclined to make any personal advance of money to the Club than he has been heretofore.

Very truly yours,

March 14, 1952

Mr. John W. Galbreath, President
Pittsburgh Baseball Club
Forbes Field
Pittsburgh 13, Pa.

Dear John:

We have sent out letters, as per copy attached, to approximately 80 negro colleges and universities. Then, about two or three days later, under date of March 12th, we sent out more than 1600 similar letters to negro high schools, copy of which is also attached. The only difference in the two letters lies in the first sentence in the third paragraph. The college letter was addressed to the head of the athletic department by name. The high school letters were addressed to the Principals.

We expect a fairly heavy mail and, indeed, the only benefit to be derived for the next three or four months will be the United States Postal Department, but I think we will make a showing within three years as a direct result of this little simple effort. In any event, we are preparing to meet a completely new scouting situation without adding any additional field expense.

I will keep you informed about the situation from time to time.

Yours,

BR/b
Encl:

PERSONAL AND CONFIDENTIAL

March 21, 1952

Mr. John W. Galbreath, President
Pittsburgh Baseball Club
Forbes Field
Pittsburgh 13, Pa.

Dear John:

-1-

On Tuesday afternoon, March 11, I talked with you over the telephone from Palm Springs, and you told me that Ralph had agreed to terms. Immediately I prepared the contract and sent it to him by hand with a longhand note, verbatim copy of which I am enclosing herewith.

Last Saturday night, March 14, after the game had started in San Francisco, he returned one signed copy of the contract. For four days he had us stymied. Bill was anxious to have a talk with the team, — his annual spring talk on, I take it, club rules, etc. During this time, Ralph was pretty largely a law to himself, — coming, going, and reporting as he pleased. I told Bill not to have the slightest disagreement with him about anything. During this time, of course, players assumed Ralph was a member of the club and subject to all the work of other players. It was a bad situation.

For example, he reported to San Diego for the night game without shoes, uniform, or, indeed, anything, — turning up as he pleased and leaving as he pleased. He had not been seen all day.

-2-

I quote Bill Meyer in a remark he made to me during the past week: "I told Roy Hamey two years ago that he (Hamey) was ruining the club by the way he was handling Ralph, — giving him special privileges on reporting, traveling as he pleased, etc." Bill states that he had many conversations with Roy about the matter, but that in effect Roy's reply always was, — "Well, I know, but he puts them in the park."

Bill felt he could hardly bring other men in line and it had gotten to the place where in 1950 his players took many little advantages; there was very little team spirit and he himself went to pot along with everything else. He doesn't at all blame Ralph for his own dereliction, but he felt then, and felt, indeed, all last year that it was very hard to get a bunch of men to devote themselves to a common task or job when the star of the club was not a part of the program, and particularly was this so when, according to Bill, so many of the players felt that Ralph was not at all a star. The players' opinion in this respect is shared by Bill. Indeed, I am inclined to go along with his judgment. If it were not for the single thing, — home run hitting, Ralph would be unable to be a member of any major league club. He cannot say this outside and never has. Neither can I say it out loud.

-3-

Of course I have had several heart to heart talks with Bill about his problems, — particularly this one, and largely my statements are based upon the information coming directly from Bill, except that I have independent opinions from my own observations. The fact is that Ralph "used to hit all the time," ahead of the practice and even stay after the game for hitting practice. Not anymore. He really had a terrible year last year. Bill came to me two or three times to discuss the advisability or desirability of benching Ralph for awhile. There was a period of one month where he contributed nothing at all even to our offense. We agreed finally that he should not be benched even for a day.

-4-

There came a time in late summer when he did not accompany the club to an exhibition game, but went elsewhere for the day on what may have been a social engagement, but seemed to be a commercial appointment, — and he joined the team at game time, having arrived via air. A few days later, I had occasion to talk with Ralph and I brought up the point of necessity of all players being subject to the same controls; that fairness to everyone, managerial difficulties with players, team morale, and other obvious factors, made it impossible to grant exceptional privileges to any one player. I recall using Eisenhower's very pointed remarks throughout his book about morale being the greatest single factor in winning a war. Inventions, equipment, logistics, manpower, superior fire, generalship, food, and indeed any of these or all of these or all of them put together could not equal as a controlling force the value of army morale. I pointed out how the General labored personally to bring it about. It was a very cordial and friendly discussion, and must have lasted the better part of an hour. To begin with, he did not agree with me at all. He seemed to feel that, first of all, he was entitled to special considerations and then I felt that he was finally driven to defend himself upon the basis that any player might be granted special privileges, but he quickly had to abandon that position, — admitting that in such case there could be no team spirit or common purpose, in fact, no team at all.

When Ralph left me, I felt that I had made some hay. I have found out since that if I made any at all, it was only temporary

-5-

Compared to other players, he has a storehouse of equipment. In establishing standards for himself, he does in fact establish extravagant standards for everybody, and it doesn't matter whether he seeks to do so or not. He is now on an extremely extravagant scale of living for himself. His homelife, both as to place and manner, and, indeed, including associates, are not possibly consistent with the life of any other player. Now, I don't object to that at all except, that, in order to point out that the carrying of these methods and practices over into his baseball relationships which has to do exclusively with other baseball players, is definitely bad, — very bad.

-6-

In no sense is he a member of the club in spring training. He commutes from Palm Springs. His constant companion is a featherhead ... with whom, I understand, he is involved in some commercial ventures. Ralph, on the other hand, is in no sense a featherhead. He is a very substantial person. But it is the Trainer's opinion that he doesn't think things through too thoroughly before he takes a point of leadership on items suggested to him by very inconsequential persons. For example, and only as an illustration, he thinks that the clubhouse should be air conditioned. Now air conditioning our clubhouse is, in the first place, impractical and secondly, very expensive, and thereby highly objectionable to the health of the players. We have more sore arms and quick

colds resulting from players going directly from a night game to air conditioned sleeping cars than from any other single source. Most certainly
it is obvious that players coming in under profuse perspiration and a bit
tired will sit down in an air conditioned place and most of them will cool
off under those conditions. I would not stand for one minute to have an
air conditioned clubhouse. An adjoining lounging room air conditioned
would be perhaps bearable, but not the clubhouse. His leadership in this
respect is unfortunate. He does have more sense than most players and
he dominates the thinking of the others. We are now in front of a club
made up, just about 90% on the nose, of men younger than Ralph, and
most of these will average ten years younger.

-7-

During this past week, our Road Secretary, Bob Rice, came to me
privately and most disturbed and said, —"Mr. Rickey, I'm on the spot,
and I don't know what to do about it." I said, "well, tell me about it."
Then he said, "I am told that Nancy is to have special seating, — with the
club officials this year; that she had nothing in common with the other
player's wives, and that she is not to sit with them. Now what am I to do
about it?"

Bad relationship between players can destroy team morale. But
when you get the wives at sixes and sevens, or twenty four to one against
the "star," we are in a helluva fix. Wives in that case will take care of this
thing called morale without any doubt whatever.

-8-

You told me over the telephone that Ralph requested a clause be
inserted in his contract in effect contractually insuring the retention of
Greenberg Gardens for the period of his contract. You assured him correctly that it was your understanding that no changes would be made this
year in Greenberg Gardens and that satisfied him. I do not refer to this
request of Ralph's except for the purpose of pointing out that the request
in itself indicated his desire to subordinate, if necessary, a major policy
of the club to what he regards as a personal advantage to himself. He
would control the physical dimension of the playing field in order to
accommodate his home run record. He might, on the same principle,
demand that the Greenberg Gardens be brought 30' closer.

Murry Dickson, in discussing his contract and the point of his allowing more home runs year in and year out than any other pitcher in the National League, stated with some justification that "Greenberg Gardens" was largely responsible for his record; that he might be the star and have a large salary instead of Kiner if the field had normal, natural, and original proportions.

Players generally and in a vast majority favor the removal of the Gardens. I believe that if a proper free vote could be held on the part of our public there would be an overwhelming majority in favor of the removal. My mail indicates it.

There is an esthetic value to Forbes Field of which we are justly proud. The artificial enclosure mars it. It is wrong in purpose and only justification finds itself in the reason for increasing income by creating a home run hitter, and it is conceivable that under a given set of circumstances park alterations could be properly considered. In any event, it would be preferable to insolvency if indeed that were the alternative.

Gus Bell, our right fielder, offered some difficulty in contract negotiations. He alleged that the park dimensions were unfavorable to him and that no consideration whatever was given to him when the club built an artificial barrier against his making home runs by placing a wire screen in a given area in right field. He could very well have said, "You make it easy for Kiner to hit home runs by bringing the fence in. You make it hard for me by artificially moving it out."

Not only do players have rights, but the club itself has rights, and surely one of them is to determine and adopt conditions and measurements and policies in general which in the opinion of the club conduces to better attendance, park attractiveness, and public comfort, and surely no one player should be consulted very much when it comes to the consideration of matters affecting the club as a whole.

The fact that some one player is even willing to advance his own interest at the expense of other players or the club itself disqualifies him as having in mind team spirit. Victory in games is subordinated to the record he keeps on his own cuff. That is not generally considered to be good.

Finally, may I say that park alterations involving the playing field is that sort of major item which the General Manager would refer to the Board of Directors before making a decision. Certainly no single player should have the right even to discuss it for the sake of his own advantage.

-9-

This thing already referred to about of some one player to suit himself about transportation is unthinkable. Of course there are exceptions, — in case of sickness of business emergency or unusual events when players are accommodated by management, but this practice must not be placed on a personal basis. It must stand on principle.

-10-

One of our players this past week went to Byron Jorgensen, our Clubhouse Custodian, and said to him, in effect, "I am going to so and so place by automobile. You tell the Manager." Byron, having no authority and being a very subordinate employee, was embarrassed and said in reply, "Don't you think you better speak to Bill (Meyer) about it?" The player got very mad and said, "you can go to hell and you can tell the Manager to go to hell," and out he went. Now I speak of this as an illustration of many little things that are happening and will continue to happen in greater number if the Manager is unable to control all the players under the same set of rules. Personally, I don't believe that this player would have ever acted as he did or said what he said if the Kiner story had not been in the background.

To the extent that any player requires or seeks special conditions for his own sake as against the other players, or as against victory, — or against attendance receipts or against public appeal is saying "to hell with other players and receipts and the pennant and everything else. All that counts with me is my home run record and the club must put in writing the physical boundaries of the park as I dictate."

This idea simply had to be in his head when he made the request to you.

-11-

The winning of the pennant in this game of competitive baseball is based upon the sound broad principle that no player is greater than his club.

Babe Ruth was a great player. He was a national character, a public idol. He was suspended, as I recall it, indefinitely by Manager Huggins for infraction of a disciplinary rule.

He was suspended three months by Commissioner Landis for undertaking to say that in effect he was bigger than the game.

THE PUBLIC SUPPORTED MANAGER HUGGINS AND ALSO COMMISSIONER LANDIS.

Babe Ruth could run. Our man cannot.

Ruth could throw. Our man cannot.

Ruth could steal a base. Our man cannot.

Ruth was a good fielder. Our man is not.

Ruth could hit with power to all fields. Our man cannot.

Ruth never requested a diminutive field to fit him. Our man does.

-12-

Kiner is in his thirtieth year. He is slowing up. His running speed is not as good as it was, and his arm is by no means the arm he once had.

-13-

Ralph does not "care" as formerly. His major interest right now seems to be in golf. He has, in my judgment, entirely too many commercial interests even for the sake of those interests themselves. Baseball must interfere with the attention he should be giving to these other interests, — broadcasting, television, personal appearances, name identifications for gain. Money investments occasion continuous conferences and take his time. For example, he is compelled to be absent from the club twice each week on the road for as much as four hours at a time.

-14-

The Manager can never be sure of his attendance at pre-game meetings or special field work and he must adjust all organization interests and conferences having in mind Kiner's schedule.

On this past Tuesday when the Pirates were scheduled to play the Giants here in San Bernardino, and the Major League All-Star-Hollywood Game was to be played in Hollywood that evening, Ralph called Bill about noontime inquiring as to whether or not he was to appear in San Bernardino for the Giant game. Of course he was scheduled to play a part of a game at Hollywood that evening. Bill told him that he was expected to report for the Giant game. He came up from Palm Springs and arrived at the game just about the time it started. Other players hereabouts played that afternoon and also appeared that night in the Kiwanis Game, — notably Alvin Dark who played the entire nine innings of the Kiwanis game and took part in the game here at San Bernardino that same afternoon.

-15-

His baseball contract calls for his appearances at the direction of the Club. This is a very valuable asset. In effect he absolutely refuses to conform and is indeed seldom.

-16-

1949 — The club's attendance was 1,500,000. Ralph made 54 home runs and had a great year. He secured at that time a two year contract.

1951— The club's attendance was under 1,000,00. Ralph made 41 home runs and was in many other respects less valuable.

The first question that occurs is this. Does attendance depend upon Kiner's home runs more than the club's standing in the pennant race? Second, is the salary out of proportion really to his ability? That brings me to

-17-

Three things determine the salary of players: First, the ability of the club to pay. Second, the ability of the players to earn. Third, comparative salaries paid to players of like age, ability, and experience. The third of these is the most important because, in addition to affecting the amount of salary, it affects team morale. The reason that pennant winning clubs have difficulty in repeating is due very often and largely to the disparity in salaries paid to players on the same team. The Pittsburgh club is surely in a vulnerable spot in this respect.

-18-

It is doubtful that at the present time more than two clubs are interested or would become interested in obtaining Kiner's contract. It is the belief of Bill Meyer and Myself that Kiner may be in front of quick deterioration. If so, the market can pass completely at the end of the coming season.

-19-

The player is tied up too closely, I think, with another person who shares a so-called bachelor apartment in Pittsburgh paying $175.00 per month, — two bedrooms. The friend is well-known for promiscuous domestic infidelity.

-20-

Ralph is the National League player representative. That in itself is bad for Pittsburgh, and again this in turn has a tendency to affect and probably does his playing ability.

-21-

Last Fall we conducted a camp for a number of young players at DeLand, Florida. Four players on the Pittsburgh roster were included. All four of these players requested that they be permitted to go to this school, and indeed, some requested that we did not take. Ralph gave us some bad publicity in this matter. He came out with the statement that these players should be paid a salary for the time they were in DeLand and it created much comment. None of the boys received anything but expenses, and in no case was any boy whether on the Pittsburgh club or otherwise urged to attend. It was purely an invitational affair. The boys were told in writing, in effect, that if it was inconvenient or expensive or an interference with school or job, they would not be expected to come and under no circumstances would their absence be permitted to affect the most friendly relationships with the club.

Ralph's press story was a very unfair and unjust attack.

Incidentally [a] ... fellow ... who is indirectly an employee of the club in a broadcasting job supported the views taken by Ralph.

It is my understanding that the facts, which Ralph could easily have known in advance, have been made known to him, nevertheless no retraction or apology has come from him, either publicly or privately at anytime.

Yours,

BR/b

Encl:

March 6, 1953

Mr. Ralph Kiner
Thunderbird Country Club
Palm Springs, California

Dear Ralph:

I am in receipt of your letter of February 23rd, received in the Pittsburgh office on February 26th, forwarded and received here in Cuba on March 3rd.

It could be that you have believed that an offer, coupled with intention to accept, makes an agreement. Ignorance of the fact that a contract is based upon an offer and acceptance is no excuse for a charge of violation of a contract which never existed.

Prior to February 1st, your contract for 1953, calling for $67,500 was sent to you. If it becomes necessary to discuss the fairness of that offer, I am prepared to do that very thing in considerable detail and without delay. However, this letter is simply an answer to yours which at least pretends to assume the existence of a contract between you and myself, made on February 13, 1953.

Branch [Jr.]has had a visit with you and on his return he advised that he believed that a visit by myself to you would be necessary. I arranged to go to California to see you. I wished very much to avoid any contract difficulty whatever. I expected to return with the signed contract and so stated to several people, for I had in mind to exceed the maximum reduction.

Our conversation lasted about three hours. In a long past, I don't recall a contract negotiation where I tried harder to sign a player. During the later period of our conference, I expressed my regret and concern by your failure to come to terms. It was, indeed, very embarrassing to me to fail in my conference with you.

You will surely recall that, finally, after I had made the offer of $75,000 with the two concessions on reporting time and transportation, you mentioned in effect that it had never occurred to you that the offer would be less than $80,000. I told you $75,000 was the top; that that figure would never be raised. You didn't wish to accept that offer. You stated you would have to give it further consideration. At no time did you directly or indirectly indicate that the offer was satisfactorily or that it ever would be. Your expression as I remember was to the effect that you didn't feel that a delay in negotiations at that time to be injurious. It was when you mentioned $80,000 that I told you that in event you were traded, I would see to it that you got an extra $5,000.

You stated two or three different times that you were willing to cooperate, or take a slight cut, but not as much as $15,000. We spent considerable time on your reasons for demanding more than $67,500. It all boiled down to a point of your gate appeal, and we spent a lot of time on that. We never did have an understanding on terms. We parted without either of us knowing what the final terms might be.

It is very difficult to express the depths of my resentment to your implied questioning of my integrity. I can only state categorically that when you claim an agreement was reached on February 13th, you state an unmitigated lie and moreover you know it very well.

You told the press that you have accepted the offer of February 13th, but you fail to tell the papers that the offer was withdrawn on February 17th, and the reason for its withdrawal.

We both wished to avoid a "holdout" situation and we both knew that that condition could not exist until after March 1st, and we wished to avoid a press story that we had reached an impasse. You heard me say to the reporters repeatedly that I was "hopeful," etc., — using that word several times. No paper anywhere in this country carried the story that we had reached an agreement. We both knew very well that subsequent negotiations were necessary. I suggested that we make a simple statement that we were hopeful that everything would be alright upon the required reporting date, and you agreed to that statement, and accordingly a concise statement to that effect was made by both of us.

That you may have intended sooner or later to accept my offer may be true, but you never, by word or action, conveyed any such intention to me.

Our meeting was on Friday, February 13th. I got back to Pittsburgh on Saturday afternoon. I was continuously interviewed by reporters regarding the possibility of a "holdout," etc. I now have information from more than one that you recently stated that no agreement was reached on February 13th. On Monday, February 16th, I dictated a wire to you withdrawing my offer. I WIRED because I wished the withdrawal of my offer to precede any acceptance by you. This wire was not sent until Tuesday because I wished Branch to see the telegram before sending it and he was not in the office. This required changing one word, — "yesterday" for "today." The wire reads as follows: "Upon returning to Pitts-

burgh, I was reminded that our agreement with Cuba requires present-
ing regular team for exhibition games beginning March 7th. This necessarily changes club requirements for reporting date for all players. You
will therefore give consideration to this matter in further negotiation on
contract. I am hopeful that we will be able to come to satisfactory terms
before March 1st. Congratulations on domestic news in yesterday's press.
Kindest regards and best wishes to Nancy and yourself."

This wire stated very clearly that you were then placed in a position to consider or demand entirely different terms from any suggested
or proposed. This telegram placed you in the position of being able to
say that your salary must be $100,000 or any other sum in order to induce
you to report on March 1st. The telegram meant exactly that and said
exactly that. That telegram bore the date of February 17th.

For many years, I have believed that spring training for major league
players who were not overweight extended over too long a period of
time; that players of well-known major league ability in good physical
shape put themselves in playing condition within four weeks. I still so
believe. That principle would apply to a half-dozen players on the Pittsburgh club at the present time and I so stated to you in our conversation at Gilmore Field and named several of the players. I pointed out on
that occasion that the objection lay in the effect of the exceptions for
reporting dates upon team morale; that it was an important feature for
the club to consider and indeed for the player himself to consider. My
arguments had no effect. What other players were required to do made
no difference to you. As an inducement, to secure an agreement with you
at that particular time, I conceded the point.

Two days later, namely on February 19th, I wrote a letter to you
referring to my wire, and stating terms, and hoping that we would not
experience a so-called "holdout," and asked you to wire acceptance if
terms were satisfactory and stated very explicitly that if the contract was
not satisfactory, 'you will understand, I am sure, why terms as now submitted will and are now withdrawn as of March 1st and it will then be
necessary to renew negotiations on terms as stated in the original contract, viz, $67,500.' You made no reply to my telegram and I did not
hear from you until March 3rd. You took about five days after receiving
my telegram before it occurred to you, evidently, that you had made a
mistake on February 13th in not accepting my offer; that the thing to do
now was to allege an understanding and even state as a fact that we had
an agreement on February 13th.

It can be true that you so fully intended to accept my offer that on the Saturday, Sunday, and Monday, intervening before you received my telegram, — you could have made certain commitments which you evidently regard as more important than a baseball career. You had no right to make any commitment prior to your acceptance of the offer and you had no right to make any commitment after the offer was withdrawn.

Our Cuban exhibition games make it important for you to report immediately in condition to play at once. If so, your salary will be $75,000. If not, your salary will be $67,000 and there will be a deduction from salary corresponding to the period of the delay. I hope I may have a telegram of acceptance upon receipt of this letter.

Very truly yours,

Branch Rickey
General Manager

BR/b

Club Nautico de Marianao
Marianao, Havana, Cuba

June 16, 1953

Mr. John W. Galbreath
Pittsburgh Athletic Company, Inc.
Forbes Field
Pittsburgh 13, Pa.

Dear John:
    I am rather anxious to hear about your conversation with Les Biederman. I have been around newspapermen all my life and I have had plenty of criticism on my judgment on how to build ball clubs and a lot of other things, but Les Biederman has caused me for the first time ever to go past the writer himself with any kind of protest. Very definitely I am not in front of any kind of compromise with this man as long as he shows malice and distrust and makes personal accusations. I have no use

for him and I will have nothing whatever to do with him and I will tell him just that, and my action will be in accordance with that position.

There are two kinds of writers. Biederman represents one kind and a man like Arthur Daley represents the other kind. Arthur Daley has had one interview with me, — a very brief one too, and one of these articles was written before I ever saw Daley. Neither Arthur Daley nor the New York Times is accustomed to reporting untruths and neither has the reputation for unfairness. I am enclosing two articles which Daley has written quite recently.

Yours,

BR/b
Encl:

November 19, 1953

(Personal and Confidential)

Mr. John W. Galbreath
42 East Gay Street
Columbus, Ohio

Dear John:

Our budget for 1954 is based upon an attendance of 450,000. At the same time this budget was made up, I estimated attendance for 1955 at 900,000 and, with that figure in mind, we estimated our needs up to the reasonableness of the 1955 attendance estimate and I wish this letter to give you the data which, in my judgment, supports my reasons for the 900,000 figure.

First of all it must be understood that I have not taken into consideration at all the so-called economic conditions of our country which may obtain in 1955. That is something which I do not control and something that the Pittsburgh Baseball Club does not control and I, most certainly, am not in position to anticipate our future economic status. It may be worse — it may be better. We may have active world-wide war and we may not have. Television may hurt us. I believe it will help. However, I have not taken television into consideration in arriving at the estimate of 900,000 for 1955. There are, say, three supporting reasons for this estimate as follows.

I.

You are somewhat familiar with the ten-year survey which I made some time ago in the Cardinal organization which showed that boys who were "regulars" in the major leagues had each served on an average of three and one-half years in the minor leagues. Those Cardinal clubs were younger than any other club in the National League by something more than one year each. Another survey made by the New York American League club covering a period of five years showed approximately four and one-half years of minor league service before a man was a so-called "regular" on that club.

Our production of approximately 450 new or different players brought into the Pittsburgh organization since I came to Pittsburgh three years ago equals the previous production records in St. Louis and Brooklyn, the two clubs where I have spent most of my baseball life. Some of the same men and, indeed, the best ones, who were with me in those productive years are with me here in Pittsburgh. This means that our standard of player qualities has not been lowered. It is the same. The quantity production averages as high as any previous similar period. Therefore, I have every reason to believe that out of our three-year production in Pittsburgh we have, by and large, the same kind of players that were produced in both St. Louis and Brooklyn.

Now, no one of these 400 odd players has had more than three years of professional baseball experience and only 86 have had that much or more. About 60 of them have had only two years and 75 have had only one year, and in the neighborhood of 40 of them have had none at all.

In any acceptable definition of a major league players, the Pittsburgh club will not have very many "regular" major league players on the basis of baseball experience until the end of another year, which, even then, will give us only a portion of the present roster with as much as four years under their belts. However, at the end of 1954 Pittsburgh will have approximately 120 men with four years professional baseball experience. If history is accorded the right to repeat itself, I have good support for my judgment that we will have a major league club on the field in 1955.

II.

Pittsburgh is a good city for baseball! There is plenty of population hereabouts. There are a great many really big industries in this community. In history of depressions in our country, Pittsburgh will show a comparatively high rate of employment. We do not have very strong sport competitors, in fact, none at all. It is a one-club baseball city. We do not have the seashore to compete against and we do not have racing in any of its many ramifications. And the city has earned the wide reputation, which it unquestionably has throughout the country, of supporting its own activities and particularly baseball.

It is possible that there is not a single franchise in either major league, everything considered, that has the market value equal to that of the Pittsburgh franchise. Then, too, it has Forbes Field. In the judgment of a great many baseball people, Forbes Field has both location value and an aesthetic value unequaled most certainly by any city in the United States. All of this means that the facilities for high attendance are already here.

III.

Figures in the past support my estimate for 1955. I have before me the National League President's report for 1953 and in this report he gives the attendance figures of all the clubs in the National League for the years 1946 to 1953 inclusive. I give you these figures from the President's report and I will add the position of the club in the race each of the last eight years:

Year	Attendance	Position
1946	749,962	7th
1947	1,283,531	8th
1948	1,517,021	4th
1949	1,449,435	6th
1950	1,166,267	8th
1951	980,590	7th
1952	686,673	8th
1953	572,757	8th

And now some brief comment on these figures:

You came into the ownership in August of 1946. A new and very expensive building program was undertaken and finished for the season of 1947. The new ownership and the new park, with several changes in player personnel, afforded quite a stimulus in every direction and attendance increased in 1947 over 1946 by something over half-million. Then, in 1948, you were in first division part of the year and finally finished fourth and made a further increase in attendance of about 235,000 and went above the attendance mark of one-million and one-half. Pittsburgh interest kept up for another year, although the team finished 6th, and continued remarkably in 1950 when Pittsburgh finished last. In 1951, my first year, the club finished 7th, and attendance fell below the million mark, but it was a most remarkable attendance considering that the club was in last place the previous year.

A frank rebuilding program based upon new and young players out of quantity production had been announced and was closely followed and, of course, the club, as explained in I. above, could not and did not improve its position and, in 1952, the club finished 8th with a reduced attendance under 700,000. And our last-place club in this past season drew approximately 570,000.

Our estimate of 450,000 for 1954 is based upon our pre-season ticket sale from year to year and not at all upon any expectation of a great team. There is in my opinion much better reason to expect more than 450,000 in 1954 than there is for any one executive less than 900,000 in 1955. I think the club will exceed both figures.

You have money in this thing and so has Tom and so have I! And it means a very great deal to me not to lose any part of my investment. My investment was made more or less recently, and proved my faith in the future of the Pittsburgh club. I would take the same investment now if I could.

You have advanced money to us and, without your help, I do not know what would have happened. Others with means, for one reason or another, do not wish to go along with you in further financial support. You are about to interview a gentleman who is a possible purchaser of the stock from Tom and Mr. Phillips. I know you like this prospective purchaser, and so do I! If this does not come about, then it is possible that we must very quickly negotiate the sale of player contracts. I know you do not want to do this and I certainly do not want to do it for it would mean an indefinite "Jerry Nugent" operation, in which case we would find ourselves anchored in a low position.

As an alternative to the compulsory sale of player contracts, I would prefer; personally, to recommend that you join with me in an effort to sell the controlling interest in the club. I do not care for any sort of continuous identification with a "loser." On the other hand, I feel that, if we can get enough money to see us through until the middle of 1955, we are 'out of the woods' and we will pay off our debts and then really make a lot of profit. I sincerely believe every bit of this, but I must add that, when I speak of "enough" money, it must be "enough" to keep us up a normal production in the free-agency field. Otherwise, we simply postponed the day of a World Series in Pittsburgh.

This is written to you having in mind that you should be as fully aware of the reasons for my beliefs about our operation in Pittsburgh as I am myself and, particularly, my reason for the 1955 estimated attendance.

Very sincerely yours,

Branch Rickey
General Manger

BR:jd

Notes

Chapter 1

1. *Sport,* "Pittsburgh and the New Pirates," Jack Sher, 8/47.
2. *Branch Rickey,* Murray Polner, Atheneum, 1982, pg. 215.
3. *Branch Rickey,* Murray Polner, Atheneum, 1982, pg. 215.
4. *The Lords of Baseball,* Harold Parrott, Praeger Publishers, 1976, pg. 31.
5. Interview, Thomas Johnson, 6/8/98.
6. *Pittsburgh Post-Gazette,* 3/19/47.
7. Interview, Thomas Johnson, 6/8/98.
8. Interview, Thomas Johnson, 6/8/98.
9. *The Sporting News,* 11/15/50.
10. Interview, Thomas Johnson, 6/8/98.
11. *Pittsburgh Post-Gazette,* 11/20/50.
12. *Pittsburgh Post-Gazette,* 11/20/50.
13. *Pittsburgh Post-Gazette,* 11/28/50.
14. *Pittsburgh Post-Gazette,* 11/28/50.
15. *Pittsburgh Post-Gazette,* Al Abrams, 12/10/50.
16. *Pittsburgh Post-Gazette,* 1/12/51.
17. *The Sporting News,* 1/10/51.
18. *The Sporting News,* 1/10/51.
19. *The Sporting News,* 12/20/50.
20. *Pittsburgh Post-Gazette,* 12/9/50.
21. *Pittsburgh Post-Gazette,* 12/9/50.
22. *Pittsburgh Post-Gazette,* 12/9/50.
23. *Pittsburgh Post-Gazette,* 4/17/51.
24. *Pittsburgh Post-Gazette,* 12/8/50.
25. *The Sporting News,* 11/29/50.

26. *The Sporting News*, 12/27/50.

27. *The Sporting News*, 2/7/51.

28. *Pittsburgh Post-Gazette*, 4/10/51.

29. The Branch Rickey Collection, Library of Congress, attachment to a letter to Galbreath, 12/18/50.

Chapter 2

1. *Pittsburgh Post-Gazette*, 1/17/51.

2. *The Sporting News*, 1/24/51.

3. *The Sporting News*, 1/24/51, Charley Young.

4. *Pittsburgh Post-Gazette*, 2/2/51.

5. *Pittsburgh Post-Gazette*, 2/18/52.

6. *The Sporting News*, 12/20/50.

7. *The Sporting News*, 2/14/51.

8. *The Sporting News*, 2/28/51.

9. *Pittsburgh Sun Telegraph*, 3/3/51.

10. *Pittsburgh Post-Gazette*, 3/2/51.

11. *Pittsburgh Post Gazette*, 3/19/51.

12. *The Sporting News*, 3/28/51.

13. *Pittsburgh Sun-Telegraph*, 3/8/51.

14. *The Sporting News*, 3/14/51.

15. *The Pittsburgh Post-Gazette*, 4/19/47.

16. *The Sporting News*, 3/28/51.

17. The Branch Rickey Collection, Library of Congress, Crosby letter to Rickey, 3/15/51.

18. *The Sporting News*, 4/4/51.

19. *The Sporting News*, 4/4/51.

20. The Branch Rickey Collection, Library of Congress, Rickey memo to Galbreath, 5/7/51.

21. *Pittsburgh Post-Gazette*, 4/6/51.

22. *Saturday Evening Post*, Myron Cope, 5/9/59.

23. The Branch Rickey Collection, Library of Congress, Rickey memo to Galbreath, 5/7/51.

24. *Pittsburgh Post-Gazette*, 4/17/51.

25. *The Sporting News*, 6/13/51.

26. *The Sporting News*, 6/13/51.

27. *The Sporting News*, 6/13/51.

28. *Pittsburgh Sun-Telegraph*, 3/21/51.

29. *Pittsburgh Post-Gazette*, 8/1/51.

30. *Pittsburgh Post-Gazette*, 9/7/51.

31. *Pittsburgh Post-Gazette*, 9/21/51.

32. The Branch Rickey Collection, Library of Congress, telegram, 9/5/51.

33. *Pittsburgh Post Gazette*, 9/21/51.

34. *The Sporting News*, 11/14/51.

35. The Branch Rickey Collection, Library of Congress, letter to Galbreath, 11/26/51.

36. The Branch Rickey Collection, Library of Congress, letter to Galbreath, 11/26/51.

37. *The Sporting News*, 11/14/51.

38. *Sport*, "Has Rickey Failed at Pittsburgh?" Arthur Mann, 6/19/54.

Chapter 3

1. The Branch Rickey Collection, Library of Congress, letter to John Galbreath, 2/26/52.

2. The Branch Rickey Collection, Library of Congress, letter to John Galbreath, 2/26/52.

3. The Branch Rickey Collection, Library of Congress, letter to John Galbreath, 2/26/52.

4. Interview, Thomas Johnson, 6/9/98.

5. The Branch Rickey Collection, Library of Congress, interview with Joe Brandis, 7/30/54.

6. *Pittsburgh Post-Gazette*, 2/2/52.

7. *The Sporting News*, 12/31/52.

8. *The Sporting News*, 1/30/52.

9. *The Sporting News*, 1/30/52.

10. *The Sporting News*, 2/20/52.

11. *The Sporting News*, 2/20/52.

12. *The Sporting News*, 2/27/52.

13. *The Sporting News*, 2/13/52.

14. *The Sporting News*, 3/12/52.

15. The Branch Rickey Collection, Library of Congress, letter to John Galbreath, 10/10/51.

16. *The Sporting News*, 3/5/52.

17. *The Sporting News*, 3/5/52.

18. *The Sporting News*, 3/5/52.

19. *The Sporting News*, 10/3/51.

20. *The Sporting News*, 10/3/51.

21. *The Sporting News*, 11/21/51.

22. *The Sporting News*, 3/5/52.

23. *The Sporting News*, 4/23/52.

24. *The Sporting News*, 4/23/52.

25. *The Sporting News*, 3/5/52.

26. *Pittsburgh Post Gazette*, 3/31/52.

27. *The Sporting News*, 4/23/52.
28. The Branch Rickey Collection, Library of Congress, 3/21/52.
29. *Pittsburgh Sun-Telegraph*, 4/15/52.
30. *Baseball Is a Funny Game*, Joe Garagiola, J.P Lippincott Company, 1960.
31. *Life*, "The Boy Buffoons of Baseball," Marshall Smith, 8/13/56.
32. *Pittsburgh Post-Gazette*, 5/12/52.
33. *Pittsburgh Sun-Telegraph*, 5/14/52.
34. *Pittsburgh Sun-Telegraph*, 5/14/52.
35. *Pittsburgh Sun-Telegraph*, 5/1/52.
36. *Pittsburgh Post-Gazette*, 4/21/52.
37. *Pittsburgh Post Gazette*, 4/21/52.
38. *Pittsburgh Sun-Telegraph*, 4/20/52.
39. *Pittsburgh Sun-Telegraph*, 5/15/52.
40. *The Sporting News*, 2/20/52.
41. *The Sporting News*, 3/12/52.
42. *The Sporting News*, 6/4/52.
43. The Branch Rickey Collection, Library of Congress, letter to John Galbreath, 11/26/51.
44. *Pittsburgh Post-Gazette*, 6/7/52.
45. *Pittsburgh Post-Gazette*, 6/21/52.
46. *The Sporting News*, 7/9/52.
47. *Pittsburgh Post-Gazette*, 8/10/52.
48. *The Sporting News*, 7/9/52.
49. *Pittsburgh Post-Gazette*, 7/3/52.
50. *Pittsburgh Sun-Telegraph*, 4/29/52.
51. *Pittsburgh Post-Gazette*, 8/7/52.
52. *Pittsburgh Post-Gazette*, 8/12/52.
53. *Pittsburgh Post-Gazette*, 9/18/52.
54. *Pittsburgh Post-Gazette*, 9/3/52.
55. *Pittsburgh Sun-Telegraph*, 9/29/52.
56. *The Sporting News*, 10/29/52.
57. *The Pittsburgh Pirates: An Illustrated History*, Bob Smizik Walker Publishing, 1990.
58. *The Sporting News*, 10/29/52.
59. *The Sporting News*, 12/24/52.
60. *The Sporting News*, 12/31/52.

Chapter 4

1. *Pittsburgh Post-Gazette*, 6/4/52.
2. *The Sporting News*, 12/10/52.
3. *The Sporting News*, 1/28/53.

4. The Branch Rickey Collection, Library of Congress, "A Few Remarks About the Camp," 3/19/53.

5. *Sport*, "Mr. Home Run," Al Stump, 6/50.

6. *Sport*, "How Kiner Got That Way," Braven Dyer and Frank Finch, 3/48, p. 23.

7. *Sport*, "How Kiner Got That Way," Braven Dyer and Frank Finch, 3/48, p. 23.

8. *Sport*, "How Kiner Got That Way," Braven Dyer and Frank Finch, 3/48, p. 23.

9. *Sport*, "How Kiner Got That Way," Braven Dyer and Frank Finch, 3/48, p. 23.

10. The Branch Rickey Collection, Library of Congress, letter to John Galbreath, 3/21/52.

11. The Branch Rickey Collection, Library of Congress, letter to John Galbreath, 3/21/52.

12. The Branch Rickey Collection, Library of Congress, letter to John Galbreath, 3/21/52.

13. The Branch Rickey Collection, Library of Congress, letter to John Galbreath, 3/21/52.

14. *The Sporting News*, 10/17/51.

15. The Branch Rickey Collection, Library of Congress, letter to John Galbreath, 3/21/52.

16. *Pittsburgh Sun-Telegraph*, 2/18/53.

17. *Pittsburgh Post-Gazette*, 1/14/53.

18. *Pittsburgh Post-Gazette*, 1/21/53.

19. The Branch Rickey Collection, Library of Congress, letter to John Galbreath, 3/21/52.

20. *Pittsburgh Post-Gazette*, 1/23/53.

21. *Pittsburgh Post-Gazette*, 1/28/53.

22. *Pittsburgh Post-Gazette*, 2/14/53.

23. *Pittsburgh Sun-Telegraph*, 2/16/53.

24. *Pittsburgh Post-Gazette*, 3/16/53.

25. *Pittsburgh Post-Gazette*, 3/16/53.

26. *The Sporting News*, 3/25/53.

27. *The Pittsburgh Pirates: An Illustrated History*, Bob Smizik, Walker Publishing Company, 1990.

28. *The Sporting News*, 2/25/53.

29. *Saturday Evening Post*, 7/30/55, "The Pirates Haven't Driven Me Nutty Yet!" Fred Haney as told to Charles Dexter.

30. *Pittsburgh Post-Gazette*, 4/28/53.

31. *Pittsburgh Post-Gazette*, 5/5/53.

32. *Pittsburgh Post-Gazette*, 5/5/53.

33. *Pittsburgh Post-Gazette*, 6/3/53.

34. *The Sporting News*, 6/10/53.

35. *Branch Rickey*, Murray Poher, Atheneum, 1982.
36. *Branch Rickey*, Murray Polner, Atheneum, 1982.
37. *The Sporting News*, 4/29/53.
38. *Dollar Sign on the Muscle*, Kevin Kerrane, Beaufort Books Inc., 1984.
39. *The Sporting News*, 4/29/53.
40. *The Sporting News*, 7/1/53.
41. *Pittsburgh Post-Gazette*, 6/24/53.
42. *Pittsburgh Post-Gazette*, 6/24/53.
43. The Branch Rickey Collection, Library of Congress, letter to John Galbreath, 6/16/53.
44. *The Sporting News*, 7/29/53.
45. *The Sporting News*, 7/29/53.
46. *Pittsburgh Post-Gazette*, 7/6/53.
47. The Branch Rickey Collection, Library of Congress, Jim Herron letter to Branch Rickey, 10/7/53.

Chapter 5

1. *Wait Till Next Year*, Carl T. Rowan with Jackie Robinson, Random House, 1960, pp. 116, 117.
2. *Voices from the Great Black Baseball Leagues*, Revised Edition, John Holway, DaCapo, 1992.
3. *Branch Rickey*, Murray Polner, Atheneum, 1982.
4. *Branch Rickey*, Murray Polner, Atheneum, 1982.
5. *Branch Rickey*, Murray Polner, Atheneum, 1982.
6. *Josh and Satch*, John Holway, Carroll and Graf, 1991.
7. The Branch Rickey Collection, Library of Congress, memo to Branch Jr., 3/17/51.
8. Interview with Joe Brown, 10/2/94.
9. Interview with Christine Roberts, 3/17/97.
10. The Branch Rickey Collection, Library of Congress, interview with Joe Brandis, 7/30/54.
11. *The Sporting News*, 3/17/54.
12. *The Sporting News*, 3/17/54.
13. *Pittsburgh Post-Gazette*, 3/2/54.
14. *Pittsburgh Post-Gazette*, 3/2/54.
15. *Pittsburgh Post-Gazette*, 3/2/54.
16. *Pittsburgh Post-Gazette*, 3/11/54.
17. *Pittsburgh Post-Gazette*, 2/3/54.
18. *The Sporting News*, 3/31/54.
19. *The Sporting News*, 3/31/54.
20. *The Sporting News*, 4/7/54.
21. *Pittsburgh Post-Gazette*, 3/13/54.

22. The Branch Rickey Collection, Library of Congress, letter to John Galbreath, 2/17/54.

23. *Pittsburgh Post-Gazette*, 4/6/54.

24. Interview with Tom Johnson, 6/4/98.

25. Interview with Tom Johnson, 6/4/98.

26. *Pittsburgh Post-Gazette*, 4/17/54.

27. *The Sporting News*, 7/21/54.

28. *The Sporting News*, 6/23/54.

29. *The Lords of the Realm: The Real History of Baseball*, John Helyar, 1994, Villard Books, p. 47.

30. *Pittsburgh Post-Gazette*, 8/3/54.

31. *Pittsburgh Post-Gazette*, 8/7/54.

32. The Branch Rickey Collection, Library of Congress, interview with Joe Brandis, 7/30/54.

33. *Pittsburgh Post-Gazette*, 8/2/54.

34. *The Sporting News*, 8/11/54.

35. The Branch Rickey Collection, Library of Congress, memorandum, letter to Branch Rickey, Jr., 10/53.

36. *The Sporting News*, 8/25/54.

37. The Branch Rickey Collection, Library of Congress, 9/14/54.

38. *The Sporting News*, 12/1/54.

39. Interview with Howie Haak, 9/3/98.

40. Interview with Clyde Sukeforth, 8/8/97.

41. *The Sporting News*, 12/8/54.

42. *The Sporting News*, 8/25/54.

43. *The Sporting News*, 12/22/54.

Chapter 6

1. *The Sporting News*, 1/12/55.

2. *The Sporting News*, 1/12/55.

3. The Branch Rickey Collection, Library of Congress, scouting report for Santurce v Ponce, 1/25/55.

4. *Pittsburgh Post-Gazette*, 2/2/55.

5. *Pittsburgh Post-Gazette*, 1/9/55.

6. *The Sporting News*, 3/25/55.

7. *The Sporting News*, 3/25/55.

8. *Pittsburgh Press*, 2/20/55.

9. *Pittsburgh Press*, 4/22/55.

10. *Pittsburgh Post-Gazette*, 2/24/55.

11. *The Sporting News*, 2/23/55.

12. *The Sporting News*, 3/16/55.

13. *Pittsburgh Press*, 3/4/55.

14. *The Sporting News*, 4/20/55.

15. *Pittsburgh Sun-Telegraph*, 4/12/55.

16. *The Sporting News*, 3/9/55.

17. *The Sporting News*, 8/31/55.

18. *Branch Rickey's Little Blue Book,* Macmillan, 1995, p. 74.

19. *Branch Rickey's Little Blue Book,* Macmillan, 1995, pp. 74–75.

20. The Branch Rickey Collection, Library of Congress, Reconstructed Radio Broadcast of Pittsburgh-Milwaukee, 5/6/54.

21. The Branch Rickey Collection, Library of Congress, comments on Bob Prince's broadcast, 6/12/53.

22. *Pittsburgh Press*, 4/26/55.

23. *The Sporting News*, 4/20/55.

24. *The Sporting News*, 4/20/55.

25. *Jackie Robinson: A Biography,* Arnold Rampersad, Knopf, 1997.

26. *Jackie Robinson: An Intimate Portrait,* Rachel Robinson with Lee Daniels, Abrams Publishing, 1996.

27. Interview, Mrs. Christine Roberts, 3/17/1997.

28. Letter from Jackie Robinson to Curt Roberts, courtesy Leith Roberts.

29. The Branch Rickey Collection, Library of Congress, scouting report, 10/29/54.

30. The Branch Rickey Collection, Library of Congress, observations of Pittsburgh-Chicago game, 3/23/55.

31. *The Sporting News*, 8/31/55.

32. The Branch Rickey Collection, Library of Congress, Inter-Club Communication, 5/26/55.

33. *The Sporting News*, 8/31/55.

34. *The Sporting News*, 8/31/55.

35. The Branch Rickey Collection, Library of Congress, letter to Fred Haney, 9/23/55.

36. The Branch Rickey Collection, Library of Congress, letter to Fred Haney, 9/23/55.

37. *Pittsburgh Sun-Telegraph*, 9/16/55.

38. *Pittsburgh Post-Gazette*, 10/22/55.

39. Interview, Thomas Johnson, 6/8/98.

40. *Pittsburgh Sun-Telegraph*, 10/25/55.

41. *Pittsburgh Press*, 10/20/55.

42. *The Sporting News*, 11/2/55.

43. *Pittsburgh Press*, 10/20/55.

44. *Pittsburgh Press*, 10/21/55.

45. *Branch Rickey,* Murray Polner, Atheneum, 1982, pp. 242–243.

Index

Page numbers in *italics* indicate photographs.